Hunger

Hunger

Food Deprivation as a Military Weapon

N.S. 'Tank' Nash

Pen & Sword
MILITARY

First published in Great Britain in 2023 by
PEN & SWORD MILITARY
an imprint of Pen & Sword Books Ltd
Yorkshire – Philadelphia

ISBN 978-1-39904-059-4

Typeset by Concept, Huddersfield HD4 5JL.
Printed and bound in England by CPI Group (UK) Ltd, Croydon CR0 4YY.

Pen & Sword Books Ltd incorporates the imprints of Aviation, Atlas,
Family History, Fiction, Maritime, Military, Discovery, Politics, History,
Archaeology, Select, Wharncliffe Local History, Wharncliffe True Crime,
Military Classics, Wharncliffe Transport, Leo Cooper, The Praetorian Press,
Remember When, White Owl, Seaforth Publishing and Frontline Books.

For a complete list of Pen & Sword titles please contact
PEN & SWORD BOOKS LTD
47 Church Street, Barnsley, South Yorkshire, S70 2AS, England
E-mail: enquiries@pen-and-sword.co.uk
Website: www.pen-and-sword.co.uk
or
PEN & SWORD BOOKS
1950 Lawrence Rd, Havertown, PA 19083, USA
E-mail: uspen-and-sword@casematepublishers.com
Website: www.penandswordbooks.com

Contents

List of Illustrations

List of Maps

Abbreviations used in notes

GGS   *German General Staff, The Franco German War 1870–1871* (London 1874–1884) (Berlin 1872–1881).

Guerre   *La Guerre 1870–71*, Publiée par la Revue d'Histoire, rédigée à la Section historique de l'Etat-Major de la Armée (Paris 1901–1913).

SHAT   Service Historique de l'Armée de Terre (Vincennes).

O.R.   The War of the Rebellion of the Official Records of the Union and Confederate Armies.

IWM   Imperial War Museum.

TNA   The National Archives.

Acknowledgements

This book takes a different approach to military history over the last 160 years. Research carried out for my previous books is now focused on the studies of selected campaigns and this volume confirms the efficacy of starvation as a weapon. However, it also shows that the imposition of food denial is not assured of success. In places, it makes for grim reading, but then war is a grim and brutal business.

I am most grateful to those who have so willingly supported my authorship. Professor Robert Tombs considered my text and has contributed the foreword that follows. Dr Herbert Meiselman, the pre-eminent food psychologist, and very old friend, has contributed a valuable scientist's view of hunger. Lieutenant Colonel Tom Gowans was, as always, my first editor.

I have drawn on the work of many historians who preceded me, as the bibliography shows. For many of them, 'hunger' was but a by-product of a much wider canvas and not a specific subject for study. It is now apparent that, over thousands of years, starvation has not only been a major cause of death but also of victory/defeat and subsequent strategic realignments.

Happily, Pen & Sword have once again appointed the outstanding Linne Matthews as my text editor. She is a joy to work with and her clinical appraisal of my work went far beyond corrections to my syntax. She questioned my judgements, debated priorities and, by so doing, strengthened the text. She made the tedious editing exercise enjoyable.

Matt Jones, and the production team he leads at Pen & Sword, combined to produce yet another handsome book – but then that is what they excel at, and this author is very grateful for their expertise.

Any errors or omissions are entirely my responsibility.

Tank Nash
Tetbury
Gloucestershire
February 2023
nsnash39@gmail.com

Foreword

by Professor Robert Tombs

Those who have lived through wars at the receiving end – and that often means civilians as well as the military – must always have been well aware of the overwhelming need to find food. When their states manage to function, this may be guaranteed, to some extent, by rationing. But even then, hunger means black marketeering and theft, and the threat, always present, of social breakdown.

If most wars are at least in part about food, there is a terrible paradox in the modern history of war – that is to say, from the mid-nineteenth century to our own day. On one hand, states became more powerful and efficient, and many of them accepted as never before a direct responsibility to look after all their citizens. Hence, they were increasingly able to secure and control available food supplies and distribute them through more or less effective systems of rationing.

In Britain – one of the world's most advanced countries – wartime rationing actually led to an improvement in public health. Moreover, advances in civilization meant that attempts were made to protect civilians from the direct

consequences of war. During the American Civil War, the Federal government's Lieber Code aimed to separate combatants and non-combatants, and
shield the latter from direct violence. The later Hague and Geneva conven-
tions went further still in trying to protect civilians and prisoners. Finally,
increased economic efficiency and improvements in transport, especially
railways, made mass hunger in normal times a thing of the past.

The terrible paradox is that as these increasingly efficient states laboured to
protect and feed their own people, they were also more able to inflict damage
on the enemy, including enemy civilians. As wars became more 'total', with
whole populations participating in the war effort by their economic labours
and by their political support, belligerent states felt it necessary and justified
to put pressure on civilians, including by depriving them of food, with the
intention of forcing them to demand that their own governments accept
defeat.

So instead of modern war becoming less devastating for civilians than it
had been in previous centuries – which many enlightened people (including
politicians and soldiers) had hoped for – they became in fact as exposed to the
dangers of war, if not more exposed, than in the terrible Thirty Years War in
Germany or the Hundred Years War in France. Civilians were increasingly
bombarded and bombed. Worse still, they were starved. So, the First and
Second World Wars, as well as other wars of the last 150 years, were in large
part fought around, and even decided by, food and hunger. Famine returned,
whether as a by-product of the conflict (as in the Bengal famine of 1943), or
even as a deliberate act, following blockade (notably that of Germany during
the First World War) or through the deliberate seizure of food supplies and
food production.

Whether as part of grand strategy, or as an inevitable aspect of counter-
guerrilla warfare, control of food became crucial. It reached its nadir as
practised by the Germans during the Second World War, in which a 'Hunger
Plan' was aimed at the racial destruction of Slavs in Eastern Europe in order
to provide surplus food to enable the Germans to withstand a world war
against Britain and America. Though they were never able to impose it fully,
they nevertheless deliberately starved huge numbers of Russian prisoners of
war to death.

There is nothing to suggest that future wars will not adopt similar strate-
gies. Indeed, Vladimir Putin is at the time of writing using food as a military
and political weapon.

So, Tank Nash's latest book could hardly be more relevant to our own day.
In looking comprehensively at the importance of food in warfare since the
mid-nineteenth century, he has given us the full perspective on this terrible
geopolitical development. In recent years, many historians have begun taking

an interest in the crucial importance of food in war, but none has tried to bring all the major examples together in a single work. Writing in accessible style, and using his own military experience as a guide, he has produced an important and sobering book.

Robert Tombs is a historian of modern Europe, emeritus professor of French history at Cambridge University, and a Fellow of St John's College. He has long taken an interest in the history of war, and has written on the Franco-Prussian War, the Paris Commune, and on Franco-British relations during the 'second hundred years war' (1689–1815) and during the two world wars. He has also written *The English and Their History*. He is an accomplished and well-informed journalist and writes for the print media as a commentator on history and politics. He co-edits the website *History Reclaimed* (historyreclaimed.co.uk).

Chapter One

On Food Denial

*Famine makes greater havoc in an army than the enemy and
is more terrible than the sword.*

Flavius Vegetius Renatus[1]

The military historian, seeking a topic, finds that today the facts of most military confrontations are well documented and of course unchanging. For example, the battles of the Somme, the Bulge and Normandy have each been the subject of hundreds of books. The anguish and misery of those campaigns and others has been laid bare in reiterative and graphic detail.

The aim of this book is to view several campaigns from a different standpoint. It is the intention to show that wars are not always won by the personal sacrifice of foot soldiers, dying by their hundreds of thousands in muddy ditches, but sometimes by the denial of food to one side by the other. On land, this is usually accomplished by siege, and at sea, by the remorseless application of a blockade with naval force. The sealing of an enemy's ports and rivers and thereby preventing the movement and, specifically, the import of vital supplies – not the least food – is a war-winning strategy.

It is suggested that although the logistics of warfare are all about 'bullets, bandages and bread', often the most important of these is 'bread'. In all campaigns, the two adversaries seek to disrupt or destroy the other's logistic chain – this is a tactic as old as war itself. However, there are examples when the aim has been, specifically, to deny the opposition access to food. When successful, this food denial tactic generates starvation to some degree, and that starvation always comes with the full range of attendant dietary diseases. Starvation is perhaps one of the most painful and miserable ways to die. It is unpleasant but, to be specific:

Victims of starvation die of nutritional dystrophy, a process whereby once the body has used up all its fat reserves, the muscles are broken down to obtain energy. The small intestine atrophies and it becomes increasingly difficult for the victim to absorb nutrients from what little foods he or she can obtain. As a defence mechanism the body reduces the activity of vital organs such as the heart and liver and the victims suffer

1

not only from muscular debility but from a more general and over-powering fatigue.[2]

Eventually, a starving person dies of multiple organ failure. The instigators of food denial tactics, over the period covered by this book, may have had no personal experience of the horror of starvation either as a victim or as spectator. The exception to that was the Germans, who had suffered under a draconian British blockade during the First World War. With that experience behind them, during the Second World War, the Germans sought to starve Britain into submission during the Battle of the Atlantic.

For a blockade to succeed, it follows that the navy conducting a blockade must first gain control of the sea around its adversary's coast and must have a force large enough to allow for constant patrolling – perhaps for several years. The effects of a naval blockade are not just felt by the military but also by civilian non-combatants who co-exist with them. These people share the hunger and suffering of the military, which do not manifest themselves in the short term. However, over time, a blockade can bring about hunger, starvation, death and the collapse of an economy, national morale, and civil governance.

Sieges on land are labour-intensive, protracted, but are generally conducted with *relatively* low loss of life. The besieged usually surrender before death from starvation is prevalent among their ranks. Vicksburg, Metz and Kut are examples to be considered here. The blockade of Berlin (1948–9) was a siege defeated by air power – a first of its genre in modern military history.

Overwhelming logistic superiority is usually a guarantee of military success and it worked for the Americans in the Pacific War. However, it proved to be irrelevant in Vietnam, where, despite its unmatched wealth and power, the USA was unable to stem the food supply to its guerrilla enemy.

There is another side to the coin and that is the need to wage war to secure a food source. The Japanese annexation of Manchuria in 1931 is an illustration of that. Similarly, the German invasion of Russia was motivated by its perceived need for food-producing territory. Food, and its acquisition, lay at the heart of the Second World War.

The first 'modern' war was, arguably, the civil war fought in the United States of America from 1861–5 – it provides ample evidence of the efficacy of food denial as a weapon of war.

Notes

1. *Military Institutions of the Romans* (trans. Clark, 1776).
2. Collingham, L., *The Taste of War* (London, Penguin Group, 2011), p. 6.

PART ONE

THE AMERICAN CIVIL WAR

Chapter Two

US Civil War:
Secession, *Casus Belli*[1]
(1861)

In 1860, the United States of America was a stable, wealthy but complex and unbalanced society. The national census of that year revealed that the population was 31,443,321. Of these, 4,441,830 were black slaves (about 14 per cent) and a further 480,070 were termed 'free black men'. Most of the latter group lived in northern states but were not given equality with the white citizens around them.

Slavery was an unremarkable feature of American life, more efficiently employed in the Southern states where its labour had resulted in the white owners amassing vast fortunes. Slavery was slowly being abandoned in the North as it was the recipient of massive immigration from Europe, which provided cheap labour and supported the move to an industrialised society.

In Massachusetts, in the period 1781–3, there was a series of judicial reviews that abolished slavery in the state. In Pennsylvania, they did not go quite as far but in 1780, the Gradual Abolition Act was passed.[2] The two objectives were to appease slave owners whilst at the same time emancipating enslaved people without making slavery immediately illegal. It was an unsatisfactory and weak compromise, not least because it permitted Pennsylvanian slave holders to keep the enslaved individuals that they already owned – unless they failed to register them annually. The act provided for the eventual freedom of individuals who were newly born into slavery, but no time frame for this was provided.

Slavery was then, and is now, an abomination, but it was not of overpowering importance at the time. On 6 November 1860, Abraham Lincoln was elected as the sixteenth president. Lincoln was not an abolitionist. In a speech in Charleston, Illinois, on 18 September 1858, he had said:

> I will say then, that I am not, nor ever have been, in favor of bringing about in any way, social and political equality of white and black races.

On his election, he refined his views and expressed the determination that, as the USA expanded further westwards, slavery should be curtailed and not

Abraham Lincoln (1809–65),
President of the United States 1861–5.

permitted in new and emerging territories. Lincoln's prime aim was to expand and preserve the Union without recourse to slavery.

The widely held presumption that the US Civil War was only about the abolition of slavery is incorrect. It was, more accurately, about limiting its use. Abolition may have been the result, but it was not the initial Union aim. Nevertheless, slavery, in general, was a significant factor, which set brother against brother, in the bloodiest war in the country's history.

What lesser issues could generate such furious and enthusiastic blood-letting? There were none worth fighting for, even in a varied American society. North and South were divided socially, politically, economically and culturally, although they did all share a common language, monetary and legal systems, and in some cases, they shared the same god.

In other countries, slavery had been increasingly abandoned. On 23 March 1807, the British House of Commons, with the insouciance that only a world power can presume, declared that the international trade in slaves was illegal. Thereafter, and for over six decades, the Royal Navy fought its longest campaign in the Atlantic and the Caribbean, where it sought to eradicate the slave trade. This unheralded, but laudable, campaign was chronicled in the magisterial history by Peter Grindal.[3]

However, Britain had no cause to be smug about this commitment, nor its cost in treasure and the lives of good men, because much of Britain's wealth, prior to 1807, had been accrued from slaving activities that were, *by the standards of the day, normal and routine*. It is a matter that, 216 years later, the British 'woke' generation of 2023 ignores in its vociferous and frequent rhetoric on the subject.

Lincoln's position on slavery in the new territories was sufficient to convince many Southerners that secession was the only viable option if their way of life was to be preserved. Proceedings moved very swiftly and by 8 February 1861, seven slave states – South Carolina, Mississippi, Florida, Alabama,

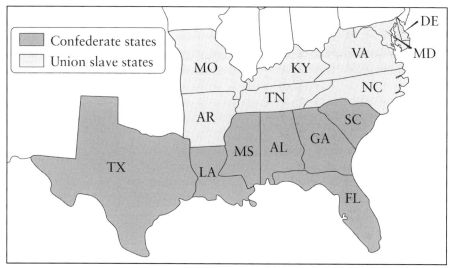

The seven-state Confederacy, February 1861.

Georgia, Louisiana and Texas – had seceded from the Union. They had appropriated Federal property including 'arsenals, forts military camp and the US Mint in New Orleans'.[4] There were eight other states in which slavery was a staple of economic life and Lincoln had to move with great care not to tip them into the Confederate camp. In the South, the appropriation of Federal property was conducted in a civil manner and without conflict. For no evident reason, the trigger for open warfare was Fort Sumter, which was a Union installation at the mouth of Charleston harbour (SC), one of the South's largest ports. The fort was held by a small detachment commanded by a Major Robert Anderson.

By March 1861, the fort was running low on food but Jefferson Davis, the recently elected president of the Confederacy, would not permit it to be resupplied – and it is the first example, in this text, of food being 'weaponised'.

Lincoln and his government were faced with a dilemma. It was argued that if the fort was evacuated it would signify the division of the nation. The fort was of little importance militarily, but it was a potent symbol of the unity of the states. Calm voices advised Lincoln to let Sumter go. Notwithstanding that, on 28 March, the Union government resolved to resupply the fort and a small fleet was despatched on 5 April. The following day, Anderson sent a note to the governor of South Carolina in which he said:

> I am directed by the President of the United States to notify you to expect an attempt will be made to supply Fort Sumter with provisions only, and that if such attempt be not resisted, no effort to throw in men, arms or

ammunition will be made without further notice, or in case of an attack on the fort.[5]

There was room for compromise here and certainly no pressing need for violence. However, before the resupply arrived, Anderson was given an ultimatum by Confederate commander Brigadier General Pierre Beauregard.

Major Robert Anderson (1805–71), commander, Fort Sumter, April 1861.

The ultimatum was simple: either Anderson surrender, or he and his men would face an artillery bombardment. This precipitate initiative flew in the face of common sense but there were sufficient individuals, thirsting for violence, to sway the decision-making. Anderson declined to surrender, and on 12 April, the bombardment threatened by Beauregard commenced.

It could be argued that the US Civil War was started by Beauregard, but he served under the political direction of Jefferson Davis. On that basis, Beauregard was just the initiator of the war. The recently digitised US census records from 1850 to 1880 show that an estimated 750,000 soldiers died in the ensuing conflict.[6]

The bombardment by the Confederates is worthy of note because 3,341 artillery rounds were fired at the stationary target of Fort Sumter. This torrent of fire, over thirty-three hours, should have reduced the fort to a pile of rubble and killed the entire garrison. Similarly, the counter-fire of approximately 1,000 rounds should have wreaked havoc in Confederate ranks. Incredibly, there was only one fatality. It was a non-combatant mule, minding its own business.[7]

The 'battle' of Fort Sumter was a major military non-event. However, the exchange of ineffective fire was sufficient to provide each side with a *casus belli* and now they prepared to fight a war for which they were unprepared and unequipped. The Union Army was only 16,000 strong and that was deployed west of the Mississippi, confronting recalcitrant Indians. There were very few professional soldiers on either side, and from the evidence of Fort Sumter, none were gunners.

The garrison of Fort Sumter was permitted to withdraw in the vessels sent to resupply them. The fall of the fort caused Lincoln to mobilise the civilian militia of Union states and his initial aim was to raise 75,000 men, but such was the martial enthusiasm of the populace, that number was rapidly over-taken. In the South, there was matching enthusiasm and a rush to arms. The State of Virginia reconsidered its position and on 17 April, it voted (88 to 55) for secession. Immediately, militia were sent to seize the arms factory at Harper's Ferry and the naval dockyard and facilities in Norfolk.

Arkansas and North Carolina both threw in their lot with the Confederacy, but Tennessee hedged its bets by merely passing a declaration of independence. The eastern borders of Tennessee had few slave owners, and the population was loath to support a cause that was not of their concern. Throughout the war, the North was to focus on separating these loyalists from their secessionist fellows and about 30,000 Tennesseans fought on the Union side. The situation in Tennessee is a graphic illustration of men fighting friend, neighbour, and brother.

Jefferson Davis (1808–89), President of the Confederate States, 1861–5.

Maryland and Delaware were geographically northern states, but they were home to a strong secessionist minority. Neither left the Union because they were at particular risk from Union armed force. However, throughout the war the loyalty of both states to the Union was problematic.

Kentucky was evenly divided, politically, and so tried to be all things to all men and declared its neutrality. Shrewdly, Lincoln bided his time and eventually the pro-Union faction had a majority, and then Kentucky joined the war on the Union side. Notwithstanding that, many Kentuckians left home and fought in the grey of the Confederacy. Missouri was also divided and in effect was administered by two separate state governments. Thus, it was not able to join formally either side.

The principal aim of the Union government was to encourage the South to abandon secession and re-join the Union. It was hoped that the device to persuade the South was the 'Anaconda Plan'.[8] General Winfield Scott, the General-in-Chief of the US Army, proposed a blockade of all Southern ports on the Atlantic and Gulf coasts, and the control of the Mississippi River. By so doing, the Union would prevent imports and strangle exports to and from the South. The economic hardship and probably hunger caused would bring the South to its senses, and thence to the negotiating table. The plan was leaked to the press, but initially, it did not find favour with the Northern public, who demanded swifter action. The taking of Richmond would do to start with, and 'on to Richmond' became a popular catch phrase.

The rush to the Colours in both North and South produced vast numbers of volunteers with aspirations to be soldiers, but there was a serious dearth in men capable of being officers and able to lead. The US Military Academy at West Point was established in 1802, and St-Cyr, France that same year. The RMA Sandhurst is of similar vintage (1801). The difference between these officer training establishments was that the two European academies were supporting large standing armies, West Point was not. The output in trained officers from West Point was limited to:

> sometimes less than a dozen a year before 1861, all of whom were engineers. In 1861, there were 239 cadets at West Point, of whom eighty came from the South. Seventy-six of these resigned or were dismissed for refusing to take an oath of allegiance to the Union.[9]

There was a pool of graduates, many now in civilian employment, but insufficient to officer two armies.

It was pressingly urgent to commission officers to fill the command gap and attention was turned to doctors, lawyers, accountants and merchants – in fact, any educated, middle-class person prepared to serve. It was soon apparent that the skills of these professional men did not readily transpose into a capacity to command and events were to show that enthusiasm was not enough. The numbers killed in any engagement, in any war, are a simplistic reflection on the quality of the leadership of the dead. The US Civil War was to be no exception.

Notes

1. A *casus belli* is an act or event that provokes or is used to justify war and it includes direct offences or threats against the nation declaring the war.
2. General Assembly of Pennsylvania, 'An act for the Gradual Abolition of Slavery' (1780).
3. Grindal, P., *Opposing the Slavers* (London, IB Tauris, 2016).
4. Smith, A.F., *Starving the South* (New York, St Martin Press, 2011), p. 1.
5. Sandburg, C., *Abraham Lincoln* (New York, 2002), p. 228. The original work, by Sandburg, was *Abraham Lincoln: The War Years*, which filled volumes 3 to 6 of a six-volume biography. The first two volumes were published in 1926.
6. Hacker, J.D., 'A Census-Based Count of the Civil War Dead' (*Civil War History*, No. 57, Dec. 2011), pp. 307–48.
7. Keegan, Sir J., *The American Civil War* (London, Vintage, 2010), p. 34.
8. The Anaconda Plan was also referred to as the 'boa-constrictor', or 'Scott's Great Snake'.
9. Keegan, pp. 38, 48.

Chapter Three

Blockade of the South (1861–5)

On 17 April 1861, two days after Lincoln's call for his 75,000 volunteers, Jefferson Davis accelerated the move to war by inviting applications for Letters of Marque. The recipients of such a document would then be authorised, by Davis and his government, to engage and destroy Union ships.

This was a bridge-burning action, and predictably, it brought a swift and punitive response from Washington. Scott's 'Anaconda' idea was endorsed, and a blockade of all nine of the Southern ports was ordered. The aim was to prevent cotton, tobacco and sugar being exported and military supplies, not least food, from being imported.[1]

To impose a blockade on 3,600 miles (5,793km) of coastline required a major force and the US Navy (USN) in early 1861 was not that force. It was of a size and strength entirely compatible with the aspirations of the, then united, country. Its assets totalled eighty-nine hulls. They were:

Ships of the Line – 10
Frigates – 10
Sloops of war – 20
Brigs – 3
Store vessels – 3
Permanent store and receiving vessels – 6
Screw frigates – 7
First class steam sloops (screw) – 6
First class steam sloops (side-wheel) – 4
Second class steam sloops (screw) – 8
Second class steam sloops (side-wheel) – 1
Third class steamers (screw) – 5
Third class steamers (side-wheel) – 4
Steam tenders – 2.[2]

Across the globe, navies were making the change from sail to steam and from wooden to ironclad hulls. The list above reflects the early evolution of the USN, especially the last eight, steam-driven categories. The ships of the line were all sail powered, and except for USS *Vermont* (1848), were at least

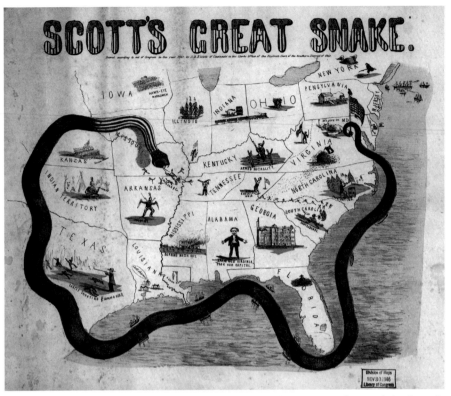

This cartoon map was created in 1861. The tail of the snake is wrapped around the flagpole at Washington DC. The head of the snake is thrust at the heartland of the Confederacy.

(J.B. Elliott, The Library of Congress/American Memory)

forty years old. For most practical purposes, large sailing ships were of limited use and increasingly obsolescent. Ships in foreign waters were recalled and merchant ships were purchased and converted into gunboats. By these means, the USN quickly expanded to 150 ships, with construction underway on a further fifty. By December 1861, the Union had 264 ships to enforce its blockade.[3]

The Confederate States Navy (CSN) was much smaller; it had taken control of any vessels in Southern ports but could still only muster about twenty assorted ships. The multiplicity of roles allocated to the CSN were to assist any ships breaching the Union blockade, the protection of Confederate ports, the defence of the Confederate coast and the repulse of invasion. This all-encompassing brief was far beyond the capability of twenty ships. The hope was that, in time, the CSN would take the war to the Union by attacking its merchant ships worldwide. The CSN was obliged to purchase vessels to supplement its navy and it sent emissaries to England to negotiate appropriate contracts. In the meantime, it was a case of 'make do and mend'. The results of this necessity were remarkable.

The sunken, wooden hull of the USS *Merrimack* was re-engineered. It was fitted with steam engines and armour plated. The result was the innovative CSS *Virginia*. This ship famously fought an inconclusive engagement with the USS *Monitor* at the battle of Hampton Roads on 8 March 1862.

The CSN was the first to design, build and send into action a submarine. This was CSS *Hunley*, which sank the USS *Housatonic*. It was pyrrhic victory because *Hunley* was destroyed by the same mine that sank its foe. Nevertheless, this was the first successful submarine attack in maritime history.

Historians are divided on the success of the Union blockade, and one view is that:

> in terms of closing off ports, capturing ships, and stopping supply lines, the blockade was ineffective. The very concept of closing off shipping on a 3,600-mile coast studded with inlets and inner channels, with a numerically insignificant navy, was a highly unrealistic goal and the Union could not accomplish it. For the first few years, there was virtually no blockade and the blockade runners entered and cleared Southern ports with minimal risks. Only very late in the war was it more effectively enforced, but by that time the war had basically been decided.[4]

This author refutes that view as simplistic and believes that the blockade must be judged on the result of the war upon which it had a major influence.

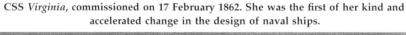

CSS *Virginia*, commissioned on 17 February 1862. She was the first of her kind and accelerated change in the design of naval ships.

Notwithstanding, it is acknowledged that the blockade was dismissed by contemporary sources. The *New York Herald* called Gideon Welles, Lincoln's Secretary of the Navy, 'a moron', the *New York Tribune* published its view that the blockade was a 'laughingstock', and the *Philadelphia Enquirer* stated that there was 'no blockade at all'.[5] The blockade of their ports was viewed in similar fashion by some Confederates. However, they did see it as being the ideal device that would cause both the UK and France to recognise the validity of the Confederacy as their trade was to be disrupted. This was naïve and took no account of the British commitment to destroy the ongoing slave trade and British rejection of slavery in all its forms.

There was an air of complacency in Confederate circles where it was perceived that all food was available in abundant measure and would continue to be so. It was thought to be inconceivable that supplies of wheat, corn, beef, sugar and rice could be affected, and on that basis, the Union blockade was dismissed from any logistic planning the Confederacy might be making.

The blockade had political and legal implications, not least for the trading partners of the Confederacy. Lord John Russell, the British Foreign Secretary, recognised the blockade as legal, in February of 1862, not because Britain believed the blockade was effective, but because she did not want to get involved in the war.[6] Britain, the paramount naval power in the nineteenth century, was well placed to assess the effectiveness of the blockade. The US Consul at Liverpool observed that:

> Members of Parliament, mayors, magistrates, aldermen, merchants, and gentlemen are all daily violating the laws of nations. Nine-tenths of all vessels now engaged in the (blockade running) business were built and fitted out in England by Englishmen and with English capital and are now [in 1862] owned by Englishmen.[7]

The disapproval of the US Consul will have carried little weight because this was a situation in which money was to be made on both sides of the Atlantic and a balance struck between 'risk' and 'reward'. It was the sort of judgement all businesspeople make daily – blockade running was just another business opportunity.

J.D. Gladney, an aide to Jefferson Davis, who did not share the complacency of some of his fellows, wrote a summation of Union strategy as he saw it. He commentated, with some prescience, that Union strategy was:

> To take our chief sea-coast cities … to cut off all supplies from foreign countries, get possession of the border states of Kentucky Missouri and Tennessee which are grain-growing states, properly belonging to the Confederacy: cut our railway connection between Virginia and the

Slaves using the first cotton gin, 1790–1800. Published in *Harper's Weekly*, 18 December 1869.
(Illustration by William L. Sheppard)

cotton states and cut the cotton region into two divisions by getting full possession of the Mississippi River ... By taking ... the sea-coast cities on one side [of the river] and the principal grain growing region on the other ... By commanding the Mississippi River, they expect to starve the people into subjection.[8]

It is germane at this point to look more closely at the economic health of the Confederacy. The territory was enormous and much of it was cultivated, but not to grow food. The two crops that drew the labours of the slave population were those of cotton and tobacco. These two products were aimed at the export market and the UK was a major customer for both. The invention of the cotton gin, in 1793, by Eli Whitney had speeded the process of preparing the cotton by removing the seeds from the cotton balls, a previously labour-intensive task carried out by hand. The quality of American cotton was internationally recognised, and the South thrived. The cost-free labour was the principal reason that, by 1860, the per capita income in the South was about double that of the North. However, the wealth being created was divided very unevenly and Southern society was stratified. The measure of wealth was slave ownership but the proportion of those living in the manner depicted in *Gone with the Wind* was miniscule.

The second social level was composed of white, rural farmers who lived off their land and cattle; some of them were slave owners. Below them there was a third level of poor white people who subsisted on what they could grow, fish or hunt. They were sometimes employed as field hands and worked alongside the fourth tier in the social scale – black slave families.

Someone once said that there are 'Lies, damned lies, and statistics'. However, as a basis of discussion, it was suggested that:

> in 1860, 1% of white Southern families owned 200 or more human beings, but in states of the Confederacy, at least 20% owned at least one and in Mississippi and South Carolina it ran as high as fifty percent.[9]

Perhaps the detailed arithmetic is of no consequence. Suffice it to say that the system was cruel, but it was fundamental to the domestic affluence of a significant proportion of the most prominent citizens in the newly formed Confederacy.

*   *   *

The agrarian South, having allocated its most productive farmland to cotton and tobacco, would have to change to accommodate wartime requirements and the growing of wheat given a higher priority. Wheat is a winter crop and after it is harvested in the spring, the ground can be reseeded with, for example, corn. However, it was necessary for the legislators to make the growing of foodstuff mandatory as many farmers were unaware of the urgency forced on them by wartime conditions.

In the event, in 1861 the Confederacy produced the largest amount of food in their history. Corn was particularly prominent, with the yield increasing from 30 million bushels in 1860 to 55 million bushels in 1861.[10] This bumper harvest was duly converted into bread and also used to feed livestock. The *Columbus Sun*, published in Georgia, summed up, saying, 'plant corn and be free or plant cotton and be whipped.'[11]

The feeding of livestock with grain is very inefficient use of a valuable commodity. The 3 to 4.5 kilograms of grain that must be given to a beast to obtain 0.5 kilograms of beef has about tenfold more calories than the half a kilogram of beef produced.[12]

In 1860, the USA slaughtered 3 million hogs, but of these only 20,000 were produced by the, soon to be, Confederate states, which imported 1.2 million annually to meet their needs. The political atmosphere in early 1861 was such that a meat-packing facility was established at Nashville to serve military requirements in the west.

Later, and despite a state of war existing between North and South, the two sides continued to trade with each other until August 1861. When this arrangement ceased, it served to highlight the enormous gap in available, salted pork and the requirement. The Confederate Commissary General, Major General Lucius Northrop, calculated that he would only be able to provision about a third of the 500,000 hogs needed per annum – and so the focus turned to beef.[13]

There were about 40,000 beef cattle in the South but, to put that into context, the Army of North Virginia consumed 1,000 of these a month and so they were a diminishing asset. By 1864, there were only 6,000 beasts left. There were practical difficulties. For example, the South had few slaughterhouses and few skilled slaughtermen. The beasts, when butchered, had to be salted, but salt was in very short supply. Once salted, the beef had then to be moved to the consumer, but the transport system was, at best, inadequate. The result was that good, salted beef often rotted in the sun while it waited for transport.

Notes

1. Moore, F., *The Rebellion Record* (New York, G.P. Putnam, 1861), pp. 1, 71, 78.
2. Register of the Commissioned and Warrant officers of the Navy of the United States, including officers of the Marine Corps and others, for the year 1861.
3. Massey, M.E., 'The Food and Drink Shortage on the Confederate Homefront' (*North Carolina Historical Review*, 1949), pp. 318–21.
4. Tans, J.H., 'The Hapless Anaconda: Union Blockade 1861–1865' (*The Concord Review*, 1995), p. 13.
5. Owsley, F.L., *King Cotton Diplomacy: Foreign Relations of the Confederate States of America* (Chicago, University of Chicago Press, 1959), pp. 239–40.
6. Tans, p. 15.
7. Price, M.W., 'Ships That Tested the Blockade of the Carolina Ports' (*American Neptune*, Vol. 8, July 1948), p. 201.
8. J.D. Gladney to Jefferson Davis, 6 August 1861 (O.R., Set 4, Vol. 2), p. 39.
9. Brown, A., 'What Percentage of White Southerners Owned Slaves?' (*The Moguldom Nation*, August 2020).
10. Smith, A.F., *Starving the South* (New York, St Martin Press, 2011), p. 31.
11. Gates, P.W., *Agriculture and the Civil War* (New York, Alfred Knopf, 1965), p. 16.
12. Collingham, L., *The Taste of War* (London, Penguin Group, 2011), p. 3.
13. Moore, J.N., *Confederate Commissary General: Lucius Bellinger Northrop and the Subsistence Bureau of the Southern Army* (Shippensburg, PA, White Mane Publishing Co., 1996), p. 59.

Chapter Four

Transport

In a country as vast as the United States the movement of people and goods was, and still is, fundamental to economic success. Getting goods to market was the name of the game; although the horse-drawn wagon remained at the heart of the transport system, the navigable rivers and canals were being increasingly exploited – not least by the Erie Canal.

The canal opened to traffic on 26 October 1825 and had thirty-four locks over its 363-mile (584km) length. The canal provided a navigable route from the Atlantic Ocean to the Great Lakes Basin. The economic impact of the Erie Canal was huge. It hastened the development of cities along its route such as Albany, Syracuse, Rochester, and most particularly, New York. Trade between the eastern states and the Midwest blossomed.

Users of the canal found that their transport costs were reduced by an incredible 95 per cent, because a mule could carry 250lb (113kg), but, when hauling a barge, that same mule could move 60,000lb (27,215kg).[1] The success of the Erie Canal encouraged a spate of canal building, and in the ten years from 1830, canal mileage increased from 1,270 miles (2044km) to 3,220 miles (5,182km). Most of this building was in the Midwest.[2]

Canals were expensive to build and maintain and topography limited their routes. The transport gaps were filled by the emerging new technology of the railway. In 1830, there were only 23 miles (37km) of track in the USA but, by 1840, there were 2,800 miles (4506km). On the outbreak of war, the North was served by 31,000 miles (49,890km) of railway. In combination, the transport systems fuelled the economy. Farmers were able to grow crops best suited to their soil and had the capacity to move their produce hundreds of miles to the point of sale. Manufacturers were able to develop markets miles from the production site. The development of canals and railways had 'rolled back the mighty tide of the Mississippi and its ten thousand tributary streams until their mouth practically and commercially is more in New York and Boston than at New Orleans.'[3]

The transport systems in the Confederate states had little changed in a hundred years, and if the North was on the way to being industrialised, then the South was by any measurement, agrarian. As both sides prepared for war, they each faced major logistic challenges. One of these was the need to find

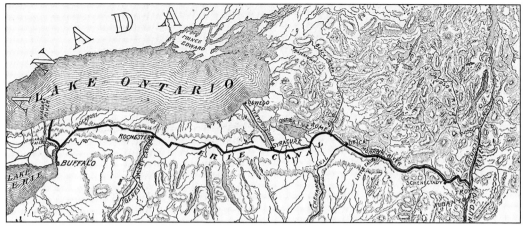

The Erie Canal, *c.*1840, which transformed the economy of the Union States. (*T.C. Clarke*)

the hundreds of thousands of horses and mules upon which to mount cavalry and haul guns, supply wagons, field kitchens and ambulances.

Transport is a logistic function and Winston Churchill, who was a seasoned soldier, remarked: 'victory is a bright-coloured flower. Transport is the stem without which it could never have blossomed.'[4] The great man will have drawn upon the American Civil War as an example that fuelled his stricture – one that has been proved to be correct time and time again and which certainly applied in this conflict.

The war was fought over a wide expanse of territory and the efficient, swift transport of men and materiel was, as always, a major factor in all military manoeuvring. The Mississippi River provided the South with a key supply line, notwithstanding its shifting sand banks and the difficulties they posed for navigators along its length. New Orleans on the Gulf Coast was the largest city in the Confederacy and was protected by several forts that were thought to be sufficiently strong to repel any Union advance from the Gulf of Mexico.

Control of the Mississippi was central to Union strategy. If achieved, it would isolate the fortress of Vicksburg and ensure the capture of New Orleans. Gladney had been correct in his supposition.

Within a year of the 'battle' of Fort Sumter, the North had 700,000 men under arms and the South approximately 400,000.[5] These huge forces had to be clothed, fed, sheltered, deployed and trained. The logistic burdens, particularly those of transport, were huge. But one man was to emerge as the master logistician, and he wore the blue coat of the Union. He was Montgomery Meigs.

He was a West Pointer and, of course, an engineer. Meigs was promoted to Brigadier General and on 15 May 1861, appointed Quartermaster General of the Union Army. He was obliged to accept the responsibility of supplying all the needs of the Union Army and was aware that the supply line only ended with the soldier in a trench or redoubt. The delivery of bullets, bread and bandages to this soldier was entirely dependent upon an effective transport

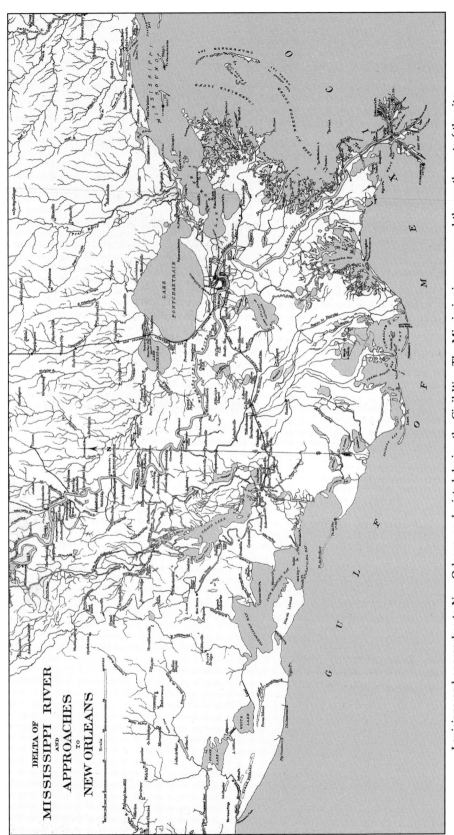

Louisiana and approaches to New Orleans, as depicted during the Civil War. The Mississippi runs around the south-west of the city, which faces Lake Pontchartrain to its north-east. (*Government Printing Office: Washington, 1904*)

system. Meigs started from scratch; his leadership ability, coupled with demonstrable hard work and complete integrity, were factors in his building a system that, arguably, made him second only to Grant as the winner of the Civil War.

The Confederacy had no equivalent to Meigs. History shows that all wars, with the exceptions of the second war in Vietnam (1955–73), and Afghanistan (2001–21), are won by the side which has the strongest logistic base. Eighty years later, General Omar Bradley would reflect sagely that 'amateurs talk strategy, professionals talk logistics'.

Meigs' contribution to the Union cause prompted James Blaine, a Republican politician from Maine, a member of the House of Representatives (1863–76), to remark that Meigs was:

Major General Montgomery Meigs (1816–92), Quartermaster General of the Union Army.
(Library of Congress)

kept from the command of troops by the inestimably important services he performed as Quartermaster General. Perhaps in the military history of the world there never was so large an amount of money disbursed upon the order of a single man … The aggregate sum could not have been less during the war than fifteen hundred million dollars, accurately vouched and accounted for to the last cent.

Notes

1. Clark, R.W., *Works of Man* (New York, Penguin, 1985), p. 87.
2. Tilden, A., *The Legislation of the Civil War Period* (Los Angeles, University of Southern California Press, 1937), p. 47.
3. De Bow, J.D.B., *The Industrial Resources of the Southern and Western States* (New Orleans, Office of *De Bows Review*, 1852), Vol. 2, p. 484.
4. Churchill, Sir W.S., *The River War: A Historical Account of the Reconquest of the Sudan* (London, Longman and Green, 1899).
5. Keegan, Sir J., *The American Civil War* (London, Vintage, 2010), p. 43.

Chapter Five

Cotton, Sugar and Salt

Initially, the Union blockade was an irritant to the Confederacy and it did not impact upon food supply to any marked extent; it did, however, affect the cotton trade. The quality of Southern cotton was universally recognised, and it accounted for about 85 per cent of manufactured cotton goods in the USA, Britain and France. In Britain, the trade had contributed to the advance of the Industrial Revolution, and it was a major contributor to burgeoning national wealth.

The Southern states were politically and economically dependent upon cotton, and after secession, cotton continued to provide the revenue for the purchase of arms. The Confederacy saw cotton as a diplomatic card to be played in influencing cotton-buying countries, not least Great Britain, then the most powerful nation in the world. The hope was that by cutting exports to Britain it would coerce the British into an alliance. The measure of the Confederate hand was that 77 per cent of the 800 million pounds of cotton (362,873,896kg) used in British mills was from the American South.

To kick-start its cotton diplomacy, the Confederacy, at great cost, burned about 2.5 million bales of cotton to create a shortage. It succeeded in that aim and exports to Europe dropped from about 3 million bales per annum to mere thousands. However, the strategy failed to consider the political judgements made by the British as they appraised the domestic strife threatening to overcome the USA. Similarly, the Confederacy was unaware of the stockpiles of cotton in Britain, built after the particularly plentiful harvests from the mid-1850s.

The artificial 'cotton famine', and the attack on the British textile industry, did not take effect until early 1863. However, when the impact of the 'famine' was felt, it had a deleterious effect on the global economy. The price of cotton rose from 10 cents per pound in 1860 to $1.89 per pound in 1863–4. The British found their cotton from other sources such as India, Egypt and Brazil.[1]

The Confederacy had not lured Britain into a formal alliance, but the two parties continued to trade, and cotton was one bartering tool that was exchanged for arms, ammunition and ships. The trade was made possible by blockade runners who made massive profits each time they breached the USN blockade. The normal practice was for the blockade runners to carry cotton to British colonies such as the Bahamas or Bermuda. Here the cotton was exchanged for the goods desired by the Southern states. This trade frustrated the Union, whose blockading was hampered by the lack of coaling stations and shipyard facilities. The last Southern port to be captured was Wilmington, North Carolina, and it was not until January 1865 that the blockade sealed off the South.

A Confederate ordnance officer considered that the armaments supplied through the blockade with 'cotton in payment' as 'being of incalculable value'. At the Battle of Shiloh, Confederate troops used weaponry and supplies conveyed from Great Britain by the blockade runner *Fingal*. During the war, an estimated 600,000 'pieces of equipment' were supplied by the British.[2]

It seems to be bizarre but, whilst the Union was fighting a savage war with the Confederacy, it was also trading with its enemy to obtain cotton for its textile mills. On that basis the Union's Treasury Department issued permits to those requiring to purchase cotton.

> The system was rife with corruption, particularly in the Mississippi Valley. Confederate cotton that was subject to confiscation by the North could not be distinguished from legitimate cotton grown by planters loyal to the Union. Cotton could be purchased for as little as 12 to 20 cents a pound, transported to New York for 4 cents a pound, and sold for up to $1.89 a pound. One observer noted that the 'mania for sudden fortunes in cotton' meant that 'Every Union colonel, captain, or quartermaster is in secret partnership with some operator in cotton'. The lure of cotton wealth would entice White Northern civilians and Union soldiers south during and after the war.[3]

The naval blockade of Southern ports had an immediate but patchy effect as blockade runners were able to penetrate the blockade with relative ease, although, at this early stage, they did not bring food. To keep its ships on station, the USN had to find new coaling facilities. Prime targets were Fort Hatteras and Fort Clark, both on the Outer Banks of North Carolina. These two installations were manned only by small garrisons and were assailed by troops commanded by the unpopular and ruthless Major General Benjamin Butler. On 28 August 1861, his troops were landed by ships of the USN and carried their objectives with ease the following day.

This modest victory helped to assuage the Union's earlier loss of the Battle of Bull Run on 21 July 1861, the first battle of the war. However, the measure of success at Bull Run was not in the head count, but the headlong retreat of the Union Army.[4] However, the Confederates were unable to drive home their advantage and assault a defenceless Washington, 'because there was not one day's rations for the entire army. The abandonment of the "onto

Washington" scheme is the first and quite probably the most important instance of the manner in which supply deficiencies shaped strategy.'[5]

Winning the battle for the Hatteras Inlet Batteries prompted the Union to repeat the process and it took Roanoke (7–8 February 1862), Elizabeth City (10 February 1862) and New Bern (14 March 1862), and a year later, Fort Pulaski (10–11 April 1863).

The Mississippi River figures large in the economic history of the USA and during the Civil War, control of the river was a military objective for both sides. However, until August 1861, traffic continued unhindered.

As there were few lines of railways running north and south during this period, the Ohio and Mississippi rivers were still the great arteries of commerce. In addition to the long-distance traffic, there was ample local trade along the rivers, the steamers often having goods for the small towns and plantations along their banks. The lower Mississippi and the Ohio rivers gradually became the most important highways for this type of commerce. Although grain was still being moved downriver, the railways and Erie Canal were drawing off trade. Cincinnati became the chief distributing centre for the Ohio Valley, and to an increasing degree, for the whole 'cotton south'. The effect was to increase the commercial traffic on the Ohio River.[6] The importance of the port of New Orleans, the largest city of the Confederacy, was consequently much reduced. Those living in the Upper Mississippi Valley, hundreds of miles from the sea, were less concerned about any closing of the outlet of the river but rather with any interference to the intra-valley commerce.

Before the secession of the Southern states, but as that became a possibility, there were strong feelings about the river; for example, Governor Yates of Illinois, in his inaugural address on 14 January 1861, asked:

> can it be for a moment supposed that the people of the valley of the Mississippi will ever consent that the great river shall flow for hundreds of miles through a foreign jurisdiction, and they be compelled, if not to fight their way in the face of the forts frowning upon its banks, to submit to the imposition and annoyance of arbitrary taxes and exorbitant duties to be levied upon their commerce? ... I know I speak for Illinois, and I believe for the northwest, when I declare them a unit, in the unalterable determination of her millions, occupying the great basin drained by the Mississippi, to permit no portion of that stream to be controlled by a foreign jurisdiction.[7]

These fears rang alarm bells and to allay concerns, on 18 February 1861, the Confederate Congress passed a law giving passage for goods free of duty.

This included practically everything that the north-west produced. In addition, everything that had previously been carried down the river in the intra-valley trade and before a tariff bill could be worked out, a free trade policy was proclaimed. This was a thinly disguised bid to win sympathy from the northern valley states.

Fort Henry and Fort Donaldson, both on the Tennessee River, were constructed in 1861 on the instructions of the Governor of Tennessee. Their purpose was to provide protection for the agricultural areas of Western Tennessee and the railways that moved the product of those areas to the far reaches of the Confederacy and to Nashville, its logistic heart. Fixed defensive positions such as these forts can at best only provide protection for their immediate area and they were little more than accommodation for the garrison-based troops. The presence of these two forts was militarily useless and both installations fell to Union forces, in February 1862, providing access to the 688-mile long (1,107km) Cumberland River. The Confederacy surrendered close to 20,000 men.

The Confederate logistic base at Nashville was evacuated but, incredibly, no arrangements were made to resite the veritable mountain of foodstuffs filling the warehouses. One must wonder why the food was not destroyed. Not so doing was a culpable Confederate own goal. Logistics do not necessarily win wars, but they can lose them with supply management of this quality.

The *New York Herald* wrote exultantly that the withdrawing Confederates had left behind 'an immense amount of flour, beef, pork bacon etc. which had been accumulating for the supply of a great army for a long campaign'. It follows that these huge losses would have to be replaced and the burden fell on the states of Alabama and Mississippi. The economic effect was to drive up food prices in accordance with the fundamental laws of supply and demand.

The Confederacy was confident that the defences of New Orleans would be able to repel any Union attack. The city's defence centred upon two brick-built forts, Fort Jackson and Fort St Philip. These were supplemented by fortifications along the banks of the river and a handful of ironclad gunboats. The city was sparsely defended by militia troops, but the situation changed when, in August 1861, the river was closed to traffic by the ever-tightening blockade by the USN. The flow of grain and food from the Midwest to New Orleans ceased, and during the following eight months, a siege situation developed. The situation became grave, and in desperation, Virginia was asked to send a trainload of grain daily to combat the famine that now existed. This was unreasonable and totally impractical.[8]

The Union determined to take New Orleans, and on 24 April 1862, a flotilla of eighteen USN ships, led by Captain David Farragut in command of the Gulf Blockading Squadron, arrived at the Mississippi Delta. Farragut's force with a combined armament of more than 100 heavy guns was a formidable threat. He engaged and subdued the two forts, and the Union flotilla forced its way past the city into the broad reaches of the lower Mississippi River.[9]

Farragut led his ships upriver and they occupied Baton Rouge on 5 May and Natchez five days later. By 18 May, he arrived at Vicksburg on the east bank of the river. Here he met determined opposition and although the first assault on Vicksburg failed, the lower Mississippi remained firmly under Union control.

New Orleans was occupied by Union forces and they were at once confronted by 'the starving people of New Orleans'. The famine conditions were attributed to the former city administration and some Northern journalists were unstinting in their condemnation.[10] Life in New Orleans was hard, and it became more so when Major General Benjamin Butler was appointed to take charge. Butler was a civilian masquerading as a soldier, and he was a stranger to compassion.

However, he raised regiments of exclusively black troops and trained them to fight; thereafter, escaped slaves flocked to the city. By late 1862, Butler had put in place a policy to confiscate or destroy agricultural activity, equipment and facilities in lower Louisiana. Levees were destroyed, plantations were razed, and all foodstuffs were seized. Union troops foraged across the state. Food production in Louisiana virtually ceased and a sugar harvest of 270,000 tons in 1861 had fallen to 5,400 tons by 1864.[11]

The closure of the Mississippi and the occupation of New Orleans and much of the Gulf Coast reduced the status of the white population and incentivised over 150,000 slaves to decamp and flee to the North, where many enlisted to fight for the Union. These were the very people upon whom Southern agriculture depended. Later in 1862, when even more trudged north, it initiated a collapse in agricultural production, the first stage in a famine.[12]

Salt is a prerequisite in the human and animal diet and up to 1861, consumption in the USA was an estimated 450 million pounds annually. Almost all of this was imported from Wales and arrived in the USA as ballast in ships employed in the cotton trade.

This salt was a multi-purpose product and used extensively in the tanning trade, where it cured the leather being fashioned into boots, shoes, bags and harnesses. When war broke out the need for leather increased, as did the need for salt. However, in a time before refrigeration, salt's prime use was the preservation of meat and:

virtually all pork and beef that was not cooked and served immediately after slaughter was preserved in brine. Salt was used to preserve fish, and other food, such as butter, had to be salted. Salt was used in cooking and offered as a condiment at the table. At the time Americans consumed more salt than any other nation in the world and more salt was used in the South that in any other region of the USA.[13]

The blockade cut off the consistent supply of Welsh salt and the stockpiles, in places like New Orleans, were rapidly reduced. Consequently, the price of salt soared and reached such a level that farmers were unable to preserve their maturing hogs. The carcases would have to be burned or buried. It is a constant that, whenever there is an unfilled demand, speculators flourish at the expense of their fellow man. A newspaper observed that:

> all the salt in New Orleans and elsewhere is now in the hands of speculators ... Something must be done in the matter and be done quickly. We are willing that speculators should reap a rich profit, but we are not willing for them to suck the very life blood out of the people if we can avoid it.[14]

The salt famine worsened, and strident voices demanded that some element of control be put in place to deter speculators and ensure a fair distribution of, what was now, a valuable commodity. The editor of Atlanta's *Southern Confederacy* made it clear, in May 1862, 'that we will be in a dreadful condition unless we get salt'. This was understating the gravity of the situation that forced Southerners to seek a home-grown solution. Salt was obtained from salt lakes, saline artesian wells, and seawater. However, salt from these sources barely scratched the surface of the problem because the demand was very large and by far outstripped supply.

> In December 1862, twenty women from Greenville, Alabama angered by the salt famine marched on the local railroad station shouting, 'Salt or Blood' and they forced an agent to give up the contents of a large sack of salt.[15]

This demonstration was well short of a riot, but it was indicative of the strong feeling that the deprivation of salt had engendered. In Florida, the extraction of salt from seawater was successful and almost enough was produced to meet the most pressing requirements of the South. However, Florida had no railway connections, and the transport of the all-important salt was dependent on horse-drawn wagons.[16]

A rich source of salt was discovered, in May 1861, on Avery Island near New Iberia. This was a salt dome and one of five similar domes on the

Louisiana Gulf Coast. This mine eventually yielded 10,000 metric tons of salt and it was a major asset until May 1863, 'when Union Colonel W.K. Kimball advanced to the beautiful little island, and without opposition, burned eighteen buildings, smashed the steam engines and mining equipment, scattered 600 barrels of salt awaiting shipping, and brought away a ton of gunpowder'.[17]

The USN made a specific target of salt-producing facilities in North Carolina and along the Floridian coast to such effect that Southerners were obliged to reduce their dependence upon salt. Seawater was used in cooking and more canned meat was eaten. Books and newspapers were published offering salt-free recipes. Salt recycling became a norm.

> Southerners collected and reused loose salt grains from cured meat. Troughs and barrels used for brining meat were dried and the salt recaptured. The floorboards of salt houses were ripped out, soaked and the brine boiled down to produce a little salt.[18]

The occupation of the Avery Island and New Iberia (about 21 miles (33km) from Lafayette) in Louisiana by Union troops had a serious impact on the inhabitants of Louisiana east of the Mississippi, who were said to be starving for the want of salt and salt meat. The phrase 'salt famine' came into common use. Efforts were made to slow or stop the rise in the price of salt but without success.[19]

The shortage of salt had led, inexorably, not only to a shortage of meat but also to a reduction in the working capacity of cavalry, artillery and transport horses. The absence of an essential electrolyte sapped their strength and led to sickness. Compounding the salt famine was the failure to exploit to the full the salt sources available and then to distribute the product efficiently.

The Union's grip-tightening blockade and its raids up Southern rivers aggravated the existing transport deficiencies in the South, which did not have the capacity to build new railways and rolling stock. It did not task blockade runners with the import of the equipment to enhance or expand the rail system. The railways that the South did have were poorly maintained and minor lines were stripped to provide spare parts. This served only to exacerbate the food distribution problem as vast stocks of food, awaiting distribution, rotted by the ton.

Southern roads were, for the most part, mere tracks. In wet weather, they became a quagmire and a major obstacle for horse-drawn traffic. Horses were getting weaker by the day and part of their burden had to be their own forage. The requisition of horses and mules for military service was at the expense of domestic agriculture. It can readily be seen that there was a series

The blockade runner *Advance*, flying the red ensign denoting British ownership, by R.G. Skerrett, 1899. (*US Navy Art Collection, Washington, DC*)

of associated factors stemming from the Union blockade that combined to put the Confederacy at a considerable disadvantage.

The riposte to the blockade was to make best use of the 'blockade runners', civilian entrepreneurs with access to fast steam cargo ships. This unregimented arrangement deployed about 300 fast steamers, which made an estimated 1,300 sorties through the blockade; of these, about 1,000 were successful. Those 1,000 shiploads pale into insignificance when compared to the 20,000 ships that had served the South in the four years before the outbreak of war.[20]

The USN was under unremitting pressure. Its ships, on constant patrol, required regular dockyard maintenance and frequent re-coaling. It faced an unarmed adversary that operated the fastest ships on the sea, many of which could move as fast as 17 knots – an amazing speed at the time. These blockade runners had a low silhouette, were painted in drab colours and were expertly captained. The loss of a blockade runner was seen by its owners as just a business expense, swiftly covered by the next voyage of a ship of similar ownership. Rear Admiral Samuel Lee, who commanded the North Atlantic Blockading Squadron from 1862 to 1864, became an important player whose most creditable exploit was to close, by blockade, Wilmington, North Carolina, an infamous haven for blockade runners.

Lee had forty-eight ships in September 1862, but by 1864, his fleet fluctuated in strength between eighty-four and 117. He deployed this larger force skilfully and in two lines. The function of his slower ships was observation; they issued warnings of the presence of blockade runners by rocket signals.[21] The faster, better-equipped ships would then pursue and detain the target.

Lee's success rate was impressive in 1861; only one in fourteen 'runners' were captured or destroyed, but by 1862, it was one in eight, and in 1865, the capture rate was one in two. The life expectancy of a runner was seven voyages, but that was still economically attractive. The wonder is that this aggressive naval activity did not provoke diplomatic anger or even retaliation. The presumption is that the Royal Navy was disinclined to involve itself when it was fully employed elsewhere in opposing the slavers.

Notes

1. Dattel, E.R., 'Cotton and the Civil War' (*Mississippi History Now*, July 2008), p. 1.
2. Mallett, J.W., 'The Work of the Ordnance Bureau of the Confederate States 1861–65' (Richmond, VA, *Southern Historical Society Papers*, Vol. 37, 1909).
3. Dattel, E.R., p. 2.
4. Eicher, D.J., *The Longest Night: A Military History of the Civil War* (New York, Simon & Schuster, 2001), p. 99.
5. Goff, R.D., *Confederate Supply* (Durham, NC, Duke University Press, 1969), p. 23.
6. Coulter, E.M., 'Effects of Secession Upon the Commerce of the Mississippi Valley' (*The Mississippi Valley Historical Review*, December 1916, Vol. 3, No. 3), pp. 275–300.
7. Reports to the General Assembly of Illinois, twenty-second session, 7 January 1861 (Springfield, 1861), p. 27.
8. Bergeron, A.W. ed, *The Civil War in Louisiana* (Lafayette, University of Louisiana, 2002), p. 92.
9. Farragut was promoted to rear admiral after his victory, the first admiral in the history of the USN.
10. *Harper's Weekly*, 6 June 1862, pp. 380, 383.
11. Pace, R.F., 'It was Bedlam Let Loose: The Louisiana Sugar Country and the Civil War' (*Louisiana History*, Autumn 1998), pp. 391–2, 396–8.
12. Litwack, L.F., *Been in the Storm so Long: The Aftermath of Slavery* (New York, Alfred Knopf, 1979), pp. 51–9.
13. Smith, A.F., *Starving the South* (New York, St Martin Press, 2011), p. 20.
14. *Daily Vicksburg Whig*, 15 November 1861.
15. Smith, pp. 20–1.
16. Ibid., p. 21.
17. Winters, J.D., *The Civil War in Louisiana* (Baton Rouge, Louisiana State University, 1963), pp. 231–2.
18. Smith, p. 22.
19. Lunn, E., *Salt as a Factor in the Confederacy* (Tuscaloosa, University of Alabama Press, 1965), pp. 43–5.
20. Tans, J.H., 'The Hapless Anaconda: Union Blockade 1861–1865' (*The Concord Review*, 1995), p. 30.
21. Merrill, J.M., 'Notes on the Yankee Blockade of the South Atlantic Seaboard 1861–1865' (*Civil War History*, Vol. 4, December 1958), pp. 389–90.

Chapter Six

Vicksburg, Gettysburg and Port Hudson (1863)

After two years of conflict, the increasing scarcity of food was affecting the operational effectiveness of the Confederate Army. On 23 January 1863, General Robert E. Lee burst into print when he wrote to his president saying that he was down to an eight-day supply of fresh and salted beef and: 'I am more than usually anxious about the supplies of the army as it will be impossible to keep it together without food.'[1]

Lee was obliged to send two divisions from northern Virginia to Suffolk in the south-east of that state, where food was more plentiful. One can only presume that it was thought to be easier to send the men to the food than transport the food to the men.

Soon after the outbreak of the Civil War, President Lincoln declared to his military advisors that 'Vicksburg is the key' and failure to capture this city meant 'hog and hominy without limit, fresh troops from all the states of the far South [for the Confederacy]'. Vicksburg was, indisputably, a vital logistical link to the resource-rich Trans-Mississippi. It was at Vicksburg that huge quantities of molasses, cane sugar, sheep, oxen, cattle, mules, sweet potatoes, butter, wool and salt were transported across the great river and on to every corner of the Confederacy. Some historians have argued that it was the Trans-Mississippi, not the Shenandoah Valley of Virginia, that was the true breadbasket of the Confederacy. It was via Vicksburg that critical war material smuggled through Mexican ports could pierce the Federal blockade and sustain the military needs of the South.[2]

The Confederacy enjoyed success in late 1862 against the Union Army of Tennessee, commanded by Major General Ulysses Grant. Despite the setbacks, Grant decided to lead his army south, through Louisiana, and with much of the Mississippi River under Union control, he had the confidence imparted by a firm, logistic supply line. Grant's intention was to land his army below Vicksburg and take the Confederate bastion from the south.

The details of this complex campaign need not detain us here, suffice it to say that, on 16 and 22 April 1863, Rear Admiral David Porter's fleet passed

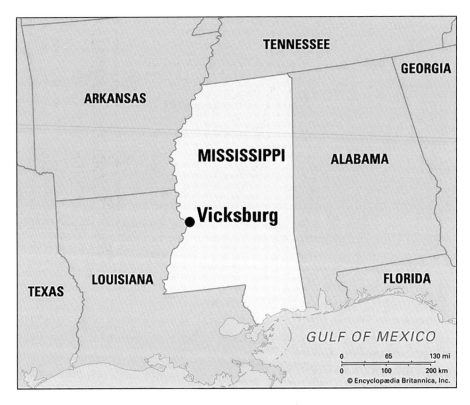

the formidable Vicksburg batteries and was able to position river transports to carry Grant's army across the Mississippi and allow the general to launch the decisive operation. Vicksburg was previously dependent upon the river and the Southern Mississippi Railroad as its supply lines but, by the spring of 1863, the Confederate Army was outmanoeuvred and out-fought by General Grant, who drove his opponent, Lieutenant General John Pemberton, and his army into the refuge of the city.

History shows that any general who withdraws to a fortress immediately cedes the initiative to his enemy and is then hostage to his logistic supply line. Vicksburg is just one such example, Metz and Kut are others, in which the besieged force had no logistic support and was eventually starved into surrender.

Pemberton had ensured that he drove all available livestock ahead of his withdrawing army together with all other foodstuffs that could be pillaged from the surrounding countryside. However, there was an abundance of food, so much so that some was burned because there was insufficient transport to move it into the city. The Southern Mississippi Railroad was still intact

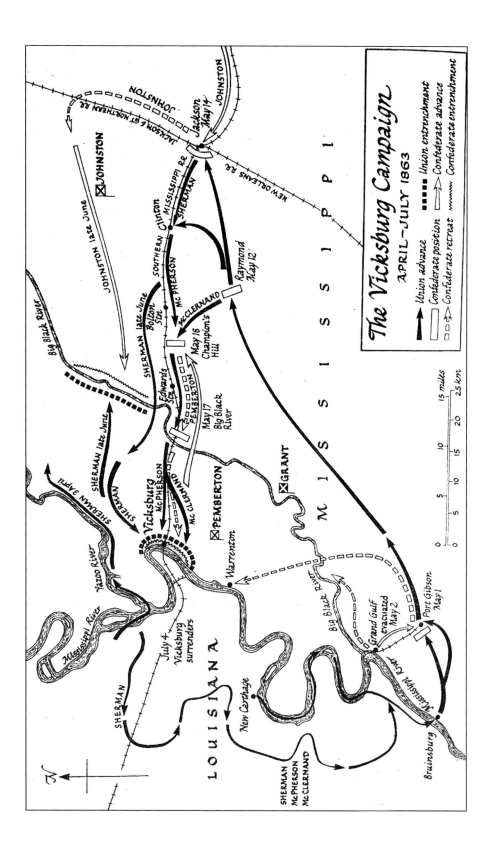

The Vicksburg Campaign
APRIL–JULY 1863

Union advance
Confederate position
Confederate retreat
Union entrenchment
Confederate advance
Confederate entrenchment

and provided a vital logistic link. The pious hope was that this railway, and the accumulated food, would provide succour until Vicksburg was relieved.

Unfortunately, the Confederate plans to march to Pemberton's aid were thwarted when, on 6 May 1863, the Union Army of Tennessee moved north-east, away from Vicksburg, in a bid to cut the railway. On this mission, the Union XVII Corps encountered the vanguard of the Confederate relief force under General Joseph Johnston heading for Vicksburg. There was an engagement, after which Johnston abandoned his plans to relieve Pemberton and withdrew. The railway line was cut, and Pemberton and his men were left to fend for themselves.

Vicksburg was a mighty fortress. The city stood on the steep Walnut Hills and the deep, wooded ravines along their flanks were a feature of the topography. The bottoms of the ravines were choked with dense under-growth and fallen trees. These natural abatis were enhanced with man-made abatis. Above these tangled obstacles, the rugged natural terrain was covered with well-designed earthworks.

In other settings, a fortress would clear its surroundings to provide line of sight and clear fields of fire. At Vicksburg, this was not possible, and the local conditions added to the 'defendability' of the city. The earthworks were improved and strengthened, artillery platforms were constructed, redoubts, redans, and lunettes built. 'These terms were all derived from the inter-national vocabulary of fortification science. Largely French in origin, which was taught meticulously at West Point.'[3]

West Point also taught that when confronted by a fortress, the infantry should advance to the outer defences and enter by storm. However, if that failed to resort to a deliberate siege, it should be accompanied by mining and bombardment.

Grant's infantry invested the city on 19 May and prepared to exercise the 'storm' option. He ordered an assault against the Stockade Redan for 19 May and committed Sherman's corps to the operation. It faced a daunting task, and as it advanced under small arms and artillery fire, the corps sustained casualties. The attack was swept aside, having achieved nothing, although 165 mothers lost a son. Recovering the 777 wounded from the difficult terrain was a further testing exercise. Inside the fortress, morale was high and the eight dead and 62 wounded had been a modest price to pay for victory. The Confederates, assumed to be demoralised, had regained their fighting edge.[4]

Grant's army started to 'dig in' around the 6½–mile (10.5km) perimeter. While Pemberton polished his already strong defences, he knew that the fortress was close to impregnable and well able to resist Grant's army, pro-viding that there was sufficient food to feed the thousands behind its walls.

Major General Ulysses S. Grant (1822–85), commander of the Army of Tennessee, later, commander of the Union Army, President of the USA (1869–77).

The capture of Vicksburg was an integral part of Scott's Anaconda Plan, and Grant, who had a numerical advantage with 35,000 troops, mounted a second assault on 22 May in a very sophisticated operation. This too was repulsed with heavy casualties on the Union side, and by assaulting a redoubt defended by 30,000 determined troops, Grant revealed poor judgement. Union casualties for the day totalled 502 killed, 2,550 wounded, and 147 missing, about evenly divided across the three corps employed in the attack. Confederate casualties were not reported directly but are estimated to have been under 500.[5]

Grant thought again. He decided, as had countless commanders through the ages, that besieging the city was to be preferred to yet another bloody assault. Later, Grant wrote: 'I now determined upon a regular siege – to "out-camp the enemy," as it were, and to incur no more losses.'[6]

The siege commenced on 25 May 1863 and Grant's troops were now dispersed along 12 miles (19km) of trenches. In Vicksburg, Confederate soldiers engaged in the customary pilfering – fruits, vegetables and livestock. This indiscipline created shortages and caused food prices to rocket. Food became scarce and civilian families subsisted on bacon and cornmeal. Salted mackerel was considered a delicacy, but stocks were soon exhausted.[7]

Food was readily available outside Vicksburg and Grant's army ate well. Inside the city walls, it was very different and despite the last-minute acquisition of a great deal of 'hog meat, some molasses, corn, salted beef and salt', there was insufficient food to sustain an army 30,000 strong and the civilian population of 4,600.[8]

Pemberton was confident that he could hold Vicksburg for six weeks, and in the event, his estimate was correct. Although Grant had settled into siege mode, he proactively pursued his aim of destroying the Confederacy elsewhere by sending Major General Francis Blair and his 2nd Division of XV Corps to wreak havoc in the agricultural district bordering the Yazoo River. Blair moved as far as 45 miles (72km) upriver, seizing or burning anything of use to his enemy.

This was the ruthless face of food denial as a weapon.

The Union force was not quiescent, and it bombarded the city constantly. Porter's gunboats provided additional firepower to the Federal forces, by lobbing roughly 22,000 shells into the

Lieutenant General John C. Pemberton (1814–81), commander of the Confederate Army at Vicksburg.

Confederate fortifications over the course of the thirty-nine-day siege – an average of 564 per day.

In the city, shelters were dug into hillsides and soon many lived a troglodyte existence, drinking 'coffee' made from sweet potatoes and wondering where the next meal would come from. Food stocks dwindled at an alarming rate. But then, 35,000 people eat a veritable mountain of food every day. The ration for a soldier consisted of 14 ounces of food per man per day. This was composed of 4 ounces each of bacon, flour or meal. The rest was made up with peas, rice and sugar. This was significantly less than the normal ration and the sickness rate reflected the debilitation among the troops.[9] On 12 June, the meat ration was halved, and that included the yield from slaughtered horses and mules.

Vicksburg did have a plentiful supply of one product – that was cowpeas, sometimes called black-eyed peas. These were ground into the consistency of flour and fashioned into 'bread'. When baked, the 'bread' was so hard that it defied the strongest jaws, and its inedibility ensured its hasty removal from the menu. Mule meat was relished by some but by no means all, although it was more attractive than the alternatives of cat, dog and rat.

Notwithstanding, Confederate Major S.H. Lockett commented that his soldiers ate rats, 'with the relish of epicures dining on the finest delicacies of the table'. Rats were hung, prepared and dressed in the market for sale along-side mule meat. The going rate for a rat was $2.50.[10]

From the middle of June 1863, the famine in Vicksburg was driving all the inhabitants to the edge of starvation. The people ate anything, they were exhausted mentally and physically, and inanition killed several. Cases of scurvy were noted. Discipline, in what was a civilian army, broke down, and men started to desert. These desertions confirmed to Grant the parlous state of Pemberton's force.

It was on 28 June that Pemberton received an anonymous letter. It was signed, 'Many soldiers'. It must have devastated the general because it read, in part:

> our rations have been cut down to one biscuit and a small piece of bacon per day, not enough scarcely to hold soul and body together, much less so to stand the hardships we are called upon to stand. If you can't feed us, you had better surrender us, horrible as the idea is … This army is now ripe to mutiny unless it can be fed.[11]

Pemberton had few options open to him. He was confined with plentiful munitions but had almost no food. The poor diet was telling on the Confederate soldiers and by the end of June, half were sick or hospitalised. In addition, scurvy, malaria and dysentery had reduced his effective fighting strength. Shoe leather became a last resort of sustenance for many adults.[12] A month earlier, Pemberton *could* have led his men from the protection of Vicksburg's ramparts and engaged Grant, but he did not. In late June, his soldiers were not only debilitated by hunger but also, apparently mutinous. The high probability was that, if ordered into action, they might refuse.

In Gettysburg, Pennsylvania, 1,047 miles (1,685km) away, the scene was set for one of the most significant battles of the Civil War, fought on 1–3 July. As Pemberton wrestled with his parlous situation in Vicksburg, he was unaware that the next week would, for practical purposes, determine the outcome of the war.

Pemberton wrote to Grant on 3 July and opened the negotiations for surrender. Grant sought unconditional surrender. However, he realised that this would generate the dilemma of how he was to manage, feed, accommodate and secure a vast host of 31,600 prisoners.

This was a situation to be repeated in many wars yet to be fought. The Prussians took 104,000 French prisoners when they captured the city of Sédan in September 1870; many died of the deprivation that followed. The British took 133,298 Italians prisoner in North Africa in 1941. The Japanese took 80,000 British prisoners in Singapore in 1942. The Russians took 3,060,000 Germans prisoner following Operation BARBAROSSA. Of these, 1,094,250 died in captivity. In every one of these cases, the prisoners gave the victors major logistic problems, the most urgent of which was food supply. The Japanese and Russians simplified the issue by starving their captives. This was not Grant's style. He was a tough negotiator but was nevertheless open to a reasoned argument. His subordinate, the 34-year-old Major General James MacPherson, suggested a solution that was pragmatic and innovative.[13]

MacPherson persuaded Grant to offer parole for all the Confederate soldiers. It was an offer that Pemberton was only too happy to accept. The conditions were entirely reasonable. Officers could retain their swords and one horse-drawn cart – the provision of the horse must have presented a difficulty as all Confederate horses had been eaten weeks before. The Confederate soldiers signed the parole papers, and a notable feature was the generous way the Union troops treated their defeated foe. They fed them and there was a marked lack of animosity. The paroled soldiers dispersed, many to their homes, but some, in violation of the parole, took up arms elsewhere.

With the benefit of 20/20 hindsight and given the success of the siege, one might speculate on the necessity for Grant to expend those 667 lives in his two abortive assaults. Starvation was a cheaper, effortless, and more effective weapon than gunfire. In effect, Grant had weaponised food and it had won him a great strategic victory. He correctly observed that 'the fall of the Confederacy was settled when Vicksburg fell'.[14]

When news of the surrender was promulgated, Major General Frank Garden, who commanded the now isolated, very hungry garrison of 6,340 men at Port Hudson, had to consider his position. He had been besieged for forty-seven days in Port Hudson, which dominated a bend in the Mississippi with its twenty-one heavy guns. In early 1863, the Mississippi River from Port Hudson, north for 200 river miles (322km) but only 137 miles as an energetic crow might fly, to Vicksburg was in Confederate hands. Garden reported to Pemberton and he, in turn, answered to General Joseph Johnston. That is a clear chain of command, but Garden had been subject to conflicting orders from his two superiors and that led to confusion.

Lieutenant Howard Wright of the 30th Louisiana Infantry Regiment was a member of the Port Hudson garrison, and he commented on the troops' diet:

the last quarter ration of beef had been given out to the troops on the 29th of June. On the 1st of July, at the request of many officers, a wounded mule was killed and cut up for experimental eating. All those who partook of it spoke highly of the dish. The flesh of mules is of a darker color than beef, of a finer grain, quite tender and juicy, and has a flavor something between that of beef and venison. There was an immediate demand for this kind of food, and the number of mules killed by the commissariat daily increased. Some horses were also slaughtered, and their flesh was found to be very good eating, but not equal to mule. Rats, of which there were plenty about the deserted camps, were also caught by many officers and men, and were found to be quite a luxury – superior, in the opinion of those who eat them, to spring chicken.[15]

General Robert E. Lee (1807–70), commander of the Confederate States' Army 1861–5.

Evidently, food was an issue but, by mid-June, it was not yet critical, although the garrison realised that the loss of Vicksburg had comprehensively altered their situation. The prospects of resupply and reinforcement were now zero. Starvation was just around the corner, and accordingly, Garden surrendered Port Hudson on 8 July. The Union was now firmly ensconced in the heart of the Confederacy, and along the Mississippi, its most potent weapon had been food denial.

Meanwhile, at Gettysburg, the Union, despite early reverses on the first day of the battle, had inflicted defeat on General Robert Lee's Army of North Virginia. The Confederate force was not well nourished, but food was not a factor in this epic engagement, in which 7,853 Americans died and there were about 50,000 wounded. It was the bloodiest battle in the entire war and seen by some as the 'turning point' and the herald of Union victory – although that was two years hence.

It was only when the defeated Confederate Army withdrew, on 4 July 1863, carrying many of its wounded in a mile-long convoy of carts that its supply situation became an issue. Nevertheless, Lee, the consummate general, conducted the fighting withdrawal, aided by the lacklustre pursuit of Mead's Army of the Potomac. The remnants of Lee's army lived to fight another day.

Notes

1. Smith, A.F., *Starving the South* (New York, St Martin Press, 2011), p. 27.
2. nps.gov/museum/exhibits/vick/significance.html.
3. Keegan, Sir J., *The American Civil War* (London, Vintage, 2010), p. 209.
4. Bearss, E.C., *The Campaign for Vicksburg* (Dayton, OH, Morningside House, 1985), Vol. 3, pp. 778–80.
5. Kennedy, F.H. (ed.), *The Civil War Battlefield Guide* (Boston, Houghton Mifflin Co., 1998).
6. Grant, U.S., *Personal Memoirs of U.S. Grant* (New York, Charles Webster & Co., 1885), Vol. 1, p. 612.
7. Carter, S., *The Final Fortress: The Campaign for Vicksburg 1861–1863* (New York, St Martin's Press, 1980), p. 76.
8. W.H. Johnson (a free African American and valet to President Lincoln) to Colonel L.B. Northrop, Commissary-General of the Confederate Army, 10 August 1863 (O.R. Ser. 1, Vol. 24, Pt. 3), p. 1052.
9. Smith, p. 102.
10. Ibid., p. 105.
11. Wheeler, R., *Voices of the Civil War* (New York, Meridian, 1976), p. 346.
12. Korn, J., *War on the Mississippi: Grant's Vicksburg Campaign* (Alexandria, VA., Time-Life Books, 1985), pp. 149–52.
13. Keegan, p. 219.
14. Grant, p. 281.
15. Wright, H., *Port Hudson: Its History from an Interior Point of View* [1937] (Baton Rouge, The Eagle Press, 1978), p. 51.

Chapter Seven

Civil Disorder in the South (1863)

After two years of war, the dearth of imported food, the destruction of Southern agriculture, the fleeing of much of the workforce, the demands of a large army and an inefficient transport system all combined with avaricious speculation in food stocks to produce a volatile mix that caused civil disorder in the South.

These, so-called, 'Bread Riots' were widespread and largely spontaneous. In Richmond, on 2 April 1863, somewhere between 'a few hundred and 5,000' women armed with knives, clubs and guns assembled at Belvidere Hill Baptist Church.[1] Their aim was to protest at their incapacity to feed their families at the prices now being charged for food. In the city, the wealthy were able to eat well, but these women were at the lower end of the socio-economic order, and for them, the present malnutrition was the precursor to starvation. Richmond was also the site of Confederate States Army (CSA) warehouses, and from here, the Army of North Virginia was victualled, but these women were, of course, precluded from this food source.

The women, under the direction of Mary Jackson, started to loot shops, taking food, clothing, shoes, and even jewellery. This was criminal conduct and unrelated to food. Order was restored by the militia, but the property stolen was valued at tens of thousands of dollars. Although there were no fatalities, several people were injured.

The incident in Richmond was the most significant, but elsewhere there was similar discontent. Four months earlier in Greenville, Alabama, a group of women had forced their way into a CSA depot and stolen sacks of salt. In Bladen County, North Carolina, six sacks of corn were taken by a group calling themselves 'regulators'. Five of the miscreants were arrested and convicted. A more serious incident occurred on 16 March, 'when about twenty women, one of whom carried a revolver went around grocery stores in Atlanta seizing bacon, meal and vegetables paying such price as they thought proper'.[2] There were many other examples of low-level felonies of this sort and the point does not need to be laboured. Suffice it to say that the situation worsened, disorder spread throughout the South and public confidence in the Confederate government was seriously eroded. The population of the

The looting during the Bread Riot. (Frank Leslie's Illustrated Newspaper)

Confederacy was experiencing the misery of food denial and the dearth of food was an increasingly negative element in their lives. Jefferson Davis implored the press not to publicise the disorder, but the press was not compliant and across the South, editors lambasted Davis and his ilk.

The reduced availability of food had caused many in the South to abandon their farms and plantations and seek sustenance elsewhere; an estimated 400,000 sought shelter in Southern cities, of which Richmond was one example.[3] This exodus further reduced food production but increased demand from the non-productive refugees. To make matters worse, the summer of 1862 was very dry and drought conditions prevailed east of the Mississippi. In Virginia, the wheat crop was only a quarter of the expected yield; Georgia, North and South Carolina were similarly affected.

It would take skilled management to counter this combination of unfortunate factors, but the Confederacy did not have anyone of the quality of Montgomery Meigs. Jefferson Davis had appointed an old classmate from West Point, Lucius Northrop, as his commissary general. Northrop was out of his depth, and he could not fall back on experience, because he had none in the leadership of large organisations. He had no background in either agriculture or food management. He was a well-meaning man and despite the logistic deficiencies that limited the operations of the CSA, Davis retained him in post. A diarist noted that Northrop was 'the most ''cussed'' and vilified man in the Confederacy. He is held accountable for everything that goes wrong in the army.'[4]

Several solutions, of varying practicality, that might ameliorate the food shortage were proposed to Davis, but he was implacable. He rejected any suggestion that, in a trade with the Union, cotton could be exchanged for food. Cotton was, in effect, the only card in the Confederate hand but Davis refused to play it. The *Daily Southern Crisis*, published in Jackson, Mississippi, commented bleakly: 'there is more to fear from a dearth of food than from all the Federal armies in existence – who can fight starvation with hope of success?'[5] The *Richmond Despatch* was specific, and it laid the ills of the South firmly at the door of food speculators. It thundered: 'the Yankees are monsters enough to starve us to death if they could, but they can't whilst speculators can and are doing it.' It continued, saying that speculators were 'rendering more aid and influence than all the combined armies of Yankeedom to accomplish the avowed purpose of this war'. This was in line with the views of Jefferson Davis.

The magnitude of the food crisis had only become manifest in early 1863 and the natural response in many quarters was to hoard whatever was available. Army quartermasters were particularly well placed to do that and Congress was passing legislations forbidding government officials (including military) from speculating in foodstuffs. The law was ignored, and some relatively junior officers made a great deal of money. A product of the scarcity of food was another rise in food prices. Price controls were imposed, but farmers hoarded staple goods and waited for further price rises. Price controls were dropped but rampant inflation followed.[6]

The Confederate government regularised the conduct of the CSA on 26 March 1863, when it legalised the practice of expropriating or impressing food where it could be found – in effect, foraging – and then paying the farmer perhaps only 10 per cent of the market price for his goods, or with a note assuring him of payment at some unspecified time in the future. The adverse effect of this measure was quickly apparent. The unforeseen consequences of impressment were a reduction in political support for the

> **BREAD RIOTS.**
> Bread riots, which the rebels were so fond of predicting in the early stages of tb national crisis, have indeed arrived; but, unhappily for the prophets, they are at their doors and not at ours.   In the very capital of the Confederacy, under the eye of Jeff. Davis and his accomplices in mischief, three thousand starving women have raged along the streets, broken open and sacked stores, and supplied themselves with food and clothing wherever they could.   A few weeks ago a similar disturbance was reported as taking place at Savannah; and a short time before the women of Atlanta helped themselves in like manner, presenting pistols at the heads of shopkeepers.   At

The *Lancaster Examiner*, 15 April 1863.

government, a spike in speculation, a slowing of the passage of goods to market and the hiding of foodstuff and livestock by farmers who only grew enough for their own domestic needs. The Confederacy recognised that it had to adapt to the situation and:

> in April 1863 it introduced a ten percent in-kind tax on agricultural products. The tax applied to foods produced during that season, which meant that it did not take effect until the fall [autumn] so it did nothing toward solving the army's immediate food problems. But the tax had the desired effect. Rather that accepting worthless Confederate currency for their crops farmers just gave a portion of their harvest.[7]

The weather was agin the Confederacy and persistent rain for forty-five days out of fifty wrote off the wheat harvest in Virginia. The impact was highly deleterious, and famine was being forecast in the press. The solution to this pressing crisis was not provided by blockade runners or the charity of foreign powers. It came from the Federal states, which cheerfully exchanged food for cotton. This commercial interaction became routine, and at the distance of 160 years, it seems bizarre that the Union, set on a policy of food denial on one hand, should act against its own best interests by providing food.

This commercial relationship was not universally popular and although there was strong opposition on both sides, it flourished, apparently to mutual satisfaction. However, the import of food from the North was too little and too late to offset the long-term deficiencies or to ameliorate the poor health of undernourished soldiers and civilians. Nevertheless, the consensus is that this trade extended the life of the Confederacy for many months and 'cost the country thousands of lives and millions and millions of treasure'. The trade was 'of greater advantage to the Confederacy than to the Union. For the South it was necessary evil; for the North it was an evil and not a necessary one.'[8]

Notes

1. Chesson, M.B., 'Harlots or Heroines? A New Look at the Richmond Bread Riot' (*Virginia Magazine of History and Biography*, 92/2, 1984), pp. 131–75. Smith, p. 49, refers to '*a few hundred women*'.
2. Smith, A.F., *Starving the South* (New York, St Martin Press, 2011), p. 50.
3. Gates, P.W., *Agriculture and the Civil War* (New York, Alfred Kopf, 1965), p. 26.
4. Chesnut, B.B.M., *A Diary from Dixie*, (eds) Martin, D. & Avery, M.L. (New York, Appleton and Co.), p. 97.
5. *Daily Southern Crisis*, 23 February 1863, quoted by Gates, P.W., p. 120.
6. Thornton, M. & Ekelund, R.B., *Tariffs, Blockades, and Inflation: The Economics of the Civil War* (Wilmington, DE, Scholarly Resources Inc., 2004), pp. 47–8.
7. Smith, p. 43.
8. Rhodes, J.F., *History of the United States from the Compromise of 1850* (New York, Harper, 9 vols, 1904), Vol. 5., p. 420.

Chapter Eight

The Confederacy Starves and the Union Triumphs (1864–5)

As the war entered its third year, the military writing was on the wall of legend. The Union, with its sophisticated industrial base, was logistically vastly superior to its Southern adversary. The Union forces were well clothed, armed and fed. The victories at Vicksburg, Gettysburg and Port Hudson had raised morale and the atmosphere in Washington was in stark contrast to that in Richmond. Union forces were now engaging Confederate garrisons in Kentucky and Tennessee and were opening a line of advance into Georgia. General William Sherman, who was leading this advance, was to write in his memoirs:

> The feeding of an army is a matter of most vital importance and demands the earliest attention of the general entrusted with a campaign. To be strong, healthy, and capable of the largest measure of physical effort, the soldier needs about three pounds gross of food per day, and the horse or mule about twenty pounds.
>
> When a general first estimates the quantity of food and forage needed for any army of fifty to one hundred thousand men, he is apt to be dismayed, and here a good staff is indispensable, though the general cannot throw off on the responsibility. He must give the subject his personal attention, for the army reposes in him alone, and he should never doubt the fact that their existence overrides the importance of other considerations. Once satisfied of this, and that all has been done that can be, the soldiers are always willing to bear the largest measure of privation.[1]

Food production in the North was complimented by an expanding railway system, which sped distribution and reduced waste and labour. The canning of food attracted innovators who adapted the manufacturing process, making the contents safer and cheaper. 'In Baltimore alone, the number of canning factories rose from thirteen in 1860 to twenty-five by 1865.'[2] The economy of scale made canned goods available and affordable for all.

Soldiers of all nations lived on canned food until deep into the twentieth century. The portability, long life and convenience of canned/tinned food was offset somewhat by the constipation that resulted from its extended consumption. Some enterprising entrepreneurs canned whisky and put a label on the tin purporting it to contain fruit or vegetables. This became so common that, especially in the USN, the authorities began inspecting cans as sailors boarded their ships.[3]

Gail Borden invented the process of condensing milk, which resolved a long-lasting scandal centred on contaminated fresh milk. His product was acceptable to the consumers and welcomed by the Federal Army. Borden won lucrative contracts with several government departments that made him a very rich man.[4] Improved transportation, the industrialisation of food processing, the mechanisation of agriculture, and superb organisation made it possible for the North to feed both its military forces and civilians and still ship a surplus to Europe during the war.

While the North's military suffered occasionally from supply difficulties, it was nothing compared to the privations of the CSA. General Lee's soldiers were starving and food deprivation across the South was further exacerbated by the ruthless way that Grant's formations conducted his scorched-earth policy, laying waste to Southern agriculture and food stocks.

General Sheridan reported to Grant that, within two months of his arrival in the Shenandoah in August 1864, he had:

> destroyed 2,000 barns filled with wheat, hay, and farming implements; over 70 mills filled with flour and wheat; have driven in front of the army 4,000 head of stock and have killed and issued to the troops 3,000 sheep.

He added that 'the valley from Winchester up to Staunton, 92 miles will have little in it for man or beast.'[5]

It was General Sherman who was the master of scorched-earth activity. During his famous five-week march from Atlanta to the sea, which started on 15 November 1864 and culminated in his capture of Savannah on 21 December, he cut a swathe 285 miles long (458km) of destruction across the state of Georgia. Sherman estimated that he had inflicted damage to the tune of $100 million ($1.8 billion at a 2022 valuation). Around 300 miles of railway (480km) were torn up and countless bridges razed. He seized 5,000 horses, 4,000 mules and 13,000 head of cattle and burned or confiscated just under 10 million pounds of corn and about the same amount of fodder. 'Sherman's raid succeeded in "knocking the Confederate war effort to pieces".'[6]

Sherman's march to the sea by Felix Darley (1822–88), engraved by Alexander Ritchie (1822–95).

Just over three months later, Jefferson Davis realised that the retention of Richmond as his capital was no longer viable. The city was set ablaze and 'thirty or forty persons' were killed when the powder magazine exploded.[7] The *New York Times* went on to comment:

> When it was made known on Sunday morning that the evacuation of Richmond was a foregone conclusion, the City Council held a meeting, and in secret session passed an order for the destruction of all the liquor in the city. Accordingly, about the hour of midnight the work commenced, under the direction of committees of citizens in all the wards. Hundreds of barrels of liquor were rolled into the streets, and the heads knocked in. The gutters ran with a liquor, and the fumes filled and impregnated the air. Fine cases of bottled liquors were tossed into the street from third-storey windows and wrecked into a thousand pieces. As the work progressed some straggling Confederate soldiers, retreating through the city, managed to get hold of a quantity of liquor. From that moment law and order ceased to exist; chaos came, and pandemonium reigned.

On 2 April 1865, Davis and his cabinet evacuated the city, soon to be a ruin. It was rapidly occupied by Federal troops and their embedded press.

Petersburg, just 24 miles (39km) south of Richmond, the main supply base and rail depot for the entire region, had been surrounded by Union forces

The ruins of Richmond, Virginia, April 1865.

for nine months. The fall of Richmond made retention of Petersburg impossible and General Lee withdrew to Appomattox. There, on 9 April, the Confederacy ended in surrender.

*   *   *

It is suggested that this was never a war between equally matched sides and given the circumstances, it is remarkable that the Confederacy fought for such an extended period. The Union was logistically, financially and numerically superior. It controlled the coast and increasingly, by a policy of food denial, the well-being of the enemy and its dependent civilian population. Food denial did not win the war for the Union, but it was a major factor in that victory.

The Confederacy plunged into a war charged with emotion but with insufficient thought to the practicalities. It suffered starvation, not entirely due to Union action but in part because of its failure to exploit its agricultural potential. In addition, it could not match the burgeoning and flexible transport capacity of the Union.

The emotions stirred by the Civil War were not quenched in April 1865 and the United States is, today, still beset with long-term social tensions. The young man, pictured above, one of 750,000, might wonder what he gave his life for.

*   *   *

In 1865, the guns were silenced, and an uneasy peace descended on the now reunited States of America. Prisoners of war on both sides were released but ugly truths started to emerge, and in the case of the Andersonville Prison, hunger was a root cause.

Andersonville was a Confederate prison that housed Union captives. It only operated from February 1864 until April 1865, and in that period, it accommodated up to 32,000 inmates at any one time. The prison camp (also known as Camp Sumpter) was not large; it measured about 540 yards (494m) by

260 yards (238m) and originally enclosed an area of about 16 acres (6.5ha). It was enlarged in mid-1864 to cover 26.5 acres (10.7ha). This prison camp had been established without any thought to the needs of the prison population or its management. The establishment was commanded by Captain Henry Wirz. This was a vast command for such a junior officer, and although he had experience of managing prison camps, this task was manifestly beyond his ability. Within three months of its opening, the camp was a veritable charnel house and a blot on the Confederate cause.

Robert Kellogg, a sergeant major in the 16th Regiment Connecticut Volunteers, recorded his thoughts on his first introduction to Andersonville on 2 May 1864 in these terms:

> As we entered the place, a spectacle met our eyes that almost froze our blood with horror, and made our hearts fail within us. Before us were forms that had once been active and erect, *stalwart men* [Kellog's emphasis], now nothing but mere walking skeletons, covered with filth and vermin … In the center of the whole was a swamp, occupying about three or four acres of the narrowed limits, and a part of this marshy place had been used by the prisoners as a sink, and excrement covered the ground, the scent arising from which was suffocating. The ground allotted to our ninety was near the edge of this plague-spot, and how we were to live through the warm summer weather in the midst of such fearful surroundings, was more than we cared to think of just then.[8]

The food denial tactics of the Union Army were keenly felt in and around Andersonville. The Confederate soldiers went hungry, and inevitably, so did their prisoners. The inmates were unable to make best use of what limited rations were available as not only was their distribution haphazard but there were no organised feeding arrangements in place. They were denied the wood needed to cook whatever food they were given. The prison was surrounded by forests. Wood, masses of it, was readily to hand but the decision not to provide it was inhuman. Andersonville was on the brink of a major disaster.

The inmates, suffering from malnutrition, were susceptible to a host of ailments. Scurvy became commonplace as there was a marked absence of fresh fruit and vegetables in their diet. Scurvy is absolutely avoidable, but it kills if the cause is not addressed. In Andersonville, it was not addressed, and it accounted for a growing number of victims. Military discipline started to break down and the prison succumbed to anarchy. However, a group of thugs who terrorised their fellows were brought to book by a further group who called themselves 'Regulators'. The miscreants were tried by an *ad hoc* court. They were severely punished and six were hanged.

Hunger was a constant issue and although an uncounted number starved to death, many did not live long enough to do so. The living conditions were so dire, so filthy, that disease was rampant. The sanitation arrangements, such as they were, contributed hugely to the loss of life. The water source was a small creek that ran across the camp. Wirz apparently made no attempt to protect this vital resource and it was used as the communal latrine. The men drank from this creek and ingested the faecal matter of their comrades. The predictable result was a very high incidence of dysentery and typhoid fever.

As 1864 drew to a close, the Confederacy offered to release prisoners unconditionally on the basis that the Union would send ships to retrieve them. This process started and it had the effect of reducing the death rate.

The prison was captured in April 1865, and Walter Whitman, the poet and essayist, wrote, of the skeletal survivors: 'the dead there are not to be pitied as much as some of the living that have come from there – if they can be called living.'

Wirz realised, in July 1864, that he was atop a social volcano and to ameliorate the situation he selected five Union soldiers and offered them parole. They were to deliver a petition, asking that the Union reinstate prisoner exchanges. His aim was to reduce the life-threatening overcrowding and relieve his charges of the insufferable living conditions. The petition was rejected. The parolees, who had given their word, returned to the prison and shared the grim news with their comrades.[9]

The combination of hunger, scurvy, typhoid fever, dysentery, exposure and hopelessness caused the deaths of 13,000 previously fit, young men.[10] They were buried without a ceremony in mass graves.

Wirz was tried, and despite a spirited defence, he was condemned and hanged as a war criminal on 10 November 1865.

Captain Henry Wirz (1822–65).

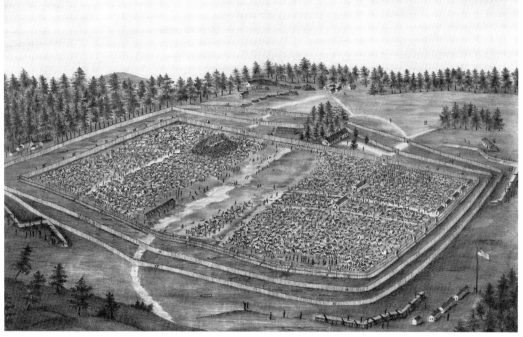

Andersonville Prison.

Summary

This long and ghastly war had ended, and wise men pored over the issues. One of the factors that led to the ultimate defeat of the Confederacy was the rate of desertion from the ranks of its army. In January 1865, one captured Confederate deserter estimated that 200 men were deserting Lee's army daily, 'partly due to the poor and irregular rations'.[11]

Confederate commander J.H. Duncan reported, on 21 January 1865, that:

> Desertions are becoming amazingly numerous ... the main cause for dissatisfaction is ... the insufficiency of rations. Our men do not get enough to eat. Unless something is done soon to remove this evil ... I fear that the number of desertions will be greatly increased during the winter.[12]

Lee, ever the realist, acknowledged the problem, and in a letter to the Secretary of War, he conceded that that the causes of desertion were 'the insufficiency of food and non-payment of the troops'. It is appropriate to give the final word to an American historian, and he judged that:

> From the first shot fired at Fort Sumpter on 12 April 1861 until the Confederate surrender four years later, food played a crucial role in the Civil War. While there were many reasons for the Confederacy's defeat, hunger is what tipped the scales in favour of the South's surrender.[13]

Notes

1. Sherman, W.T., *Memoirs of General William T. Sherman* (New York, D. Appleton and Company, 1889).
2. Smith, A.F., *Starving the South* (New York, St Martin Press, 2011), p. 82.
3. Collidge, R.H., *Report* (11 September 1862, O.R. Ser. 1, Vol. 19, Pt. 2), pp. 260–2. Quoted by Smith, p. 82.
4. 'Startling Exposure of the Milk Trade of New York and Brooklyn' (*Frank Leslie's Illustrated Newspaper*, 8 May 1858), pp. 353–4, 359.
5. P.H. Sheridan to Grant (7 October 1864, O.R. Ser. 1 Vol. 43. Pt. 2) p. 308.
6. Hattaway, H. & Jones, A., *How the North Won: A Military History of the Civil War* (Urbana, University of Illinois Press, 1983), p. 655.
7. *New York Times*, 4 April 1865.
8. Kellogg, R.H., *Life and Death in Rebel Prisons* (Hartford, CT, L. Stebbins, 1865).
9. Linder, D., 'Scopes Trial Home Page', UMKC School of Law (http://law2.umkc.edu/faculty/projects/ftrials/scopes/scopes.htm).
10. 'Camp Sumpter/Andersonville Prison', US National Park Service (https://www.nps.gov/ande/learn/historyculture/camp_sumter.htm).
11. Smith, p. 202.
12. Lonn, E., *Desertion during the Civil War* (Lincoln, University of Nebraska Press, 1998), p. 13. Power, T., *Lee's Misérables: Life in the Army of Northern Virginia from Wilderness to Appomattox* (Chapel Hill, University of North Carolina Press, 1998), pp. 236, 308.
13. Smith, p. 203.

PART TWO

THE FRANCO-PRUSSIAN WAR

Chapter Nine

The Franco-Prussian War
(1870–1)

In Europe, events in America between 1860 and 1861 had been observed with interest, but only those with any financial commitment were affected. The cotton famine was 3,000 miles (4,800km) and a lifetime away, just a fading memory. The focus now was on the *Exposition Universelle d'art et d'industrie de 1867*, to be held in Paris.

Paris considered itself to be the centre of the world in 1867, and at the time, it probably was. It was undeniably chic, sophisticated, elegant and exciting – at least for some. Emperor Louis Napoleon III reigned, and it was his ambition that the world and his wife should come to Paris to marvel at the wonders of the age. Most nations had a pavilion to display their wares and accomplishments. The British sent a state-of-the-art steam locomotive. The USA displayed a Military Field Ambulance, having developed some expertise in that area. The Prussians offered for public approval Herr Krupp's new, steel field guns.

Louis, the expansive host, invited foreign soldiers to view the defences of Paris and arranged tours of the massive fortifications that ringed the city, then home to 2 million citizens. Prussian officers took a particular interest in the tours and made notes.

The exposition was a success, it enhanced the image of France, and it fuelled the ambition and hubris of the emperor. He was described as having 'outrageous audacity and great personal courage [that] wrestled with timidity, astuteness with almost incredible fallibility'.[1] He was, perhaps, a mixture of Machiavelli and Don Quixote.

The success of the exposition fed the ambition of Louis Napoleon, who harboured aspirations to be the military overlord of mainland Europe. He was painfully aware that Prussia, ruled by Kaiser Wilhelm, advised by his chancellor, Otto von Bismarck, was a major obstacle, as was the Chief of Staff of the Prussian Army, General (later Field Marshal) Helmuth Karl Bernhard Graf von Moltke. Moltke was a man ahead of his time. He had created, in Prussia, a professionally adept, flexible, modern army, and formed the first General Staff in which officers, the best of the best, were rigorously schooled in all aspects of the conduct of war. They were expert in logistic management,

Louis Napoleon III (1808–73), the last emperor of France, photographed in 1872.

and not least, the supply and distribution of food. Moltke had produced an elite, unmatched in the world. He led an army that had been tested and won a stunning victory when it defeated Austria in the 'Seven Weeks War' in 1866. This victory had established Prussia as the dominant German state. It was also a force to be reckoned with in wider European politics.

Students of military history will have noted that it is always politicians, not soldiers, who start wars. Men who hold high political or constitutional office often have an interest in military affairs, but few have commanded large formations in the field. The exceptions who spring to mind are Ulysses Grant, Dwight Eisenhower, and Tōjō Hideki. Many others with brief, low-level military service dabble in their country's military activities, Adolf Hitler, Winston Churchill and Vladimir Putin among them. Louis Napoleon III was of that same ilk.

In 1866, and following the Prussian success in Austria, the French Army calculated the military strength of Prussia to be 1.2 million strong and that of France 288,000.[2] Following this meeting, Louis Napoleon sought parity but settled for an army of 1 million. This host had still to be recruited, trained, clothed, accommodated and fed. The building of the larger French Army took time and in the face of public opinion and political opposition, but by 1870, the task was, ostensibly, completed.

Napoleon quite correctly viewed Prussia as a threat but there were no major issues that provided a *casus belli*. Then, fortuitously, the occupation of the Spanish throne arose. It was a minor issue, but France decided to challenge the occupant proposed by Bismarck, a Prince Leopold of Sigmaringen.

There was posturing on both sides, and early moves to mobilisation, during which the candidate for the throne withdrew. This was a diplomatic win for France, but it went too far when the French ambassador, Count Vincent Benedetti, irritated King Wilhelm of Prussia by insisting that Prince Leopold's candidature never be renewed. The rhetoric got louder, and Louis Napoleon perceived that the situation suited his needs.

France had a numerically strong army but, to the shrewd observer, it was evident that it was not a match for the armed might of Prussia. In the face of common sense, subject to absurd hubris, in an act of the utmost military lunacy, and without any adequate logistic plan, Napoleon declared war on Prussia on 19 July 1870.

The French Army was equipped with the excellent breach-loading *Chassepôt* rifle and the *mitrailleuse* machine gun, but its logistic deficiencies were overwhelming. The problem lay in the lack of horses and every sort of transport. Many vehicles, when they were brought out of store, were found to be unusable and corps commanders had to rely on local purchases to fill the gap. Medical equipment and medications were stored centrally, and distribution was tardy in the extreme. The campaign was well advanced before ambulances were available. The French soldiers were expected to live in the field in the inadequate, two-man tents (*tents-abri*). There were insufficient cooking pots. Incredibly, there were no maps and officers had to scour bookshops and schools seeking atlases. To add to the mix there was no money to pay the soldiers.[3] All in all, this was gross incompetence of heroic proportions, and it set the scene for a succession of heavy French defeats once battle was joined.

The French took the city of Saarbrucken in August 1870. It was thinly defended, of no military importance, and the victors then withdrew behind their frontier. Thereafter, the Prussians invaded France and inflicted a succession of defeats on the French at Wissembourg, Spicheren, Froeschwiller, Colombey and Vionville. At Borny, the result was inconclusive. Nevertheless, the Prussian advance had been checked, albeit temporarily. For Louis Napoleon III, it was all going horribly wrong and it rapidly got worse.

Hitherto, Marshal François Bazaine, commanding the Army of the Rhine, had avoided defeat but, when engaged between Gravelotte and St Privat, on 18 August, his army was faced by the Prussian 2nd Army commanded by Prince Frederick Karl (known as 'Charles'). The Prussian force was supplemented by the 1st Army under the command of General Karl Friedrich von Steinmetz.

In the area of Gravelotte, Marshal Bazaine occupied a strong position, but he was outflanked on his left and the ferocious fighting which ebbed and flowed eventually centred on St Privat. Here, there was ferocious, hand-to-hand fighting around the village cemetery in which the Prussians eventually gained the upper hand.

Bazaine withdrew his 154,481-strong army to the sanctuary of the fortress city of Metz. It was a serious mistake. His army was badly bruised but not vanquished. However, he had ceded the initiative to the Prussians and never regained it. The city was promptly surrounded and a state of siege existed from 19 August.

Prince Frederick Karl of Prussia (1828–85), commander of the Prussian 2nd Army.

General Karl Friedrich von Steinmetz (1796–1877), commander of the Prussian 1st Army.

Bazaine was an unusual man. He started his military life in 1831 as a fusilier in the ranks. He was commissioned in 1835 and went on to rise to the very pinnacle of the French Army. He had campaigned for years, with modest success, but his investment at Metz exposed him to a series of pressures with which he could not cope. The Prussian 1st and 2nd armies, 168,435 men, swarmed around the city, dug in and awaited developments.

Meanwhile, on 17 August, the 130,000-strong French Army of Châlons was formed and its command was given to General (later Marshal) Patrice de MacMahon. The emperor accompanied the army as it marched to relieve Bazaine. However, on the way, it was halted by the Army of the Meuse under the Crown Prince of Saxony and the Prussian 3rd Army at Beaumont. The Army of Châlons retreated, in bad order, to Sédan and was deployed on the high ground behind the city.

It was an unsatisfactory arrangement and Major General August-Alexandre Ducrot, a corps commander, remarked to de MacMahon, '*Nous sommes dans un pot de chambre, et nous y serons emmerdés.*'[4] This might be translated as: 'We are in a chamber pot and now they are going to shit on us.' Ducrot was coarse, concise, and correct.

The juxtaposition of Sédan and the Iges peninsula. (*Howard, 2001*)

Moltke confronted de MacMahon, and so confident was Moltke in a forth-coming victory that he arranged for political, diplomatic and military digni-taries to view, from high ground on the other side of the river, his artillery barrage on a concentrated French target.

The Prussian gunnery was devastating. The loss of 3,220 French lives with a further 14,811 wounded obliged the French, now commanded by Baron Emmanuel Félix de Wimpffen (de MacMahon having been wounded), to surrender on 2 September 1870. The Prussians took 104,000 prisoners, 1,000 wagons, 6,000 horses and 419 guns.[5] Louis Napoleon III was captured and taken to Prussia as a prisoner of war. The impact on the French nation was immense, and with no emperor, the monarchy fell, and was swiftly replaced in Paris by a republican form of government.

The French prisoners were moved to a temporary camp in the loop of the Meuse on the Iges peninsula (*see* page 63). The captors were unprepared for such a large bag of prisoners and were overwhelmed by the logistic burden that they presented. The area of the camp was low-lying, and the autumn weather was inclement. There was no cover, no cooking equipment and very little food. This was not food denial, but it was food unavailability. The Prussians sought to ameliorate the situation, but it took time.

It is argued, by some, that the fall of Sédan was the single issue that decided the result of the war. However, at Metz, a well-equipped, rested French Army was a potent tool available to wrest the initiative back. Morale in Metz was damaged when, from the ramparts, long columns of French prisoners, ex Sédan, were marched past. Some were released to pass on the bad news to the besieged.[6] Despite this, an officer wrote: 'we were all ready to resume the campaign.'[7] He was one of many frustrated at the inaction of the commander.

The Army of the Rhine, incarcerated in Metz, needed a robust, innovative, and capable leader – but it had Bazaine. He was not merely lacking in talent. His incompetence was supplemented by indecisiveness and a lack of urgency. How he had risen to the top of the French Army by 1870 was inex-plicable then, and remains so today.

Notes

1. Horne, A., *The Fall of Paris: The Siege and Commune, 1870–71* (London, Macmillan, 1965), p. 4.
2. Figures presented by General de Castelnau to a meeting convened by Louis Napoleon III on 11 September 1866.
3. Bazaine-Leboeuf, 30 July 1870 (*Guerre* III), p. 49.
4. Sarazin, C., *Récits sur la Dernière Guerre Franco – Allemande* (Paris, 1887), pp. 114–15.
5. Howard, M., *The Franco-Prussian War* [1961] (Abingdon, Routledge, 2001), p. 222.
6. Wawro, G., *The Franco-Prussian War: The German Conquest of France in 1870–1871* [2003] (New York, Cambridge University Press, 2010), p. 240.
7. Patry, L., *La guerre telle qu 'elle est* [1897] (Hachette Livre, BNF, 2014), p. 16. Quoted by Wawro p. 43.

Chapter Ten

The Siege of Metz
(1870)

The fall of Sédan released sufficient troops for King Wilhelm I, accompanied by General Moltke, to march on Paris, and the city was invested on 19 September 1870. General (later Field Marshal) von Blumenthal was given command of the besieging troops.

France was now in a dire situation. Its effectively self-appointed government had relocated to Tours and there the nominal head of this government was Léon Gambetta. He was a capable politician, but no soldier. Nevertheless, he raised armies to confront the Prussians but made the mistake of directing operations. He was aided by his acolyte Charles de Freycinet, to the fury of the few competent generals available to him.

The Franco-Prussian war now hinged on the two besieged cities of Paris and Metz. In the latter, the Army of the Rhine was expected to break out and relieve the siege of Paris. However, in Metz, conditions for the French were bad, and after a month of siege conditions, they were getting worse. Initial calculations of the food stocks were inaccurate, and the presence of the entire Army of the Rhine limited the survivability of the fortress.

Moltke was applying a food denial strategy on both Paris and Metz, and in Metz, it was already having a deleterious effect on morale, discipline and health. Earlier, on 26 August, when advised of the approach of de MacMahon, Bazaine had issued orders for an offensive on the east bank of the Moselle. To move a large body of troops from a congested city required high-grade staff work to commit the units in the desired order with the appropriate logistic support. In this case, no attempt was made to coordinate movement over the Moselle bridges and no bridging equipment was carried to enable the army to negotiate rivers on its way.[1] The evening before the operation, two senior officers warned the commander of the lack of preparation and the consequence of failure. The next morning, at 0400 hrs, it was raining hard when the hungry soldiers set off. At that point, Bazaine cancelled the operation. It is difficult to move an army and even more so to reverse it, in the dark and torrential rain. Total chaos reigned. It is not difficult to imagine what the soldiers thought and said!

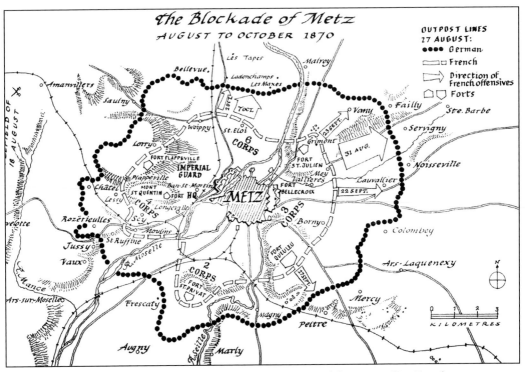

The French-held trench line around the city, and that of the surrounding Prussians. Most of Bazaine's forays (open arrows refer) were to the east but, for many of his force, it involved a crossing of the Moselle.

It was decided to try again, and a new operation was launched on 31 August; it is now known as the Battle of Noisseville. The planning was a little better, but it availed the French nothing because the Prussians repelled the assault, which cost the French 3,379 soldiers and 145 officers. It had been hard fought and the Prussians did not escape lightly, losing 2,850 soldiers and 126 officers. Thereafter, there were several low-level, local and abortive French forays, on 22, 23 and 27 September and 7 October. The breakout on 7 October was the most significant. It led to the Battle of Bellevue, in which the French were defeated, with a loss of 1,257 soldiers and sixty-four officers. Prussian losses were a little higher, but they still held the ground and continued to deny food to the beleaguered enemy.

On 23 September, an anonymous soldier, certainly an officer and probably of middle rank, wrote to Bazaine, delivered the letter to his door, and slipped away. The letter was preserved in the French National Archives, and one wonders why Bazaine did not destroy it, because it was damning. It read:

You are aware of the rumours coursing through the army with regard to your inaction in the face of the enemy over the past twenty-two days … This inaction has ruined our cavalry and will soon ruin our artillery which will reduce our army to impotence. The tragedy at Sédan and the army's continued ignorance as to the plans of its generals, makes it susceptible to the rumour that it is being prepared for delivery *pieds et poings* [feet and fists] to the enemy. And yet the enemy outside is inferior to us in every way; you must be aware of that fact. Surrender the army to the enemy when you have 130,000 elite troops in hand, it is unthinkable.[2]

This letter (shades of Vicksburg) had no discernible effect on Bazaine, although his soldiers were committed to aggressive action on 27 September and again on 7 October. Famine was now the spectre that haunted the demoralised garrison in Metz. Rations had been gradually reduced, food prices in the local shops had risen to levels far beyond any except the wealthy, and none of these were soldiers. Inexplicably, when the hay and oats provisioned for the horses was consumed, Bazaine ordered that wheat be fed to the animals. The beasts then ate the entire bread supply in a single sitting.[3]

These horses were being slaughtered at the rate of forty per day. They were the only source of meat. The effect of this was to reduce the transport capacity of the Army of the Rhine and thus its mobility. By 20 September, half of the horses had been eaten, but horsemeat alone does not make for a healthy diet. The need for food was overwhelming, and in the foray of 23 September, 200 French soldiers were killed attempting to gather potatoes. The Army of the Rhine was wasting away, it was without purpose and its only aim, by late September 1870, was survival.

The effects of famine were glaringly evident. Weapons went uncleaned and officers unsaluted. Typhus and smallpox appeared and relations between the military and civilians broke down. The fortress held thousands of men wounded in previous engagements; their care did not include nourishing food and malnutrition hastened the death of uncounted hundreds.

The situation beyond the walls of Metz was not easy for the Prussians either. The weather was now cold and wet. Winter in this part of the world is harsh, and that was just around the corner. There had been 197,326 fit and active Prussians when the siege commenced on 19 August, but a month a later, about a quarter of those men had no tentage. They existed in the open in wet clothes and slept under wet blankets. The impact was to swell the sick list. There were 22,090 men ill with gastric flu and typhus; of these, 1,328 died. A further 27,959 suffered from dysentery and 829 died. In addition, the wounded from previous engagements had to be kept under cover and treated. Local village houses were seized and used as hospitals. The feeding of this mass, distributed in penny packets over a large area, was a logistic problem.[4]

It is not relevant to a text exploring food denial, but it is germane to note the political significance of Marshal Bazaine. Bismarck was loath to negotiate with the Government of National Defense (GND, *Gouvernement de la Défense nationale*), which was, briefly, the first government of the Third Republic of France. This body was formed to fill the gap left by the absence of Louis Napoleon, captured at Sédan. It was representative of Paris but not of France and it functioned, after a fashion, between 4 September 1870 and 13 February 1871 while Paris was under siege.

Bazaine was a Bonapartist by conviction; he did not recognise or owe any allegiance to the GND. In the eyes of some, he was the only choice to re-establish the monarchy. Bismarck viewed him as the only legitimate representative of France. Predictably, Bazaine warmed to such an idea and conducted himself accordingly. Space does not permit detailed discussion of the political machinations of September/October 1870, other than to say that they availed France, Prussia, Bazaine and Bismarck nothing.

Meanwhile, the Army of the Rhine continued to starve.

Bazaine now had no other option but capitulation, although he still had the opportunity to preserve his dignity and that of his army. He had spent a lifetime in the army and had been imbued with its standards and its culture. Inexplicably, Bazaine, in this moment of defeat, ordered his regiments to surrender their Colours to the Prussians – Wawro refers to these as 'flags'.[5] They were so very much more than just 'flags'. The Colours were the embodiment of the regiment's soul. They reflected the regiment's service and sacrifice, and they were treasured. In the British Army the Colours are presented by the sovereign and are revered and saluted. They are never destroyed but 'laid up' in a place of worship until they disintegrate with age. It was similar in the French Army then, and no doubt still is.

Bazaine's aberrational order, coming after weeks of misery and starvation, raised white-hot anger among the regimental commanders, many of whom burned their Colours rather than comply. To a civilian it may all seem to be a bit over the top, but Bazaine was probably at physical risk from his officers at this point. Later, Bazaine claimed that the Colours were demanded by Prince Frederick Charles, and he had no choice. Nevertheless, this issue alone earned Bazaine the unbridled contempt of tens of thousands. One hundred and fifty years later, Colours are not carried into battle but their importance to those who have them is unchanged.

Bazaine had 600 guns in his fortress, and notwithstanding the imprecations of his officers, he did not spike them but directed that they be handed over to the enemy in good order. A significant number of soldiers considered this order to be treasonous and they rioted. Somewhat illogically, they set fire to the cathedral.

Prince Charles Frederick, ever the gentleman, offered Bazaine the opportunity to surrender with full military honours. This would have entailed

Bazaine parading his men, officers mounted, if they could find a horse. Then, with bands playing, the Army of the Rhine, *with its arms* would march to the Prussian lines. With singular ill grace, Bazaine declined the courtesy. He made a number of weak excuses after the event. 'It is hard to avoid the conclusion that his real fears were for himself, the leader whom the troops had barely seen since the beginning of the siege and whose incompetence had betrayed them.'[6]

27 October was a cold, bleak day with driving rain. In these depressing conditions, 6,000 officers, including 3 Marshals of France (Le Boeuf, Canrobert and Bazaine) and 173,000 soldiers, surrendered, together with 622 field guns, 876 fortress guns, 3 million rounds of gun ammunition, 16 million rounds of rifle ammunition, 72 *mitrailleuses* and 53 regimental Colours from a total of 84.

The fall of Metz is an ineradicable stain on the military history of France. It was an abject episode and has led historians to seek an explanation for Bazaine's conduct. The consensus is that he was an inadequate individual who lacked the intellect, leadership ability and personal qualities required of any officer – a lieutenant, let alone a Marshal of France.

Summary

Prince Frederick Charles saved many lives by not assaulting Metz and his strategy of food denial delivered victory relatively cheaply. He was now able to redirect his army to Paris and reinforce the cordon around that city, where food denial was also starting to have an impact.

The fall of Metz was, without doubt, the inevitable result of a combination of inept French leadership and hunger. The one led to the other and the need for strong leadership in siege conditions was never more evident.

Notes

1. Bazaine, F.A., *Procès Bazaine* (Capitulation of Metz) (Versailles, Paris, 1873), p. 179. Bazaine explained that he had given no orders that that bridging equipment should NOT be taken.
2. SHAT Lt, 12, Metz, 23 September 1870, *'un member de l'armée'*.
3. SHAT Lt, 12, Metz 31 October 1970, Major F.A. Léveillé.
4. *GGS*, Vol. 3, pp. 176–9; Vol. 5, p. 221.
5. Wawro, G., *The Franco-Prussian War: The German Conquest of France in 1870–1871* [2003] (New York, Cambridge University Press, 2010), p. 250.
6. Howard, M., *The Franco-Prussian War* [1961] (Abingdon, Routledge, 2001), p. 282.

Chapter Eleven

The Siege of Paris
(1870–1)

In late 1870, as the Franco-Prussian War laboured towards its inevitable con-clusion, the capital of France, and its 2 million citizens, was besieged by a formidable Prussian force of 235,000 well-trained and experienced regular soldiers. Moltke was far too wily to assault the imposing city walls, which ran for 21 miles (34km). He had learned from Grant's mistakes at Vicksburg only seven years earlier. Moltke deployed his army in a continuous first line of trenches that linked strongpoints. He occupied and fortified the outlying villages, which gave his troops a modicum of security and shelter as they rotated spells in the trenches. Curiously, there was a measure of social contact between the two adversaries. The Prussians took no action against civilians scavenging for the remains of their potato crop and the two sides patronised the same bakers and taverns, albeit at different times. Prussian soldiers exchanged their rations, slanted information, and newspapers for brandy.[1]

In the period preceding the investment of Paris, there had been energetic attempts to enhance the fortifications and 12,000 men laboured in construct-ing earthworks and strongpoints. A barrage was placed across the Seine and approach roads to the city were either torn up or mined. To give unimpeded lines of fire, forests, houses and barns were cleared. All possible entry points to the city were reinforced.[2]

Notwithstanding these defensive works, the railway line to Orléans was severed, and on 19 September, the Prussians captured Versailles and it became the headquarters of the Prussian 3rd Army.

Negotiations between the two sides had been fruitless and some senior Prussians were considering bombarding the helpless city to bring matters to a conclusion. Otto von Bismarck was particularly enthused by this option. General von Blumenthal opposed his political master, arguing that unaimed fire into a city would cause civilian casualties and prove to be not only counterproductive, but also violate the accepted rules of engagement. The impact on international opinion would probably be negative.

Within the walls, the Governor of Paris, Major General Trochu, had about 513,000 men under arms. These were an assortment of regular soldiers, *Garde Nationale*, *Garde Mobile* and sailors. The *Garde Nationale* had originally been

70

formed as a counter-revolutionary militia, but in these new circumstances, it personified the People of Paris in arms.[3] It had significant political clout, and the Trochu government recognised the need to manage it with care. The *Garde Mobile* was notoriously ill disciplined and its military value in a serious engagement was, at best, problematic. Most of the non-regular soldiers had had only rudimentary training. Their leadership was of a commensurate, low standard. However, they did have the protection of the forbidding city defences and around 2,450 artillery pieces.

On 14 September, a mass review of Parisian troops had been held amid wild enthusiasm, and with strident voices calling for aggressive action against the advancing Prussians. Trochu was a realist, and he knew full well that his enthusiastic amateurs were no match for Moltke's forces in the field. Nevertheless, Trochu realised that it would be politically expedient to mount forays into what was now Prussian territory, albeit at great cost.

Moltke's food denial strategy did not have an immediate effect, but on the wealthy, it had no effect at all. Restaurants continued to provide a service – to those who could afford it. Ostensibly, Paris was a glittering European capital city, but the well-polished image concealed social inequalities that were now exacerbated by the drastic reduction in available, inexpensive food. Trochu was under pressure from all sides to break the siege, but he was served by a collection of indifferent generals, not least Auguste-Alexandre Ducrot, who was a courageous man but a poor commander. There followed a series of forays from the city, all of which failed but caused great loss of life on both sides.

The Battle of Chevilly was the first, on 20 September 1870. The planning was nonsense from the start as it was termed 'an attack reconnaissance'. This was a unique and absurd military ploy, which was doomed to failure because its aims were so imprecise and arguably contradictory. General Vinoy, the French commander, was up to that point one of the more credible French generals. In this encounter, he committed 20,000 men but they were outmatched and 2,120 were lost. The Prussians lost only 441.[4] Soon after, on 13 October, the French tried again and fought on the high ground of the plateau of Châtillon under the command of General Ducrot. He was faced by the Prussian II and V corps and his 28,000–40,000 untrained and inexperienced soldiers were again outmatched. They broke under fire and surrendered that critical high ground. Losses on both sides were modest but the psychological impact of defeat on the French was significant.

On 29 October, the small and strategically unimportant village of Le Bourget was assaulted and taken by the ambitious Brigadier Cary de Bellemare. It was an unnecessary operation, which cost lives and produced, for the French, an immediate logistic burden, as they now had to supply the village garrison. de

Bellemare, ever the optimist, demanded an immediate promotion for his feat, but he was lucky not to face a court martial. The victory gave a short-term boost to public morale in besieged Paris and, to some small extent, muted the general air of discontent, but this was short-lived, as de Bellemare had created a deathtrap. The Prussians had no pressing need or desire for Le Bourget but conceding the village to the French was unacceptable and the decision was taken to repossess it. The battle that followed, for a valueless objective, involved 6,000 Prussian troops, of whom 500 were killed, and 1,200 Frenchmen were taken prisoner.

By now, food denial was starting to bite. It affected those at the bottom of the social scale, and it resulted in rising civil discontent. The authority of the Government of National Defence was questioned and Trochu found himself under pressure.

Following the news of these military reverses, on 31 October, a dissident faction of 15,000, some of whom were armed, and led by Louis Auguste Blanqui, Félix Pyat and Louis Charles Delescluze, demonstrated at the Hôtel de Ville. They demanded the resignation of General Trochu and the GND. Shots were fired, the dissidents took control of the building and naïvely went about the organisation of a new government.

This potentially explosive situation was resolved when *Garde Nationale* and *Garde Mobile* troops loyal to Trochu recaptured the building – incredibly, without bloodshed. On 3 November, the GND mounted a plebiscite seeking a vote confirming confidence in the GND; this was carried by about 9:1 although only 620,000 voted.

There were further breakout operations; one on 28 November was termed the 'Great Sortie'. It was a military calamity, cost thousands of lives, achieved nothing but destroyed any residual faith the population had in the GND. The public perception of the *Garde Nationale* was that of a vibrant, energetic and capable force. That view was out of kilter with the reality – it was in fact an untrained, ill-disciplined rabble. To placate public opinion, the GND planned for a further foray and based its plans around the *Garde Nationale*. The action was planned for 19 January; it was to be the last roll of the dice.

Negotiations for an armistice had been in progress for several weeks but Bismarck held all the cards, and he was going to ensure that France was soundly punished for initiating this war. The French still entertained wildly optimistic aims despite the losses of Sédan, Le Bourget and Metz. These military reverses did nothing for morale in the city where the food denial imposed by Moltke was having entirely predictable results. The flocks of sheep and cattle that had been harboured within the city walls were rapidly consumed and meat rationing was imposed early in October. 'But bread, though its quality deteriorated remained unrationed until the last weeks of the siege; and the prices of all food stuffs rose so steeply that the poor of the city faced a serious prospect of starvation.'[5]

Just as in Vicksburg and Metz, horses, cats, dogs and rats appeared in butchers' shops. In December, beasts in the Paris Zoo were all slaughtered, as there was no fodder for them. This gesture attracted considerable attention, but it had no practical effect on the diet of the vast citizenry. One enterprising restaurateur compiled and printed a menu for Christmas Day. One wonders just how much consommé is produced from one elephant? In this case there

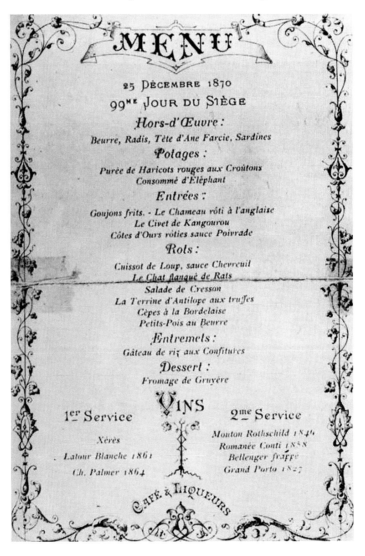

were two, Castor and Pollux. These two magnificent denizens were reduced to soup, pâté or stew.

Fresh vegetables and milk were unavailable. The besieged queued for everything and life became increasing bleak. Fuel was short, winter bared its teeth and the biting cold added to the misery. The café society that gave Paris its attractive persona ceased to exist. The men of the *Garde Nationale* were accorded priority for food and the Government of National Defence gave financial support to the unemployed.[6] However, social order started to collapse. The need for fuel led to the wholesale destruction of wooden structures, regardless of ownership. Lawlessness increased, and predictably, so too did public anxiety.

This anxiety morphed into anger, which was redirected from the invader to the GND, which was incapable of meeting the demands of a virulent, largely uninformed press. The newspapers printed as fact the wildest and most unlikely rumours, and fed the burgeoning social discontent. Ernest Pickard, a leading light of the GND, proposed the suppression of the press. He was opposed by colleague Jules Favre, although the latter admitted that firm government was impossible.[7] Paris was a very unhappy, hungry place.

The final sortie by the Army of Paris was executed on 19 January 1871. The coordination of the attack was poor and as a result, momentum was lost. The assault stalled all along its front.

> General Trochu demonstrating his ample courage rode to Montretout to inject some backbone into his faltering national guardsmen. He was very exposed and set a fine example, but no one responded to his encouragement. The lack of training esprit and commitment among the GN and GM became painfully evident as they refused further action …
>
> Trochu … ordered a general withdrawal … the infantry had to struggle to get through the jam of supply wagons, gun limbers and ambulances. All roads were choked. Unit cohesion disappeared and the Army of Paris degenerated into a heaving aimless mob.[8]

Moltke, writing after the event, commented that his defending army had suffered the loss of 40 officers and 570 men; the French, 145 officers and 3,423 men killed and wounded, with the addition of 44 officers and 458 men taken as prisoners.

This devastating, but entirely predictable, defeat was the final straw and French resistance was at an end. Military failure, combined with food denial in Paris, eventually forced the surrender of the city and of France to Germany on 28 January 1871. A few days later, the German Army exercised its right to march through Paris in accordance with the terms of the armistice. The

Germany Army occupied Paris for two days and by so doing heaped further humiliation on France and the French.

The Government of France was vested in Adolphe Thiers who, recognising the volatility of Paris, chose to base his administration in Versailles – this was a tacit admission that the local conditions were difficult and indicated a degree of mistrust in his citizens. Thiers made several decisions that fuelled the fires of discontent, not least his banning of six demonstrably left-wing newspapers on 11 March. At the same time, four of the main players at the uprising of 31 October were sentenced to death, in absentia. This was a travesty of justice and raised the atmosphere in Paris to 'inflammable'.

Thereafter, events moved swiftly. Thiers was disinclined to deal with the dissidents or to consider their demands, and by 17 March, violence had broken out. The Commune of Paris was declared on 18 March, and it was a demonstration of, what would later be labelled, 'communism'. The Commune had the wholehearted support of Karl Marx and Friedrich Engels. The latter described it as 'dictatorship by the proletariat'.[9]

The Commune was led by a committee; it was inept, lacked military skills and in late May 1971, the Versailles government took Paris by storm with considerable bloodshed. Communards were summarily executed; others were tried and then executed. By 28 May, Thiers had taken control of Paris. The number of Communards killed attracted all manner of wild guestimates. These ranged up to 30,000, but the sober scholarship of Professor Robert Tombs provided a range of between 5,700 and 7,400.[10]

The Franco-Prussian War was a disaster for France. It was comprehensively defeated on the battlefield, was obliged to cede Alsace and Lorraine to what was now Germany, and pay reparations of 5 billion francs – about US$ 24 billion in 2022. The outcome gave rise to German militarism that, in turn, led inexorably to the Great War.

Summary

It is argued, by this author, that food denial had an impact far beyond the fortified walls of Paris and for many years thereafter.[11] The war had been a self-inflicted wound for the French, who lost 138,871 killed, 143,000 wounded and an astronomic 723,556 prisoners. French losses during the siege were 28,450, of whom fewer than 4,000 were killed. In the city, there were 6,251 deaths from all causes. Of these, the demise of an uncounted number was hastened by malnutrition and the cold.

However, it cannot be argued that hunger was the decisive factor in the surrender of Paris, although hunger was one of the constituents of acute social discord and the rise of the Commune.

Notes

1. Bronsart, S.P., *Geheimes Kriegstagebusch 1870–1871*, (ed.) Rassow, P. (Bonn, 1954), pp. 183, 189.

2. Howard, M., *The Franco-Prussian War* [1961] (Abingdon, Routledge, 2001), p. 319.

3. Horne, A., *The Fall of Paris* (London, Macmillan & Co., 1965), p. 62.

4. Frederick III, *The War Diary of the Emperor Frederick III, 1870–1871* [1927], (ed.) Allinson, A.R. (Worcestershire, UK, Home Farm Books, 2006), p. 143.

5. Howard, M., *The Franco-Prussian War* [1961] (Abingdon, Routledge, 2001), p. 326.

6. Desmarest, J., *La Defence National* (Paris, 1949), p. 335.

7. Favre, J., *Gouvernement de la Défense Nationale*, 3 Vols (Paris, 1871–5), Vol. I, p. 297.

8. Nash, N.S., *The Siege that Changed the World: Paris 1870–1871* (Barnsley, Pen & Sword, 2021), p. 196.

9. Rougerie, J., repeating remarks by Frederick Engels, in London, on the twentieth anniversary of the Paris Commune, 18 March 1891, and quoted in his book *Paris Libre 1871*, reprinted in 2004, pp. 264–70.

10. Tombs, Prof R., 'How Bloody was La Semaine Sanglante of 1871?' (Cambridge University Press, *The House Journal*, Vol. 55, No. 3, September 2012), pp. 619–704.

11. Nash, N.S., *The Siege that Changed the World: Paris 1870–1871* (Barnsley, Pen & Sword, 2021), p. 282.

PART THREE

THE FIRST WORLD WAR

Chapter Twelve

The British Blockade of Germany, and the 1917 French Army Mutiny (1914–19)

An American, Alfred Thayer Mahan, won the approbation of Sir John Keegan, who described him as 'the most important American strategist of the nineteenth century'.[1] It was Mahan who had a profound effect on the Royal Navy (RN), and by extension, its role and performance during the First World War.

Mahan, having reviewed naval history between 1660 and 1783, concluded that it was naval supremacy that allowed empires to thrive, and that Britain's control of the sea was vital to its role as a world power and its economic health. Mahan pointed out that empires lacking overwhelming sea power such as Hannibal's Carthage and Napoleon's France were unable to compete with their contemporaries. Mahan's book was seen to be a blueprint for naval planners across the globe, and in part, fuelled the arms race that started soon after its publication.[2]

In 1900, at the apogee of the British Empire, the Royal Navy was the instrument of imperial power. It was the largest, smartest, and most powerful armed force on Earth. But its ships were obsolescent and inefficient. The 'bright work' sparkled but it was just show. The RN dominated the seas of the world although it was never called to account, which was probably as well because it was, in reality, a paper tiger.

The standards of gunnery were abysmal and in 1905, Rear Admiral Percy Scott was appointed 'Inspector of Target Practice'. Scott was an outstanding innovator but his practical solutions to poor gunnery were anathema to the RN establishment and he met vigorous opposition during a long and uphill struggle to effect change. Scott was a visionary; he predicted the development of ships carrying aeroplanes and the demise of the battleship. He encouraged the building of submarines and was eventually promoted to admiral. However, retired in 1913, aged 60, he played no active role in the First World War.

Scott was able to enhance the performance of HM ships, such as they were, but the individual who transformed the RN was Admiral Sir John Fisher (always known as Jackie). Fisher was a pragmatic, forceful, self-confident

(*Left*) **Rear Admiral Alfred Thayer Mahan (1840–1914).**
(*Right*) **Admiral of the Fleet Sir John Fisher (1841–1920). Photograph from 1901,
taken when he was C-in-C the Mediterranean Fleet.**

man and, in some views, he ranks with Nelson as a contributor to British naval history.

During his tenure as First Sea Lord, Fisher executed changes in the organisation of the fleet, the administration of naval dockyards, ship construction and the development of submarines. It was in this latter area that he failed. One of his major misjudgements was his insistence that the fleet needed the fast, accident-prone, oil-burning K-class submarine. This class of twenty submarines killed 318 British sailors in accidents, but a K-class boat never fired a shot in anger.[3]

However, Fisher's decision to convert all the ships of the RN from coal to oil burning was well judged and entirely correct. He supported Scott in his gunnery crusade and:

> to counter the rapid expansion of the German navy, he reinforced the British naval forces in home waters and, by scrapping obsolete ships, released men to provide the nucleus of crews for ships in reserve. He was also responsible for the creation of the battleship *Dreadnought*.[4]

Launched in 1906, *Dreadnought* was a new class of battleship and without equal. Fisher then turned his attention to a new class of ship, designed to combine the firepower of a battleship and the speed and agility of a cruiser. This new class was termed 'battlecruisers' and there were three: *Indomitable*, *Invincible* and *Inflexible*. At 8,200 tons, they were heavier and 5 knots faster than *Roon*, the pride of the German Navy. The three ships carried 12″ guns and were very fast – 27 knots is on the quick side of rapid. However, to achieve their speed they had to reduce the weight of the ship and so armoured plate was much reduced – with catastrophic effects, to be evidenced at Jutland in 1916.

The pre-war naval arms race led to both Britain and Germany building warships of previously unknown size and power, followed by the other powers: United States, France, Italy and Japan. Britain's naval dockyards and commercial shipbuilding industry outproduced those of Germany, with big-gun capital ships, cruisers, smaller warships, support vessels, depot ships and lesser craft numbering more than any other power, and the Royal Navy was also able to draw reserve strength from the world's largest merchant navy and fishing fleet.[5] The Germans, too, were influenced by Mahan, and embarked on an extensive and intensive ship-building programme and identified, quite correctly, that Fisher was a hostile opponent.

HMS *Dreadnought*, 1906.

Britain and Germany were at risk from a blockade as both countries imported much of their food. The British Admiralty had put in place plans, as early as 1907, when it revised the naval rules of engagement. It extended the definition of an 'instrument of war' to include food and to allow RN ships to seize neutral shipping if a ship was carrying supplies to an enemy.[6] This was to prove to be a highly contentious policy when hostilities started. The Admiralty perception was that a blockade would, first, oblige the German High Seas Fleet to come out and engage Jellicoe's Grand Fleet, and second, it would be an effective economic weapon to disrupt German commerce and starve it into submission. In 1908, the blockade of Germany was noted in the war plans, and these were revised constantly until 1914. The modernisation of the RN in those pre-war years was to produce a rich dividend.

The enhanced Royal Navy of 1914 had a major deficit – 'it had no suitably situated, fully prepared, and fortified bases on the East coast.'[7] Its ships concentrated in three Scottish locations: Rosyth on the river Forth, which was secure but with limited facilities and about 25 miles (40k) from the sea; and Cromarty Firth and Scapa Flow in the Orkney Islands, which were undefended. This extraordinary state of affairs had passed unnoticed. 'There was no public outcry, no shrieks of scandal from the sensationalist press.'[8]

The development of Rosyth was inexpertly handled and there was constant friction between the Admiralty and the War Office. The base was 'work in progress' and the RN had to look elsewhere in the short term. It was eventually agreed that Scapa Flow should be the war anchorage for light forces and Cromarty the main fleet base.

It was anticipated that on the outbreak of war there would be a main fleet action of Trafalgar proportions, with the likelihood that the Royal Navy would emerge as the victor. In the event, after war was declared on 4 August 1914, the first battle was that of Heligoland Bight. On 28 August, a powerful British fleet encountered a smaller German fleet. It sank three light cruisers and damaged six others. German losses were 712 killed, 149 wounded and 226 captured. The RN lost 35 killed and 55 wounded. It was British tactical success but by no means was the naval action decisive in strategic terms. The significant strategic success followed soon after, when the Kaiser issued orders for his fleet to remain in port.

Thereafter, Allied naval strategy focused upon tenacious, long-term efforts to blockade the Central Powers, depriving them of raw materials and foodstuffs. The Central Powers had to make every effort to break that blockade and proactively impose one of their own on Britain and France. The German submarine service was employed to this end. Notwithstanding the Kaiser's order, German warships were not entirely confined to port. They attacked Great Yarmouth in November 1914, and bombarded Scarborough, Whitby and Hartlepool on 16 December 1914. In addition, they made surface attacks on the Kent coast at Margate in February 1915 and Ramsgate in May 1915.

The German ships fired 1,150 shells into Hartlepool, striking targets including the steelworks, gasworks, railways, seven churches and 300 houses. People fled the town by road and attempted to do so by train; eighty-six civilians were killed and 424 injured.[9] Seven soldiers were killed and fourteen injured. The death of Private Theophilus Jones, who was 29, was the first death of a British soldier from enemy action on British soil for 200 years.[10] Eight German sailors were killed and twelve wounded.

*   *   *

In continental Europe, the national diet had undergone a considerable change during the late nineteenth century as the emphasis moved from wheat to meat. In 1870, the average German ate 16 kilograms (35lb) of meat per year but, by 1914, this had increased to 50 kilograms (110lb). Today it is about 77 kilograms (170lb).[11] These dietary changes were the result of a developing new global food economy. The expansion of railways was one factor, and another was the switch from coal to oil in steam ships, which served to reduce transport costs, making the range of foods wider and cheaper.

In Britain, the domestic production of food had been reduced by a deliberate policy to move the labour force from agriculture to manufacturing – a matter willingly embraced by the workforce, which having moved into heavy industry was paid more and offered an enhanced lifestyle. Germany recognised the vulnerability of Britain, and predictably, it mounted operations to blockade the British Isles and starve the British into submission. Sir Arthur Salter (later Lord Salter) commented:

> It was as much a war of competing blockades on the surface … Behind these two blockades the economic systems of the two opposing groups of countries were engaged in a deadly struggle for existence, and at several periods of the war the pressure of starvation seemed likely to achieve an issue beyond the settlement of the entrenched armies of the immobilised navies.[12]

Britain had a free trade policy and did not erect tariff walls. It was firmly believed that the Royal Navy was sufficiently powerful to protect imported food supplies in time of war and great reliance was placed on the capacity of the colonies to fill the gap. 'By 1914 Britain was reliant on imports for over half its foods (measured by value) and was Europe's major importer of grain.'[13] The vulnerability of the British Isles and the importance of the Royal Navy to protect its imports needs no emphasis.

Notwithstanding the capability of the Royal Navy, it was evident that, given the acute pressure on the food supply system, domestic measures were needed. David Lloyd George, speaking in the House of Commons in December 1916, averred that 'every available square yard must be made to produce food'. This was hardly an original thought, because a year before, Walter Brett had published a booklet entitled *War-time Gardening: How to Grow Your Own Food*. In his 64-page booklet he cajoled his fellow citizens, saying, 'The most urgent need for all who are not in the fighting line and who have land is to make the utmost use of it.'

The allotment scheme was founded, in which novice gardeners were encouraged to grow their own. Model allotments were set up in public parks to demonstrate how a small area of cultivated ground could produce fresh vegetables at modest cost. Staff and volunteers worked to inspire and train people to grow food, while providing advice on organic food growing techniques. Greenwich Park in London was one of many public spaces that were utilised, and in this case, about 4 per cent of the park was converted to allotments. The charge for an allotment was 7/6p per year (about £35 at 2022 prices). The allotment holder was expected to fund his own seed, tools and fertiliser.

In the York area, for example, and in accord with the Defence of the Realm Act 14 (DORA), the Ministry of Agriculture and Fishing gave power to the local authorities to take over unused plots of land for allotments. The aim was to create about 470 allotment plots in total, each about 300 square yards. It was specified that two-thirds should be for potatoes. The availability of allotment space proved very popular, and 516 applications were made by January 1917. Local bylaws were suspended, and people were allowed to keep pigs and chickens on their plots, if they were properly housed. The *Yorkshire Gazette* went as far as to claim that the cultivation of an allotment was an act of patriotism.

In 1917, the national government of David Lloyd George passed the Cultivation of Lands Order Act and York Corporation set up War Allotments throughout the city. It was estimated that over 65 acres in total had been allocated to allotments, a tenth of the area of city, with 1,091 plots. This was estimated to be a greater proportion than any other northern city.

'Allotmentitis' – the catching condition that is growing your own vegetables – significantly eased the food crisis in the First World War and paved the way for the creation of allotments across the country after the war ended. The success of allotments also paved the way for the 'Dig for Victory' campaign in the Second World War.[14]

In 1914, the British diet exhibited a pronounced preference for soft, moist bread made with hard wheat grown in Minnesota and New York State. The grain had to travel across 3,000 miles (4,828km) of sea, and by 1914, in the face of armed opposition, the consumption of plant carbohydrates had dropped in favour of imported sugar. By 1914, average individual consumption was 79 pounds (36kg) of sugar in various forms, and it was the major source of energy for working men. The British diet 'combined with urban poverty meant that hunger and malnutrition haunted the poorer sections of the working class'.[15] A product of Britain's reliance on imported food did have one positive result in that it acted as a stimulus for the world's commerce and provided markets for British manufactured goods, which in turn paid for the imported food.

* * *

Prior to the war, scientists of several nations worked to establish the necessary calorific value of food provided to their soldiers. There was a discrepancy and that was a measure of availability, food preference, national cultures and wealth.

Soldiers of the USA were the best fed in calorific terms and their system provisioned 4,714 calories per man, per day; the French had 4,446, the British, 4,193, and the Germans, 4,038 calories. However, the practicality was that often a soldier of any nation could not be reached with food, and when he could, the quality of the cooking and condition of the food became a factor in acceptability. The function of these calorific standards was solely to provide the logistic chain with targets for food acquisition. The calorific standard was not related to the food delivered in the trenches where, more often than not, soldiers of all nations went hungry.

From this author's point of view, it is the context in which one is fed that is important. The finest meal I ever had in my thirty-four years of service was a hot 'Full English' breakfast served at dawn, one bitter December morning, on the wind and snow-swept Essex marshes and after a sleepless and freezing night. I savour it still. The calorific value was of indifference to me and also to that of the cook – bless him.

Soldiers in the trenches then, now and in the future place great value on simple things like hot water to shave in or a hot cup of tea. In the field, fine dining is never required but simple and effective food production is. It follows that the better the quality of the rations provided, the better and more acceptable the finished product should be, but that is not a guarantee. It is the skill of the soldier cook that makes the difference.

* * *

In Germany, its protectionist economic policy that favoured farmers had slowed industrialisation and it could not match the volume of exported

British goods, although the German diet was marginally healthier than that of the British. That would change once the Royal Navy blockade took effect. Germany did not make any counter-blockade arrangements as, in peacetime, it was 80 per cent self-sustaining. Hitherto, much of the balance was provided by European countries such as the Netherlands and Scandinavia, which would not involve transport by sea.

The German Navy was generally thought to be inferior to that of the RN although the Germans led the way in submarine warfare. Whilst the RN struggled to establish a viable *modus operandi* for its own submarine fleet, which included the cordially loathed K-class, the Germans wreaked havoc on the Royal Navy in the early days of the war with its modest force of fifty-seven submarines.

Naval warfare was about to enter a new realm and Jackie Fisher had warned, in 1913, that merchant and all neutral ships were likely targets for submarines in a war between two maritime nations. His view was unpopular, but he emphasised that submarine warfare was barbarous and that 'war is

violence and moderation in war is imbecility'.[16] Prime Minister Asquith did not permit his view to be circulated but, in the event, Fisher was proved to be correct.

So, in 1914, both countries were intent on blockading the other and in the early exchanges Germany established a naval supremacy – if only under the sea. Its submarines sank HMS *Pathfinder* in early September 1914. Only a few days later, the three old, heavy cruisers *Aboukir*, *Hogue* and *Cressy* were all sunk off the Dutch coast by *U-19*, commanded by Leutnant Otto Weddigen, with the expenditure of only six torpedoes; 1,459 officers and men were lost. The backlash led to the resignation of the First Sea Lord, Prince Louis of Battenberg.

Then *U-19* struck again, and HMS *Hawk* went down with 500 men on 15 October. This single German officer, Weddigen, was now a much-feted national hero and he had had an

Leutnant Otto Weddigen (1882–1915).

impact on the Royal Navy out of all proportion to the size of his boat and the number of men under his command.[17]

Nevertheless, the Royal Navy was superior in numbers and had the assets to patrol and dominate the surface of the seas across which the British Empire was spread. Its adversary, the German *Kaiserliche Marine* (surface fleet), was mainly restricted to the German Bight. It deployed commerce raiders and practised unrestricted submarine warfare in operations beyond the Bight.

The Germans adopted submarine warfare in early 1915 and made it clear that all merchant ships, including the shipping of neutral countries sailing around the British Isles, were, in their view, legitimate targets. They hoped that the denial of food to the British Isles would bring them victory.

The sinking of the British merchantman *Lusitania* on 7 May 1915 became a *cause célèbre*. It was carrying munitions. That fact, in the not unreasonable view of the German Navy, made it a combatant vessel. However, it also carried a number of civilian passengers, of whom 1,201 were killed. Among those were 128 Americans. American President Woodrow Wilson reacted strongly and demanded an end to Germany's attacks on unarmed merchant ships. This protest bore fruit and in September 1915, the Germans abandoned the policy but began to suffer under the efficient British blockade of all German ports and the curtailment of imported goods. Initially, the British blockade had been slow to take effect, but it succeeded in cutting Germany off from 'direct imports from five enemy nations that in 1913 had provided 46 percent of that country's total imports'.[18] The Royal Navy started to stop and search neutral ships, which gave great offence to other maritime nations (*see* image on page 88).

A convoy system was introduced that drastically reduced the losses in merchant ships sailing to the UK from across the world. The principles behind the convoy strategy were really very simple. On the surface, a U-boat could sight a single ship about 12 miles (19km) away, and if the ocean was covered in single ships sailing independently, there were ample target opportunities. However, if ships were grouped, then although that U-boat could still identify a target at 12 miles, there were vastly fewer groups than single ships and thus fewer targets.

> A single convoy of forty ships, meant there was only a few hundred square miles where a U-boat could spot a target at all, and so many more submarines spent their patrols combing empty ocean.[19]

A U-boat attacking a convoy had to evade the protecting screen of escorts and then survive the inevitable counter-attack. Convoys worked, and the skills of the escorts were polished so inexorably that the attrition in U-boats increased and the battle against the German submarine force swung towards Britain.

The blockade attracted little public attention in Britain as that was firmly focused on the astronomic losses being suffered in the trenches of the Western Front. However, by the middle of 1916, the constraints imposed by the blockade were impacting on the German population. Food was scarce.

German officials had not planned for consumer shortages, preferring to count on a brief and victorious war. Once the war began, civilian officials deferred to military demand, which rapidly diminished domestic agricultural production through the conscription of fixed nitrogen, draft horses, and farm labour.[20] Food shortages caused the most desperate and enduring crisis of basic goods. Scarcity of consumer necessities, such as fuel for cooking and heating, however, was interrelated with these shortages and intensified the negative effects for many Germans.

THE CHALLENGE
"Halt! Who comes there?"   "Neutral."   "Prove it!"

From *Mr Punch's History of the Great War* (*London, Cassell, 1919, p. 73*).

Shortages hit individuals on the battle and home fronts with varying degrees of severity, depending on their socioeconomic position, geography, and other factors. Grave scarcities were integral to the German experience of the war overall, from early on. The deficiencies of the first months escalated to crisis level by early 1915, as a complete lack of potatoes in some parts of the country followed months of severe wheat shortage.

Frustration and fear rose to the fore. Civilians often had to spend hours standing in a queue waiting for goods that frequently ran out. The police grew fearful of the constant unrest, which they struggled to control.

This daily experience dragged on for five years, as the ability to obtain basic goods continued to diminish, and the effects were cumulative and lasting. Likewise, soldiers began to express their dissatisfaction. They deplored the limited rations and the expectation that they should live off the land in conquered territory. Infantrymen voiced rising resentment of the distinction between their own meagre rations and those of officers. Finally, they decried the hunger their families back home suffered, proclaiming that officials had broken the unwritten agreement to care for these families while they risked their lives on the front line.[21]

* * *

Briefly, a digression to consider the matter of 'living off the land'. This means of feeding invading and occupying armies is a practice of very long standing. The Romans, who invaded Great Britain 2,000 years ago, had no other option. They had no viable food supply chain and so they took food wherever they could find it. Similarly, during the formation of the British Empire, the colonialists, be they military or civilian, were dependent on local resources.

This text will make further references to 'living off the land'. Sometimes the policy worked, but when it did not, military disaster followed.

* * *

On 31 May 1916, the German High Seas Fleet ventured into the North Sea and engaged the Royal Navy's Grand Fleet at the Battle of Jutland. The battle was a pyrrhic victory for the Royal Navy. Fourteen of its ships were sunk and 6,094 men were killed. The Germans lost eleven ships, with 2,551 men killed. However, war is not an arithmetic matter, and the German fleet broke off the engagement, turned tail and returned to its home ports, from which it never stirred again. To quote an American journalist, 'In May 1916, the German fleet assaulted its gaoler and then fled back into its cell.' The effect of this retreat on the morale of the German sailors was deeply damaging, exacerbated by the constant hunger.

In Germany, rationing was an imperative because the shortages were wide-ranging. Bread, potatoes, butter, fats and meat were often unavailable and by late 1916, the domestic situation in Germany was dire, and that period was termed the 'Turnip Winter'. The population was obliged to eat foodstuffs previously fed only to livestock. It was bitterly cold and heating fuels were scarce. All Germans lost weight, the birth rate fell, and the mortality rate rose. Deaths from pneumonia and tuberculosis increased significantly, a strong indicator of malnutrition and poor sanitary conditions. As many as 750,000 died – not to mince words, they starved to death.[22]

In 1916, Countess Blücher was an Englishwoman living in Germany. In her diary, she wrote of a conversation with a friend who had been shopping, and had reported that:

> her butcher was thinking seriously of closing down. She could get no potatoes, no sugar even. The shopkeepers told her that the soldiers don't get meat more than three times a week now and even vegetables are scarce ... the magistrate forbids the selling of butter, sugar etc., until all has been bought up and distributed equally and justly ... it is all terrible, and what it is going to lead to no one knows.[23]

This is, of course, a second-hand account, but the diarist was writing for her own purpose and so it has authenticity, and the effect of the widespread hunger is widely documented. The hunger was cumulative, and in January 1917, the military leaders confronted their Kaiser and proposed that unrestricted submarine warfare be recommenced.

This momentous change of tack was made when it was calculated that, if the U-boat fleet were to be unrestrained, the tonnage of shipping it could sink would so severely damage Britain that its food deficiency would cause it to capitulate by August 1917. It was the hope that by this means Germany could reverse the military balance, which was starting to swing, albeit slightly, towards France and Britain. The Chancellor, Bethmann Hollweg, did not favour the strategy because he saw that it might antagonise the USA and could bring that country into the war – but on the wrong side. Kaiser Wilhelm was the decision maker; he was facing rising public discontent and there was a groundswell demanding aggressive action against Germany's enemies. It was on this basis that Wilhelm backed his military men.

The lack of surface opposition gave the Royal Navy full reign, and the blockade tightened the noose. In Germany, strict food rationing regulations had been imposed. American newspaper correspondent George Schreiner observed that 'among the 300 ... queueing for food there was not one who had had enough to eat for weeks. In the case of the younger women and children the skin was drawn hard on the bones and bloodless.'[24]

'Swooping from the West – It is the intention of our new ally to assist us in patrolling the Atlantic.' From *Mr Punch's History of the Great War.* (*London, Cassell, 1919, p.147*)

In January 1917, the British intercepted and deciphered an encrypted message from the German Foreign Minister Arthur Zimmermann to the German minister to Mexico, Heinrich von Eckhardt. In this letter, Zimmerman suggested that Germany would ally itself with Mexico and actively support any Mexican invasion of the Southern United States if the USA entered the war against Germany.

London sat on the letter until 24 February, and it became public on 1 March. Predictably, there was outrage in the USA. On 4 April, the Senate voted 82 to 6 to declare war. Two days later, on 6 April, the House of Representatives voted 373 to 50 in favour of a declaration of war against Germany.

By the end of June 1917, the first American soldiers had arrived on the Western Front. Thereafter, an influx of 10,000 American soldiers were arriving every day. Their very presence was sufficient to further degrade the low morale of the German military and public alike. There was a recognition of the vast manpower resources of its new enemy, its boundless wealth and logistic strength.

The American commander General John J. Pershing was determined to fight his own personal war and declined to accept any advice from British and French officers who had spent years in trench warfare. Pershing's hubris cost lives, not least on the last day of the conflict when there was a conservative total of 320 Americans killed and more than 3,240 seriously wounded in the last hours of the war.[25] All quite unnecessary American casualties. Pershing had doubted the good faith of the Germans and accordingly instructed his army to continue with aggressive operations. Douglas MacArthur, then a brigadier, served under Pershing at this time, and may well have shaped MacArthur's mindset in later life.

It had been on 28 May 1918 that the American Army fought its first engagement, at Cantigny, in which 318 were killed. During the war, 63,114 of the million American men sent to France died of disease, and 53,402 were killed in action.

The arrival of the US Navy in late 1917, with its five dreadnoughts, had moved the scales even more in the Allies' favour. The cooperation between the RN and USN was remarkable for the goodwill demonstrated by both sides, and the American commander Admiral William S. Sims was, in large part, responsible. His force and its publicised arrival were sufficient to further unnerve the Germans.

*   *   *

Throughout the war, the attrition in the trenches was enormous and all of the combatant nations counted their dead by the hundreds of thousands. The flower of French youth had been destroyed at Verdun and public morale

General Robert Nivelle (1856–1924).

reflected the losses. In May 1916, General Robert Nivelle replaced General Petain in command at Verdun and he led successful counter-attacks on German positions later in 1916. These successes came at a high cost and Nivelle was roundly criticised.

Nivelle was a fluent English speaker, a polished and charming companion, and a very persuasive orator. His muted success at Verdun was followed by his promotion to Commander-in-Chief of all the French armies on the Western Front. It was from this appointment that he planned and initiated a disastrous offensive against the formidable German defences of Chemin des Dames, on 15 April 1917. There was widespread opposition to his plan, of which the Germans were well aware.

Nivelle ignored his detractors and committed his soldiers to frontal attacks into massed machine guns defended by belts of uncut barbed wire. The inevitable result was horrific casualties to set against minimal gains. The 'Nivelle offensive' ceased on 9 May 1917, by which time the French had suffered 187,000 casualties.[26] From 29 April 1917, there followed a series of mutinies in French infantry formations. The soldiers refused to go into the trenches and mount a further attack at objectives surrounded by belts of wire:

> Mutiny was in the air. No one spoke of it, for an army mutiny is like a horrible malignant disease and the chances that the patient will die an agonising death are so great that the subject cannot ever be mentioned aloud. Yet the imminence of revolt was obvious. It was apparent to the company commander who dared not even speak to his slovenly troops when they passed him by without a salute.[27]

France was in a crisis situation. The Germans were within 100 miles (160km) of Paris and only two loyal divisions were in their path. Fortunately for the French, the Germans were unaware of the chaos in the French lines.

The grievances of the French soldiers were many and justified. They complained that they had insufficient leave, poor food, worn-out clothes and equipment, and uncaring leadership, and they sought peace.

The mutiny was handled with remarkable insensitivity. The collection evidence against individual mutineers was difficult if not impossible and so men were selected at random and some were summarily shot. This served only to feed the discontent.

Food and its availability were factors in the limitations of the mutiny. Ambitions to march on Paris and to seize railway trains to get there foundered on the unavailability of food. For example, the 310th Regiment, given orders to leave Coeuvres, realised that they were headed back to the front line. Their commanding officer, Colonel Dussange, commented later that there were 'no acts of violence occurred just determined obstinacy'. He added that some soldiers saluted him but 'they intended to march on Paris. Other regiments were waiting for them in the Forest of Compiègne.'[28]

The mutinous 310th established an armed camp, elected leaders, posted sentries, blocked roads and spent four days discussing their situation.

Finally, their food supplies were exhausted. And then they carefully shaved, washed, and formed into impeccable columns of four and marched out of their camp to surrender to the cavalry.[29]

This was not an isolated case, but it is quoted here as being indicative of the criticality of food in any, and all situations. Nivelle paid a high price for his intransigence and was moved by the French Government to be the Commander-in-Chief of the French Army in North Africa. In effect, he was sidelined. His career was at an end.

* * *

By 1918, the German population was a people at its wits' end. In France, its young men were being killed in multiples of 10,000. One estimate is that 1,773,700 had died and 4,216,058 were wounded. The fate of a further 1,152,800 taken prisoner was uncertain.[30] Most households in Germany were directly affected by these, over 7 million, individual casualties.

Soldiers, returning from the trenches on leave, left no one in any doubt as to the privations suffered on the front. They were reduced to 'stealing the barley meant to be fodder for the horses and grinding it in their coffee mills to make flour for pancakes'.[31] The unfed horses died and were eaten.

There was a growing realisation among the German hierarchy that the combination of failure on the battlefield, compounded with the starvation conditions and rising social disorder at home, could only be resolved with an armistice. Nevertheless, the war dragged on until November, by which time the denial of food had generated severe social unrest and given rise to the German Revolution (*Novemberrevolution*). This lasted until August 1919, when the Weimar Constitution was adopted. The revolution was triggered by a decision of the Naval Command that, on 24 October 1918, the navy would

Empty stomach can make you 'hangry', scientists find

By Joe Pinkstone
SCIENCE CORRESPONDENT

HUNGER really does cause anger and an empty stomach can be responsible for more than a third of your foul mood, researchers have found.

"Hangry" has become a buzzword for irritability as mealtime approaches, but the phenomenon had never been studied before researchers from Anglia Ruskin University (ARU) tackled it.

In a study, published in the *Plos One* journal, participants reported their hunger and moods on a phone app. Of the factors influencing mood, more than a third were tied to food.

Viren Swami, professor of social psychology at ARU, said: "Ours is the first study to examine being 'hangry' outside of a lab. By following people in their day-to-day lives, we found that hunger was related to levels of anger, irritability and pleasure."

The authors say acknowledging one is hangry may be a way of fighting it.

emerge and fight a final, climactic battle with the RN. The plan was never launched; instead, on 29 October, sailors of the High Seas Fleet mutinied. This unrest was contagious, a republic was proclaimed and Emperor Wilhelm II, an instigator of the war, abdicated and fled from his country. War had caused the downfall of his monarchy. He was not alone, and Austria-Hungary, Lithuania and Russia all followed suit in deposing their monarchies.

The protracted hunger of the German people had made them 'hangry' and the press cutting indicates that to some extent it is a factor in human behaviour and draws attention to the findings of Professor Viren Swami and his team.[32] Later, the professor refined his view in saying:

> our work on hanger was very much focused on individual responses in terms of emotionality and I'd be very careful in generalising what we found to broader social and political outcomes … psychologists have spent a lot of time trying to understand social disorder – termed 'crowd behaviour' in the psychological sciences.[33]

In researching this book there was empirical evidence that deprivation, in all its many forms, was more often than not a factor in the breakdown of social order. Chapter 5 referred to the turbulence caused by the salt famine in the Southern United States. Hunger was at the root of ill discipline in Metz (*see* Chapter 10). Hunger was an issue in Paris and led to the most extreme response – the Commune uprising. Hunger triggered the mutiny in the German Fleet and the fall of the monarchy in November 1918.

Dr Herbert Meiselman also suggested caution and he observed that an investigation into anger and its relationship with eating showed about 20,000 references and advised that there is 'some discussion in the literature whether hunger causes anger or anger causes hunger'.[34]

The war was at an end, but the British did not lift its blockade. With 20/20 hindsight, that can be seen to have been unduly oppressive, and it was to have a catastrophic, long-term effect. The object of extending the blockade was to suppress any communistic ascendancy and to force the Germans to accept the ruthless terms of the Treaty of Versailles.

The continuing blockade achieved its aims in the short term but, during the bleak winter of 1918/19, a 29-year-old German corporal (pictured below) watched the effect. In his book *Mein Kampf*, he commented on the civilian administration of German life. He noted that, in many local councils organised on soviet lines, Jewish people played a prominent role.[35]

He endured the humiliation of defeat and readily understood the need for his country to be self-sufficient in food. He believed that to achieve autarky, Germany would require an expansion of its food-producing territory. He determined to make best use of the democracy that the Weimar Constitution provided.

Corporal Adolf Hitler (1889–1945), pictured *c.*1917, aged 28. His experience of hunger in the First World War shaped his policies in the Second.

Summary

It is suggested by some historians, not least Richard Gough and Basil Liddell Hart, that the First World War was decided at sea, and not in the mud of Flanders.

> It was the blockade that finally drove the Central Powers to accept defeat. At first mild in its application, the blockade's noose gradually tightened, all restraint cast aside. Increasingly deprived of the means to wage war or even to feed her population the violent response was insurrection.[36]

The strategy of food denial had been a major factor in the American Civil War and similarly so in the Franco-Prussian War but, in this far larger conflict, it had been decisive. Liddell Hart wrote that:

> no historian would underrate the direct effect that semi-starvation of the German people in causing the final collapse of the 'home front'. But leaving aside the question of how far the revolution caused the military defeat, instead of vice versa, the intangible all-pervading factor of the blockade intrudes into every consideration of the military situation. The blockade was clearly the decisive agency in the struggle.[37]

The consequences of the British blockade were far-reaching. It cost 750,000 German lives and it motivated and shaped the history of, not just Europe, but the wider world. It underscored the fact that food is, was, and will always be a vital component in military operations at any level.

Notes

1. Keegan, Sir J., *The American Civil War* (London, Vintage, 2010), pp. 209, 272.
2. Mahan, A.T., *The Influence of Sea Power Upon History, 1660–1783* (Boston, Little Brown & Co., 1890).
3. Nash, N.S., *K-Boat Catastrophe: The Full Story of the Battle of the Isle of May* (Barnsley, Pen & Sword, 2009), pp. 132–3.
4. Britannica, The Editors of Encyclopaedia, 'Dreadnought', *Encyclopedia Britannica*, 5 March 2020.
5. Cant, S. & Dunkley, M., 'The Naval War' pdf (*Logistics of the First World War*), p. 36.
6. Davis, L.E. & Engerman, S.L., *Naval Blockades in Peace, and War: An Economic History since 1750* (New York, Cambridge University Press, 2006), p. 211.
7. Hough, R., *The Great War at Sea* (New York, Oxford University Press, 1983), p. 56.
8. Ibid.
9. Marder, A., *From the Dreadnought to Scapa Flow, The Royal Navy in the Fisher Era, 1904–1919: The War Years to the eve of Jutland: 1914–1916*, Vol. II (London, Oxford University Press, 1965), p. 149.
10. 'Casualty record, Theophilus Jones', Commonwealth War Graves Commission, archived from the original, 7 November 2018.

11. Davis, B.J., *Home Fires Burning: Food Politics, and Everyday Life in World War 1 Berlin* (London, University of North Carolina Press, 2000), p. 69.
12. Salter, J.A., *Allied Shipping Control* (Oxford, Clarendon Press, 1921), p. 1.
13. Belcham, J., *Industrialisation, and the Working Class: The English Experience 1750–1900* (Aldershot, Scolar Press, 1990), p. 208.
14. Royalparks.org.uk.
15. Standish, M., *A Life Apart: The English Working Class 1890–1914* (London, Thames & Hudson, 1977), p. 81.
16. Quoted in *Hoyt's New Encyclopedia of Practical Quotations* (1922), pp. 841–60.
17. Weddigen was killed in 1915. Then in command of *U-29*, his boat was rammed and sunk by HMS *Dreadnought*.
18. Davis, L.E. & Engerman, S.L., *Naval Blockades in Peace and War: An Economic History since 1750* (New York, Cambridge University Press, 2006), p. 201.
19. Adam, P., *How did the Convoy System help in the War against U-boats?* (www.Quora, 9 April 2022).
20. Wagner S.C., 'Biological Nitrogen Fixation' (*Nature Education Knowledge*, 2011), 3 (10): 15. It is an essential tool for agriculture and the manufacture of fertiliser.
21. Davis, B., *Food and Nutrition* (https://encyclopedia.1914-1918-online.net/article/food_and_nutrition_germany).
22. Collingham, L., *The Taste of War* (London, Penguin Group, 2011), p. 25.
23. Blücher, Princess E., *An English wife in Berlin* (New York, Button & Co., 1920), p. 122.
24. Vincent, C.P., *The Politics of Hunger: The Allied Blockade of Germany 1915–19* (London, Ohio University Press, 1985), p. 45. Quoted by Collingham, p. 24.
25. Persico, J.E., 'November 11, 1918: Wasted lives on Armistice Day' (*Army Times*, 10 November 2017).
26. Jukes, G., Simkins, P. & Hickey, M., *The First World War: The War to end all Wars* (London, Osprey Publishing, 2013), p. 131.
27. Watt, R.M., *Dare Call it Treason* (London, Chatto & Windus, 1963), p. 152.
28. Allard, P., *Les Énigmes de la Guerre* (Paris, Editions des Portiques, 1933), p. 198.
29. Jolinon, J., 'La Mutinerie de Coeuvres' (Paris, *Mercure de France*, 1920), p. 83.
30. *World War I Casualty and Death Tables*, Public Broadcasting System (USA), based on US Justice Department statistics (http://www.pbs.org/greatwar/resources/casdeath_pop.html).
31. Vincent, p. 131.
32. *Daily Telegraph*, 7 July 2022, 'Hangry in the field: An experience sampling study on the impact of hunger on anger, irritability, and affect', Swami, V., Hochstöger, S., Erik Kargl, E., Stefan Stiege, S. (*Plos One*, July 2022).
33. Email from Professor Swami to the author, 29 September 2022.
34. Meiselman to Nash, email of 22 August 2022 refers.
35. Hitler, A., *Mein Kampf* (Munich, Franz Eher Nachfolger GmbH, 1925).
36. Hough, p. 321.
37. Liddell Hart, B.H., *History of the First World War* [1934] (London, Cassell, 1970), p. 588.

Chapter Thirteen

Mesopotamia: the Fall of Kut (1914–16)

Military history is replete with ignorance, poor judgements, incompetence and vaunting ambition. All of these were available in abundance during the British campaign in Mesopotamia (now Iraq) in 1914–16. It provides another example of food denial, but to put that into context it is necessary to provide the background to one of Britain's greatest military defeats. The political and military events leading to the siege of Kut-Al-Amara are sufficiently unusual to merit their recitation, albeit briefly. Nevertheless, they show the inexorable, but entirely avoidable, passage to disaster.

The British invasion of Mesopotamia was a direct result of the decision by the Admiralty, on 27 November 1912, to accept the recommendation of a Royal Commission, headed by Admiral Lord Jackie Fisher, that ships of the RN should be powered by oil. Britain may have been resting on a foundation of coal, but the technology had moved on and the limitations of coal had been addressed by a singularly robust and capable personality. There is no doubt that 'providing the fleet with coal was the greatest logistic headache of the age'.[1]

That decision having been taken, one logistic burden had been replaced with another. Britain had no oil and securing a source that would keep the largest navy in the world at sea became a priority. There was an abundant supply of oil in Mesopotamia at Abadan, where the Anglo-Persian Oil Company had a flourishing facility. His Majesty's Government (HMG) had a major share in this company and thus an abiding interest in the island of Abadan (not shown on the map overleaf), situated at the confluence of the Karun River and the Shatt al Arab.

The Shatt al Arab at Basrah was about 800 yards wide (731m) and 7–12 feet (2–4m) deep. However, Basrah had no port facilities. The Royal Navy had been policing the Indian Ocean, the Gulf of Persia and the Shatt al Arab for decades. It had suppressed piracy in these waters with the tacit consent of the Turkish and Arab states along the shores. The Shatt was technically in Ottoman ownership.

There was a pressing need for Britain to secure this source of oil and the closest military force available for that task was the Indian Army. This army

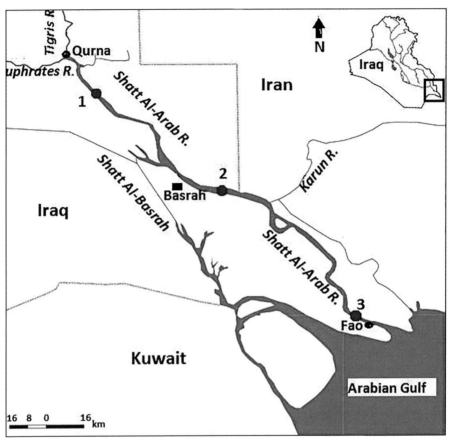

The confluence of the rivers Tigris and Euphrates, which, in combination, form the
Shatt al Arab. (*Abdul-Razak M. Mohamed, University of Basrah*)

was specifically formed, organised and equipped for operations in India.
It was never envisaged that the Indian Army would be deployed outside that
country.

In the summer of 1914, Britain's relations with Turkey were cool but getting
cool enough to be described as frosty. Two warships were being built in
Britain for the Ottoman Navy. These two, dreadnought quality vessels, the
Reshadieh and *Sultan Osman*, were diverted to the Royal Navy as HMS *Agin-
court* and *Erin*. This was an entirely reasonable decision as it would have been
nonsense to supply a likely/probable enemy with two powerful ships.

In India, the head of the Indian Government (IG) was the Viceroy, Lord
Hardinge. He was a career civil servant and before his appointment and
peerage, he had been the Permanent Under-Secretary of State for Foreign

Affairs. He was vastly experienced and at the pinnacle of public life. It did not necessarily make him infallible. He was probably the most decorated public servant in British history. By his life's end, he had attracted most of the honours possible.

> Military operations in Mesopotamia began in a modest and legitimate manner and Lord Hardinge's initial role was cautious and wholly commendable. As early as 17 August 1914 he stressed to the home government that for the sake of Muslim opinion in India any breach between Britain and Turkey must clearly be seen to be the result of Turkish actions.[2]

Hardinge had no illusions as to the capability of the Indian Army, which was composed of indigenous Indian troops led, in the main, by British officers, and supplemented by a leavening of wholly British units.

Prior to the outbreak of war, Hardinge was dedicated to reducing the cost of the Indian Army. Like generations of civil servants, then and now, faced with defence issues, but with no experience of soldiering, he sought to limit the numerical strength to the absolute minimum. He was unaware of the cruel fact of military life, that you cannot have effective defence on the cheap. It is argued that savings made today are paid for in blood tomorrow.

The lacklustre performance of General Creagh, the Commander-in-Chief of the Indian Army, over a protracted period obliged Hardinge to replace him. The new C-in-C selected was General Sir Beauchamp Duff. However, events would show that he, too, was a man of limited ability, lacking in any sort of vision and no improvement on the departed Creagh.

In London, the India Office was painfully aware of the importance of maintaining British prestige among the multiple tribal leaders of the British protected sheikhdoms of the Arabian Peninsula. It was on this basis that the Secretary of State for India, Lord Crewe, negotiated with the IG to arrange the despatch of a significant formation to the Shatt al Arab to reassure any wavering local allies of continuing British support whilst, at the same time, making it clear that Britain was prepared to use force to protect its interest in the Anglo-Persian Oil Company, and its installations and pipelines that terminated at Abadan Island.

Initially, Hardinge and Duff resisted the provision of Indian assets to secure the much-needed oil. They saw their duty to be the defence of India and the wider requirements of the Empire as of secondary importance. The RN made an exploratory excursion, on 29 October 1914, when it despatched HMS *Espiègle* and two other small ships to the northern Persian Gulf. *Espiègle* sailed up the Shatt Al Arab and this provoked a strong, diplomatic, Turkish response, which was ignored. A week later, 16 Indian Infantry Brigade

Charles Hardinge, 1st Baron Hardinge of
Penshurst, KG, GCB, GCSI, GCMG, GCVO, ISO,
PC, DL **(1858–1944)**

General Sir Beauchamp Duff, GCB, GCSI,
KCVO, CIE, KSt.J **(1855–1918),**
C-in-C The Indian Army 1913–16.

invaded Mesopotamia and took Basrah, a town of 60,000 people. Resistance was slight and the oil facilities at Abadan were secured.

The stated aim had been achieved and there the matter could, and should, have rested. However, 17th and 18th brigades quickly followed and the force of 15,000 was designated Indian Expeditionary Force 'D' (IEF'D'). The disembarkation of these 15,000 soldiers at Basrah was a minor epic as all had to be downloaded into bellums, the local small boat, rowed to the banks of the Shatt and then helped to scramble ashore.

The troops were accompanied by 1,600 camels. It quickly became apparent that there was a total absence of grazing for these beasts and 800 were promptly returned to their previous shipboard stables. The remaining 800 camels were the central element of the transport system now available for IEF'D'.

Basrah was a most unattractive place. It had little changed in the previous 300 years. The only water source was the fouled Shatt. There were no sewage arrangements, and the town was a hazard to health. There were no warehouses and no buildings suitable for the billeting of soldiers. A tented city sprang up outside the town, but the insanitary flies tormented everyone. The smell, filth and squalor repelled those new to this part of the world. It was in this deeply unsavoury place that Lieutenant General Sir Arthur Barrett, KCB, KCVO established his headquarters.

Three years later, the Mesopotamia Commission (MC) was formed to enquire into the exploits and defeat of IEF'D'. It commented that:

> The provision of adequate and suitable river transport above Basrah and of sufficient wharfage and unloading facilities at Basrah was necessary if effective military operations were to be carried out. An expeditionary force must be sea-borne, sea supported, and sea victualled.[3]

This is of course a statement of the blindingly obvious, and as already noted, a breakdown in logistic support is the first ingredient in any food denial strategy. By mid-November 1914, the Indian Army had embarked on the early stages of what was to become a massive 'own goal' and a logistic nightmare.

One of the aims of IEF'D' was to cement relations with the Arab population. Although entirely laudable, the aim was impracticable as the Indian and British soldiers held the Arabs in the lowest possible regard. They knew them to be masters of larceny who would steal anything and everything. Screwing things to the ground did not deter the thieves who would cut a throat if confronted. This was no place for a 'hearts and minds' initiative.

The India Office agreed with Hardinge and Duff that it made strategic sense to advance beyond Basrah and take Kurnah (Qurna) at the confluence of the Euphrates and Tigris rivers (*see* map on page 104). The occupation of the confluence would give control over the whole of the navigable waterway to the sea and the richly cultivated area around Kurnah.

Kurnah was every bit as repellent as Basrah; its inhabitants fouled the waters of the Tigris, and it was prudent to take drinking water from the middle of the stream because the daily defecation of countless Arabs decorated the banks and the shallows.

It was alleged that Kurnah was the site of the Garden of Eden, but that seems to be unlikely, as it is set in one of the most hostile environments on Earth. An Arab proverb avers: 'When Allah made hell, he did not find it bad enough, so he made Mesopotamia – and then he added flies.' Despite the oppressive heat and the trillions of flies, Kurnah was duly taken, with a loss of 29 killed and 242 wounded. Ottoman losses were over a thousand killed, wounded, and captured.[4]

This minor Indian/British advance was the first example of 'mission creep' instigated by the Indian Government. However, at about this time, Hardinge,

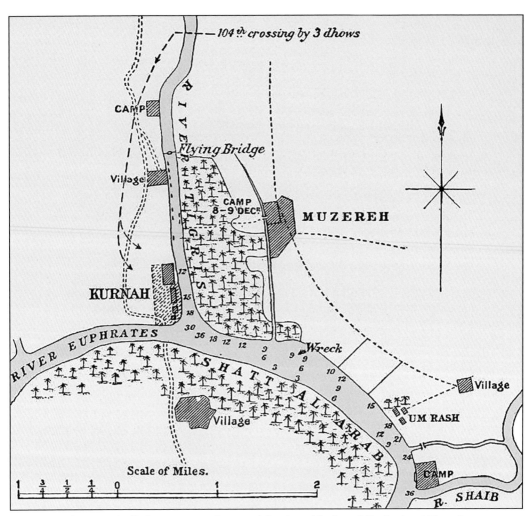

The strategically important confluence of the rivers Tigris and Euphrates at Kurnah.
(World War 1 at Sea)

with Duff's tacit support, decided that he would annex the whole of Mesopotamia, take the capital Baghdad, and add the entire territory to the Indian Empire. Hardinge did not advertise this vaulting ambition, which was wholly inappropriate for an unelected public servant. The relatively easy victory at Kurnah, on 19 November, served to bolster the outrageous hubris of Hardinge and Duff. A little later, when HMG in London heard of the Hardinge plan, it was 'peremptorily swept aside'.[5] It was at this point that the aims of HMG and the IG started to diverge. On 23 November 1914, a conference was held in Basrah at which Commander A. Hamilton of the Royal Indian Marine recommended to the General Staff that it should, as a matter of urgency, place orders for twelve of the *Medjidieh* class of river steamer. Hamilton was a subject matter expert with years of experience working on the Tigris, but his advice was rejected out of hand. The Mesopotamia Commission later commented that:

> There is reason to believe that had Commander Hamilton's foresight, knowledge and advice been acted upon subsequent difficulties would have been mitigated, if not altogether avoided.[6]

Hardinge visited Mesopotamia in late January 1915, and he was accorded all the deference and military honours to which his exalted rank entitled him. It fed his ego, and notwithstanding the quite specific wishes of the Secretary of State for India, it refuelled his territorial ambitions.

Intelligence reports indicated a likely Turkish attack on Abadan, and Duff was asked by HMG to send a reinforcing brigade to Basrah. Duff demurred and it was necessary for HMG to issue a direct order. On 1 April, and without reference to London, the IG decided to reorganise its troops in Mesopotamia into an army corps and Lieutenant General Sir John Nixon was appointed as its commander. General Barrett left the theatre on spurious health grounds, one of only two general officers to leave that place with his reputation still intact.

Nixon hit the ground running and was fully supportive of Harding and Duff's aspirations. He was armed with written orders from Duff that charged him with 'reporting on the requirement for river transport and on the desirability of building a railway with 137 miles [220km] of track'. In addition, he was to 'plan an effective occupation of Basrah Vilayet and plan for a subsequent advance on Baghdad'.

Nixon at once initiated a robust plan to take Baghdad. His corps consisted of two divisions. The first of these, and the cutting edge, was 6 (Poona) Indian Division commanded by Major General Charles Townshend, CB, DSO. This formation was deficient in a wide range of personnel and equipment. Its medical element was not geared to the medical needs of a division on active service in such an intimidating environment. The personnel issue was worsened when Nixon removed soldiers from 6 Division to staff his headquarters and his mess. Townshend was vastly aggrieved, and he recorded in his memoirs that he made repeated efforts:

> to induce Headquarters at Basrah to send back to my battalions the scores of British soldiers … who were employed in every imaginable kind of billet in Basrah – as police, clerks, batmen for officers of the Indian Army (who were not entitled to British soldiers as servants), chauffeurs for a regular fleet of motor launches, marines on gun boats, extra hands to strengthen reservist crews of blue jackets – all taken from the bayonets of my division.[7]

Lieutenant General Sir John Nixon, GCMG, KCB (1857–1921),
GOC-in-C Mesopotamia 1915–16.

The second of Nixon's divisions was 12 Indian Division commanded by Major General G.F. Gorringe, DSO (later Lieutenant General Sir George Gorringe, KCB, KCMG, DSO). This was a weak formation, and initially, it had no artillery. It played only a small role in this period.

Operations in Mesopotamia from April 1915 were led by Townshend. He was the key player, and it is necessary to explore his personality. Townshend was known throughout the army as 'Chitrál Charlie' for his successful defence of an obscure fort on the north-west frontier of India in 1895. He was a captain at the time, and for six weeks, Chitrál was a focus of international attention as it was besieged by dissident tribesmen.

Townshend did no more than his duty but, when the siege was lifted, he was made a Companion of the Order of the Bath (CB). This was an award usually given to general officers (colonel and above) and it was without precedent for a captain to receive such a decoration. A bar to his DSO would have been more appropriate. On his return from India, he was feted by the great and the good. It all rather went to his head and further inflated his ego, as did his sobriquet, 'Chitrál Charlie'.

Townshend was a gregarious, positive personality, a capable, articulate individual, who played and sang to his banjo and had demonstrable personal courage. He was a student of the business of arms and an admirer of Napoleon. Indeed, he believed that he had Napoleonic characteristics and

Major General C.V.F. Townshend, CB, DSO (later Sir Charles KCB, DSO) (1861–1924), GOC 6 Indian Division 1915–16.

was given to lecturing his senior officers on military history. He was unreasonably ambitious, and impossibly immodest. One of his less attractive traits was his constant criticism of his superiors but, with notable lack of moral courage, he never confronted any of them. Townshend was admired by his soldiers but not by his brother officers.[8] Few men are heroes to their biographers and this writer concluded that Townshend was probably the embodiment of 'the military shit'.[9]

Notwithstanding Townshend's personal characteristics, he was an innovative and single-minded individual who led 6 Division with skill and resolve.

His objective was to be Baghdad, 279 miles (450km) away, and the only way to get there was by ship up the Tigris River, which wound its sinuous course for 502 miles (808km) north from Basrah. Along the way, 6 Division would have to sweep aside the Turkish opposition along the riverbanks.

Marching along the riverbank was shorter but, over the centuries, irrigation ditches had been constructed from the Tigris. Some of these ditches were formidable obstacles to the traveller on foot or in a wagon. Mesopotamia was a land without building material. There were no suitable trees to provide timber and neither bricks nor stone. Bridging ditches, hundreds of them, was a logistic issue.

The Tigris was navigable, but passage was slow as uncharted sandbanks had to be circumvented and the depth of the river was variable. The river provided the communications and logistic route. It was also the only evacuation route for the wounded. However, it was very vulnerable along its 502-mile length, and at any point, this vital line of communication might be cut.

Nixon was described by Hardinge as being 'a keen hard soldier [who] revelled in responsibility'.[10] That might be the case, but he was also logistically illiterate, and had responsibility for a campaign that would be totally dependent on the full gamut of logistic support. Nixon was the wrong man in the wrong job.

The progress of 6 Division towards Baghdad is testament to the resilience, courage and commitment of its Indian and British soldiers. The dead were buried on the spot. However, for the wounded, the first part of an excruciating journey was their carriage to a 'hospital ship'. The MS commented:

> no satisfactory reason has been assigned for the failure to provide the ordinary form of land ambulance for these operations ... The usual form of ambulance transport has been the army transport cart, that is a small springless cart made of wood and iron and drawn by mules or ponies and ordinarily employed for the carriage of supplies. When the evidence of the suffering caused by this means of conveyance, particularly in the case of fracture or severe injury ... it is difficult to avoid criticising those responsible.[11]

The 3–5-day journey back to Basrah, in river ships wholly unsuited to the task, was a living hell. Lying in their excrement in temperatures of 115°F, tortured by trillions of flies and with scant food, many died along the way. The medical support of 6 Division was a public scandal that was a feature of the entire campaign.

On 25 September, Townshend received a signal from General Duff that said, 'No going beyond Kut-al-Amara' (*see* map on page 111). Townshend

This is the infamous army transport cart. The men in the photograph are smiling. But if, and when, any of them were wounded they would have suffered horribly as they were moved several miles to the riverside in the un-sprung, un-upholstered cart.

mused in his dairy, 'When was Sir Beauchamp Duff induced to change his mind and who persuaded him to do so?' The message arrived just as Townshend was making final preparations for his assault on Kut. He had General Nixon for company who had come upriver to spectate at the coming battle and take a share in any glory that might follow success.

Townshend's plan was bold, innovative and successful. The capture of Kut, on 29 September, was a high-water mark for the Indian Army. Townshend did not know but it also marked the apogee of his career. The MC commented:

> This part of the campaign was brilliantly executed by General Townshend … And the whole series of military operations during the past three months had been so extraordinarily successful that it is not surprising that a spirit of optimism and over-confidence as to what could be achieved overcame General Nixon and his Headquarters staff.

Townshend had anticipated 6 per cent casualties, but the 'butcher's bill' was 12 per cent. However, of his 1,229 casualties, incredibly only 94 were killed. The Turks lost 1,700 killed and wounded and 1,289 taken prisoner. Surgeon General Hathaway's medical arrangements were inadequate and General Nixon was witness to the medical incompetence and the deficiencies in the river fleet. He took passage in a ship back to Basrah.

6 Indian Division had set out on its odyssey in April 1915, it had been in action for five months and was now depleted. The attrition in its ranks caused

A British hospital ship on the Tigris, 1915.

by a combination of heatstroke, exhaustion, assorted diseases, and military action had now reduced the capability of the division. On 3 October, Townshend sent a politically critical telegram to Nixon. In this he outlined his situation, pointing out that the Turks had established a strong blocking position at Ctesiphon and casting doubt on the practicality of proceeding further upriver to Baghdad. Townshend knew his military history, and he was a seasoned soldier with years of campaigning behind him. The nub of his telegram was in his recommendation that he stay where he was and consolidate the division's position at Kut.

Major General George Kemball, DSO, Nixon's Chief of Staff, replied on the same day and said, patronisingly, that Townshend had clearly not considered Nixon's 'appreciation of the situation'. The army commander had calculated that Townshend was confronted by only 4,000 bayonets, 500 sabres and 20 guns. Quite where and how Nixon obtained his intelligence was never explained. Kemball sweetened the pill by adding that it was Nixon's intention to open the way to Baghdad and that he understood that another division was to be sent from France. This statement had all the authenticity of the plaque often seen in British pubs that avows 'Free beer tomorrow'.

Townshend's telegram found its way into the public domain. The author, who was already a household name, found himself the subject of discussion in both Houses of Parliament. Nixon denied ever having seen the telegram and in his evidence to the MC he said, 'If he says he sent it in, I suppose he did … Personally I have no recollection of that appreciation and I'm not sure that it arrived. I never saw it.' Duff also denied knowledge of the telegram.

Townshend kept a diary, and he recorded his response to the 'another division' and clearly saw it as nonsense.

Townshend stood at a moral crossroads. He could refuse to move towards Baghdad, and had he done so, he would have been summarily sacked, and his career finished. His moral courage would have won him huge respect. However, Townshend chose the easy way out and said that, as there was another division on the way, he rescinded his previous advice. It was a craven decision with dreadful consequences.

Townshend continued his advance for 40 miles (64km) to Ctesiphon and there, over three days of ferocious fighting, he won a pyrrhic victory against a strong, determined, well-entrenched Turkish force 18,000 strong. Nixon's appreciation was wildly incorrect and 4,600 soldiers of 6 Division paid the price for their divisional commander's lack of moral backbone. The Turks suffered 6,200 casualties and when they withdrew on 24 November, Townshend had won valueless territory soaked in blood. Any Nixonian aspiration to take Baghdad evaporated.

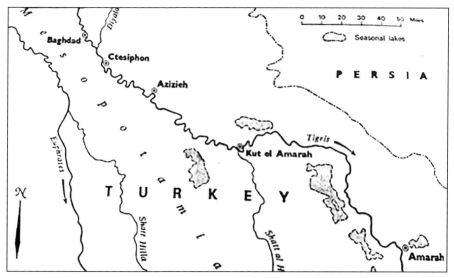

The area of later operations by 6th Indian Division. It shows the sinuous Tigris River, upon which Townshend and his soldiers were totally dependent.

Townshend executed a very professional fighting withdrawal back to Kut. He was pursued by the Turks and by predatory Arabs who would butcher any stragglers. Nevertheless, Townshend withdrew the remnant of his division in good order. As they trudged into the town the 10,398 tired men of 6 Division arrived in Kut, but it was no haven – merely a defendable position. The cavalry brigade of 1,505 sabres could play no useful part in any forthcoming siege and so Townshend quite reasonably sent it back to Basrah. British and Indian soldiers entertained aspirations of hot food, clean bedding, pretty nurses, cold beer (for non-Muslims) and a catch-up on their sleep. They got none of these because Kut was a town as equally obnoxious as Basrah and Kurnah. It offered no facilities, and the first priority was to 'dig in' and prepare defensive positions. The 6 Indian Division would have to exist in and around the town until reinforced, and more importantly, resupplied.

It has taken time for the patient reader to have reached the critical point when, on 3 December 1915, the Turkish forces, under the German General Baron von der Goltz, cut the umbilical cord that connected 6 Division to Basrah. Baron von Goltz had spent many years in Ottoman service, and he was a formidable adversary.

Townshend had seemed to accept that a siege was inevitable, and history shows that sieges are invariably the result of an earlier defeat. The siege of Kut is no exception to the rule. It has been suggested that Townshend expected to reprise his success at Chitrál, but the situations were vastly different and Winston Churchill, writing about twenty years later, said, 'Every great operation of war is unique … There is no surer road to disaster than to imitate the plans of bygone heroes and fit them to novel situations.'[12]

Townshend had 8,980 defenders, of which, 7,411 were infantry. He had to defend a trench line 2,700 yards (2.47km) long and he determined that he needed to deploy three to five men per running yard; on that basis, he was undermanned. He had to garrison Woolpress village (bottom left of map on page 114) and he had to exercise control over the indigent Arab population. Townshend had no illusions about the hostile civilian Arabs he now had, unwillingly, under his aegis. He realised that they constituted a fifth column and had no doubt that there were weapons and food concealed in the town. It was Townshend's instinct to expel the entire civilian population, but he was restrained by the political agent who pointed out that such a measure would result in the deaths of women and children in the deserts outside the town either from hunger, exposure, or the depredations of fellow Arabs.[13] Militarily necessary perhaps, but politically impossible.

Townshend looked for some middle ground and expelled about 700 Arabs who were not householders. He took twenty hostages from the balance of 5,000–6,000 as surety of good behaviour. Action had to be taken against those stealing from his soldiers. To emphasise his determination to end the looting, he caused twelve men, caught red-handed, to be tried by a court martial. They were all shot. Townshend took the view – *pour encourager les autres*.[14]

While 6 Division worked furiously digging trenches, in India, Hardinge, their political master, was declaiming that the Battle of Ctesiphon had been 'a blessing in disguise'. He argued that it had 'given the Expeditionary Force the opportunity to inflict a good beating upon the Turks'. He added:

> Talk of Townshend being trapped in Kut is total nonsense. I ridicule the idea that he should want relief for, with his 9,000 men he is supposed to be surrounded by 10,000 Turks and can break out whenever he chooses. It's really like one man surrounding another.'[15]

The extraordinary, actually absurd, views expressed by Hardinge were those of a man unversed in military matters, far from the scene and dependent upon dangerously misleading advice.

Relations between Austin Chamberlain, Secretary of State for India since May 1915, and Hardinge were weakening as the latter resented any suggestions made by his superior. Chamberlain did not share the Viceroy's view of Nixon and advised the Prime Minister, Asquith, that his 'confidence in Nixon's judgement is seriously shaken by his complete miscalculation as to changes in Baghdad'. He added that Kitchener, the War Minister, also thought that Nixon should be replaced.[16]

Hemmed into the Kut peninsula were over 22,000 people of various persuasions, 1,000 horses, 2,000 mules and ponies, and 100 bullocks. All those mouths had to be fed and Townshend was fully aware that von der Goltz, his adversary, held the all-powerful food denial card. Surprisingly, given his grasp of military history, he did not measure his food stocks and thus was unable to calculate, accurately, the endurance of his command. This oversight was to have serious consequences.

The river Tigris provided the sole means of resupply. It was insecure and traffic along it was now very vulnerable to enemy action. Any relief of the Kut garrison would require the taking and holding of both banks of the river along its length.

Undaunted, Townshend wrote, 'My former experience of sieges had shown me the great advantages of keeping up the spirits of my troops by means of instilling belief in the arrival of succour from without.'[17] Over the following four months, Townshend's *communiqués* were a source of intelligence for the enemy and self-inflicted wounds to his reputation. In them, he pleaded with his soldiers for sympathy and denigrated those seeking to come to his rescue. He presented a very poor image of a British officer and a commander.

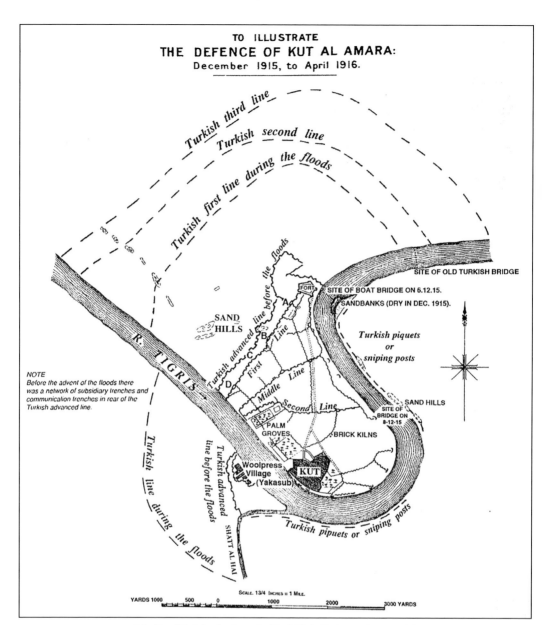

TO ILLUSTRATE
THE DEFENCE OF KUT AL AMARA:
December 1915, to April 1916.

6 Indian Division's stronghold at Kut. (*Ordnance Survey 1924*)

On 10 December, Lieutenant General Fenton Aylmer vc, kcb, an old acquaintance of Townshend, arrived in Basrah to take command of the relief force, the Tigris Corps, 20,000 strong. Aylmer was a Royal Engineer, and his VC was testament to his value as a warrior. He was an exemplary officer.

At Kut and for three days, 10–12 December, von der Goltz mounted major assaults on the British first line and concentrated on the mud fort (middle of the map above). An artillery bombardment preceded savage hand-to-hand fighting. Turkish casualties were very high and when the fighting subsided, 948 (someone counted) corpses lay in front of the British trenches. The probability was that there were at least 2,000 others licking their wounds. Licking was probably the only option because the Ottoman Army was badly served, medically. On 24 December, von der Goltz tried again; 315 defenders were killed and wounded, but again, Turkish casualties were far greater and losses of 2,000 were later confirmed. Since the opening of the siege, the 'Kuttites', as they now called themselves, had suffered 926 casualties, and of these, about 300 had been killed.

von der Goltz reached the same conclusion as Grant had done at Vicksburg, Crown Prince Charles at Metz, and Moltke outside Paris – he sat back and played the food denial card.

Turkish prisoners from the 39th Division revealed that the 35th, 38th, 45th and 51st divisions were all present in the cordon around the town. The 52nd and 26th were on their way. Townshend was surrounded by at least 40,000 Turks and his options were very limited. The Turks were accomplished snipers and there was daily attrition to headshots. This gave rise to the 'Kut stoop'. Counter-sniping teams were formed, and they had the desired effect. Early in the new year, the Turks approached under a white flag and asked if they could remove their recent dead. This was to be welcomed but, when Townshend made it clear that any attempt to use this as a ruse to refill their trenches would attract heavy fire, the Turks left their dead unburied and putrefying. The stench was stomach-turning, and after three months' exposure to burning sun, freezing nights, driving rain and the close attention of trillions of insects, the bodies decomposed. They could only be moved by dragging them with long poles fitted with hooks, and then they were tipped into pits. Many Turkish bodies fell apart; there was no dignity in death for these men – all some mother's son.

Aylmer, anxious to get to Kut and lift the siege, found himself a victim of Nixon's logistic policy. Aylmer had a dearth of bridging and signalling equipment and he found that he had to cope with a bizarre reinforcement policy. This involved sending each draft of reinforcements on foot on the fourteen days' march to the north, with their equipment following them. The second-line transport, which included such trifles as blankets and medical supplies, came on last. Under these extraordinary arrangements the men, quite unnecessarily, spent fourteen very cold, hungry nights in the desert. The rigours of this march contributed to some of the reinforcements being medical cases before battle was joined.

Chamberlain signalled direct to Townshend and asked him how long he could hold Kut. Townshend, in an act of disloyalty and deceit, replied, 'ten or fifteen days'. Townshend's motive was to inject urgency into the relief operation, and he succeeded, but it forced Aylmer to act precipitously, and lives were lost consequently.

A little later, Townshend admitted to Nixon that he had food for two months. The weather broke, and as they always did, the Euphrates and Tigris rivers burst their banks and flooded thousands of square miles of desert. Ironically, wounded men drowned in this desert. It was across this flooded wilderness that Aylmer and his soldiers struggled. They fought a series of battles against determined opposition and despite poor logistic and medical support. It was a desperate venture conducted in haste as Townshend continued to mislead his rescuers as to his food state.

On 20 January, Townshend put everyone on to half rations. He offered gratuitous advice to Aylmer on how to proceed and addressed the pressing matter of his promotion to lieutenant general. In Kut, the soldiers were hungry; horses and mules were providing meat but lack of vegetables in any form was affecting health.

Ill health is no respecter of rank, and in late January 1916, General Nixon was invalided back to India. He was not missed and was replaced by Lieutenant General Sir Percy Lake, who was appalled by the legacy left to him by Nixon. In his previous job, Lake had been Chief of Staff to General Duff, and in that capacity, read all communications. He realised how deeply he and Duff had been misled by Nixon.

A minor first in military history, on 31 January 1916, was the delivery by air of newspapers, mail and small items to Kut. From 15 to 29 April, 30 Squadron, Royal Flying Corps delivered 16,800lb of food to the besieged town.[18] It was not enough, but thereafter the aeroplane changed siege warfare for ever.

On 23 January, Townshend produced another of his 'appreciations of the situation' and in it he offered three alternatives:

(a) Break out with as many men as possible.
(b) To defend Kut to the last round.
(c) Negotiate with the enemy to give up Kut in exchange for free passage for his garrison.

With his tongue firmly in his cheek, he recommended (a) but favoured (c). To his consternation, Lake endorsed his recommendation of (a). Townshend would have to vacillate to ensure that it did not happen. He re-evaluated his food stocks and said he had thirty-four days' food remaining. This would feed his garrison to very early March.

March came and went. By April, the garrison was starving, and men were dying. Townshend visited the hospital but gave all his attention to British soldiers and scant attention to the majority of patients, who were Indian.

By the middle of April, the garrison of Kut was in dire straits and it was evident that the end was near. Townshend wanted to negotiate with the Turks, but his opposite number, the Turkish General Nureddin (von der Goltz had died), was well informed, and he was not prepared to make any concessions. He demanded unconditional surrender.

Meanwhile, Aylmer had been dismissed. His Tigris Corps had fought valiantly in appalling conditions, incurred losses of 23,000, but was nowhere near to relieving Kut. Command of the corps passed to Major General George Gorringe, who was promoted to lieutenant general. When Townshend heard the news, he wept on the shoulder of one of his officers. Gorringe had been his junior, and for Townshend, being 'passed over' was more than he could bear. It was an unsoldierly, inappropriate response and an indicator of his unrealistic ambition. He was patently in no position to assume the duties of a Tigris corps commander or a corps commander anywhere else.

Kut surrendered on 29 April 1916. It was defeated by hunger and the Turkish food denial strategy had been entirely successful. It was the blackest day in British military history since the fall of Kabul in 1842. During the siege, 1,513 had been killed, 721 died of disease or starvation, 1,958 were wounded, and 72 men were 'missing'. Most of the missing men were from 67th Punjabi Battalion and had been killed on 9 December 1915, outside the confines of the garrison. Their bodies were not recovered. The unmeasured balance were deserters.[19]

The civilian population of about 6,000 did not get away unscathed; 247 were killed and 663 wounded. The final 'butcher's bill' for operations in Mesopotamia between September 1914 and May 1916 was 40,000. All this achieved was possession of unlovely Basrah, no political advantage, the destruction of reputations, and enormous misery and suffering.[20]

Amid this surrender the Turks summarily hanged a considerable number of civilians whom it termed 'collaborators' – those who lived in the township had no other option but to collaborate. Turkish ruthlessness now extended to the starving British and Indian soldiers, many of whom could hardly walk. Townshend was treated with fawning courtesy by the victors, who returned his sword and revolver. The general moved among his men and pronounced, 'I'm going to get you all parole.'[21] He did nothing of the sort.

The Turks assembled their prisoners on the riverbank and there dumped a heap of rock-hard biscuits. Men whose teeth had been loosened by food deprivation could not eat these fibrous biscuits. They soaked them in the waters of the Tigris, and this made them more digestible but no less unpalatable. Soon thereafter, men started to froth at the mouth, their bowels loosened, and their stomachs rebelled. 'A green slime' was produced and in short order, death followed for many. The doctors called it 'enteritis'. The ghastly march to captivity followed in which stragglers were bayonetted. It was the start of an extended and protracted war crime. 'Of the British and Indian rank and file ... over seventy percent died in captivity or have never been traced.'[22]

Townshend could and should have worked to protect his men. Instead, he took passage with his entire personal staff in a ship and sailed away to very comfortable house arrest, where he was made a welcome guest until the end of the war. During those two and a half years, he espoused the Turkish cause.

Townshend's complete abandonment of his officers and men was the most heinous offence a British officer could commit. It transcends mere treachery, and it earned him widespread contempt, but no indictment. He died in 1924 and his grave is covered with a moss-encrusted stone slab upon which is inscribed 'Townshend of Kut'.

The toxic trio of Harding, Duff and Nixon, who were responsible for the abortive drive on Baghdad, were subject to excoriating criticism when the MS reported in June 1917. It concluded, in a minority report, that Hardinge and Duff 'had shown little desire to help and some desire to actually obstruct the

This group of Indian soldiers were photographed having survived imprisonment by the Turks. Indian soldiers had made up two-thirds of the garrison at Kut, and after the surrender, they were subjected to starvation and brutality by their captors. The effects of food denial are plain to see.

energetic prosecution of the war'.[23] Nixon was also chastised for his abject performance. However, incompetence, poor judgement and lack of commitment are not criminal offences, and the three men were not prosecuted.

Duff committed suicide in January 1918. Nixon retired from the Army in 1916, had a mental breakdown and died, in 1921, of natural causes. Hardinge went on to greater things and ended his career as HM's Ambassador to France. He wrote his memoirs and covered the entire Mesopotamian debacle in less than three pages. He expressed no regret or remorse for the lives he caused to be lost, and died, much decorated, in 1944, aged 86.

Summary

The fall of Kut, the surrender of 6 Indian Division, and the later deaths of so many soldiers in Turkish hands was, indisputably, the result of von der Goltz's highly effective siege and the starvation it generated.

von der Goltz had died on 16 April 1916, and just two weeks later, General Nureddin accepted the capitulation of Townshend and his division. The division was defeated not by force of arms but, arguably, by the ineptitude of Nixon and the absurd ambition of Hardinge, which, in combination, failed to put in place a functioning defendable logistic chain to feed Townshend and his men.

Notes

1. Dahl, E.J., 'From Coal to Oil' (Washington, *Joint Force Quarterly*, Winter 2000/1), p. 50.
2. Gould, D., 'Hardinge and the Mesopotamia Commission' (Cambridge University Press, *The Historical Journal*, December 1976), pp. 919–45.
3. Report of the Mesopotamia Commission, 1917, p. 9.
4. Barker, A.J., *The First Iraq War, 1914–1918, Britain's Mesopotamian Campaign* [1967] (New York, Enigma, 2009), p 36.
5. MC, p. 15.
6. Ibid., p. 32.
7. Barker, A.J., *The First Iraq War, 1914–1918, Britain's Mesopotamian Campaign* [1967] (New York, Enigma, 2009), p. 144.
8. Nash, N.S., *Betrayal of an Army* (Barnsley, Pen & Sword, 2016), p. 36.
9. Nash, N.S., *Chitrál Charlie: The Rise and Fall of Major General Charles Townshend* (Barnsley, Pen & Sword, 2010).
10. Gould, D., pp. 919–45.
11. MC, p. 105.
12. Churchill, W.S., *Marlborough: His Life and Times* [1933] (University of Chicago Press, 2002).
13. Townshend, Maj Gen. C.V.F., *My Campaign in Mesopotamia* (London, Thornton Butterworth, 1920), p. 227.
14. Ibid.
15. Hardinge to Chamberlain, 31 December 1915 (*Hardinge papers*). Hardinge to Cox, 28 December 1915 (*Hardinge papers 94*), No. 155.
16. Chamberlain to Hardinge, 9 and 16 December 1915 (*Chamberlain papers, 62/2*).
17. Townshend, p. 222.

18. Molkentin, M., *The Centenary History of Australia in the Great War Vol. 1* (Melbourne, Oxford University Press, 2014), p. 8.
19. Moberly, F.J., *The History of the Great War: The Campaign in Mesopotamia* (London, HMSO, Vol. 2), p. 459.
20. Nash, *Betrayal*, p. 215.
21. Eato, H., quoted by Braddon, R., in *The Siege* (London, Jonathan Cape, 1969), p. 259.
22. Moberly, p. 460.
23. MS *Report*, para 47, p. 131.

PART FOUR

THE SECOND WORLD WAR

Chapter Fourteen

Germany and the Hunger Plan
(1939–45)

In the Second World War, there were several distinct areas in which the provision of food, although of paramount importance, was not available, as later chapters will chronical. However, there was one campaign in which a new benchmark of barbarity was set. It shaped German attitudes towards the production, acquisition and distribution of foodstuffs to the indigenous population in its captured territories.

During Hitler's rise to power, the Nazi leadership never tired of informing its population of the pressing need for Germany to address the shortage of land for agriculture.

> Germany was more densely populated than France and lacked the colonial outlets available to Britain. In comparison to other west European countries Germany was indeed land poor. Compared to Britain, Germany had more land, but its rural population was disproportionally larger.[1]

Germany was able to relate its per capita GDP to Britain, France and the United States. However, in purely agricultural terms, it was a Third World country and more akin to Bulgaria or Romania. In 1937, a study was conducted, and the results are shown overleaf.

The table illustrates the juxtaposition of Germany in agricultural terms, and ostensibly, explains the Nazi claims of being short of land. However, the solution lay not in waging war across the globe but in restructuring German agriculture. In a nutshell, the available farmed countryside in Germany was insufficient to support the agrarian population.

In 1933, 7,000 estates of more than 500 hectares, just over 0.2 per cent of all farms, controlled 25 per cent of German farmland. By contrast, 74 per cent of all farms in Germany, 2.26 million in total, farmed only 19 per cent of the land in often widely dispersed holdings of between 0.5 and 10 hectares.[2]

The majority of the population who farmed lived at about subsistence level and the need for reformation of the agricultural system was evident. The land reform option had been debated in Germany for decades and was first implemented in 1919 when the Weimar Republic made a start by breaking up

Results of the 1937 study showing Germany's position in agricultural terms.

	Farming population 000s	Arable land 000 ha	Arable ha per farmer	Arable ha per farmer, Germany = 100
Canada	1,107	23,120	20.9	1,009.5
United States	10,752	137,333	12.8	617.4
Denmark	561	2,663	4.7	229.4
Britain	1,413	5,329	3.8	182.3
Soviet Union	71,734	223,916	3.1	150.5
France	7,709	21,386	2.8	134.1
Irish Free State	678	1,484	2.2	105.8
Germany	9,388	19,422	2.1	100.0
Poland	10,269	18,557	1.8	87.3
Italy	8,008	12,753	1.6	77.0
Romania	9,207	13,866	1.5	72.8
Bulgaria	2,464	3,711	1.5	72.8
British India	179,947	125,397	0.7	33.7

Source: SRA *Statistisches Jahrbuch für das Deutsche Reich 1937* (Berlin, 1937).

the great eastern estates of 500 hectares or more (an acre is 0.405 hectares, and 1 hectare contains about 2.47 acres) and creating many smaller, but efficient holdings. Nowhere in the Third Reich was any land holding to exceed 10 per cent of the arable landscape.

Land purchase was pursued, and local committees were charged with buying up estates and transferring the land to peasant settlers. This measure was expensive and fiercely resisted by the land-owning families. Progress was slow and 'in the period 1919–1933 only 939,000 hectares were transferred to new settlement'.[3] Land reform had a long way to go before it was efficient, and the unhappy conclusion reached by the Nazi leadership was that German territory was still insufficient to provide for a disproportionally large agricultural population.

Hitler had experienced the hunger of his country during the First World War, shared its humiliation, and was resolved never to permit a recurrence. His philosophy of *Lebensraum* (living space) called for territory in which Germany could populate and farm, and by so doing ensure abundant food in perpetuity. It was Russia that could provide Hitler's answer and that country lay at the heart of his strategy. However, like everything in his life, the strategy was overlaid and dominated by his racial ideology. Operation BARBAROSSA, launched on 22 June 1941, 'unleashed an unprecedented campaign of genocidal violence' and it epitomised the Nazi creed.[4]

The invasion was an opportunistic land grab to provide that 'living space' for Germans. It was also intended to reap the benefits of Russian agriculture, and importantly, to allow social engineering on an epic scale. There was to be the clearance 'of most of the Slav population and the settlement of millions of hectares of eastern *Lebensraum* with German colonists'.[5]

The planning for BARBAROSSA had recognised that the limited Russian railway system was incompatible with that of Germany and Poland and that there was a dearth of all-weather roads running west to east. Transport, always a key logistic component, was going to be an issue in the forthcoming operation and a likely shortage of fuel compounded the problem. The German Army could only function in the east if it fed itself by living off the land it had captured in the west. The western regions of Russia and Ukraine were perceived to be available 'breadbaskets'.[6] As early as 2 May 1941, it was acknowledged that the invading army, living parasitically in Russia, would cause the deaths of tens of millions of people.[7]

The Hunger Plan made clear the criticality of the plan by saying, 'The war can only be continued if the entire Wehrmacht is fed from Russia in the third year of the war.'[8] In Germany, the National Socialist Party had prepared for the coming war, and two officials were the prime movers in the making of food production and distribution policy. Walter Darré was the Minister for Food, and his acolyte was Herbert Backe. Between them, they had marshalled their country's agriculture and established a culture that nothing was to be wasted. Both realised that Germany had to win a short war if it was to depend on home-produced food, and given its swift advance across Europe in 1940, that seemed to be a realistic aim.

As it happens, the farmers of Germany, with the forced labour of subject people, sustained their country for over five years. The country was not self-sufficient, and neither were its conquered territories; for example, pre-war, Norway imported 57 per cent of its food and France 17 per cent. There were no plans to help in the feeding of those countries. The ambitious plan to depend upon imported food from Russia, under the terms of the 1939 Treaty of Non-Aggression, did not meet German needs. To add to its food issues, the RN was blockading German ports, a reprise of 1914. The importation of food ceased and only twelve ships breached the blockade in 1941–2.[9]

In Germany, a solution had been found to any projected shortage of food. It was all so chillingly simple. The German civil servant Herbert Backe concluded that the answer was to reduce the numbers to be fed. It was the 'Hunger Plan' (HP), and an integral part of Operation BARBAROSSA and of the Holocaust. The plan required the elimination, by starvation, of millions of 'useless eaters'. The deliberate creation of famine was the weaponisation of food at its most extreme.[10] This went far beyond the food denial scenarios that this text has touched upon so far. The scale of this inhuman plan dwarfs even the industrial scale murders of 6 million Jews. It was anticipated that

Obergruppenführer Herbert Backe (1886–1947). He cheated the hangman by committing suicide.

20–30 million would die under German aegis and the plan became known as 'Göring's Green Folder'. The philosophy of the HP was widely advertised, and all participants in BARBAROSSA were enjoined:

> to understand and commit themselves to its strategic logic. The geno-cidal plan commanded such wide-ranging support because … it was obvious to all … the need [was] to secure the food supply for the German population at the expense of the population of the Soviet Union.[11]

Backe was responsible for the implementation of the plan that would be enforced by the Wehrmacht. The killing of people by bomb or bullet usually draws a robust armed response but, in this case, there could be no response. The victims did not resist, and consequently, for the Germans the HP had little or no physical risk.

Backe was a bureaucrat, he drove a desk and pushed a pen, but he was as evil as any of those who ran extermination camps. Backe was of course assisted by many others, and not the least of these was Hans-Joachim Riecke, who died peacefully in his bed in 1986. The Hunger Plan did not meet its multi-million target in full but was, nevertheless, responsible for about 4.7 million deaths. However, there is no intention to dwell on the grotesque behaviour of the Germans in Eastern Europe. That is a topic that has been examined, judged and reported upon at great length by battalions of other historians. This text will avoid the bayonetting, gassing and shooting of millions and instead focus on the management of food in the territory occupied by the Germans.

General Eduard Wagner (1894–1944), Quartermaster General of the Wehrmacht 1939–44. An enthusiastic supporter of the Hunger Plan, he committed suicide having been involved in the plot against Hitler.

It was assumed, in Berlin, that the German Army would be fed from the resources of the territory it occupied and Russia and Ukraine would provide surplus grain for the domestic German market. The Quartermaster General, Eduard Wagner, an enthusiastic supporter of the HP, noted that 'extensive exploitation of the land' would have to be implemented immediately.[12]

Commanding officers were charged with the responsibility of feeding their soldiers from local sources. It was not a satisfactory arrangement and it produced patchy results. It was also an ad hoc, spontaneous system that rapidly got out of control as the plundering of villages was undirected and inefficient. Indiscriminate pillaging was eventually stopped, and a little late in the day, a 'well thought out plan' was produced.[13] The initial assumption proved to be overly optimistic and took no note of the attitude of the captive, hostile but quiescent millions.

It was difficult to impose a policy of restraint over mere potatoes when there was carte blanche for German soldiers to kill members of the civilian community at will, and on a whim. The 'well thought out plan' did not work and the mayhem continued unabated.

Army Groups North, South, and Central were composed of approximately 1.5 million men and a further 500,000 staffed the logistic tail. This vast host consumed 120 tons of meat daily and the draught horses who dragged guns and vehicles ate a veritable mountain of fodder.[14] Transport is key to logistic success in all wars and the impact of the upcoming, savage Russian winter, which would hinder movement, had not yet been factored into the logistic plan.

The German aim was 'nutritional freedom' and schemes were established to develop sources of protein and oil-rich plants. However, a constant deficiency was that in butter, margarine, and vegetable oils, pre-war, 95 per cent of the latter was imported, but this ceased, as did supplies of whale oil – a major constituent of margarine. For the domestic German farmer:

> one of the greatest challenges was the maintenance of both potatoes and pig production. The German pre-war diet was heavily dependent on potatoes and Germans displayed a marked preference for pork ... The problem with pigs is that they compete with humans for food as they are usually fattened on grains, potatoes, and sugar beet. A reduction in the number of pigs has the undesirable effect of reducing the amount of animal fat in the diet, as pigs produce the most fat of all farm animals ... a decline in the number of pigs leads to a vicious cycle. As meat and fat become less available humans eat more potatoes which in turn takes fodder away from pigs.[15]

The pig and potato relationship was a matter of importance, in Germany, throughout the war. In January 1940, the potato harvest was reduced by bad weather, and that had a knock-on effect on pig numbers and health. Similarly, in 1943, and by 1944, German pig herds had fallen to 60 per cent of pre-war levels and the amount of potato available for each pig had fallen by half.[16]

The impact of German militarism during the 1940s was felt across the face of Europe and a ruthless policy of food denial, firmly implemented, caused the deaths of millions. Greece, Belgium, Holland, Poland and the Ukraine were just some of the places in which the indigenous people suffered the torment of starvation.

In the first half of 1941, a confident Berlin expected to defeat Russia within two or three months but understood that the provision of food was an impending issue. However, the public position was: 'On the endless fields of the East surge waves of wheat, enough and more than enough to feed our people and the whole of Europe ... This is our war aim.'[17] Optimism is one thing, but this verged on fantasy. There were critics; one such was Gebhardt von Walther, a diplomat serving in the embassy in Moscow. He warned that the aspiration was unrealistic, and his view was endorsed when the apparent product of the Ukrainian harvest of 1941 was far below expectations.

The Hunger Plan got off to a disorganised start in its arrangements to starve the target 20–30 million, but the lethality deficiency was, in part, ameliorated by the presence of four *Einsatzgruppen*, each of about 3,200 men who got on with more immediate forms of murder. They were reinforced by battalions of armed German police, and by the spring of 1942, just *Einsatzgruppen* 'A', alone, and operating in the Baltic States, had killed more than 270,00 people.

Backe and his acolytes had anticipated that mass starvation would quickly follow the requisition of all grain and the closure of resupply systems supporting Russian cities. It was a naïve supposition.[18]

The most vulnerable were the recognisable minorities and the prime target was the Jews who had survived, so far, the attention of the murder squads. Jews were banned from food markets and from buying directly from farmers.

> They were also banned from purchasing the scarcer forms of food such as eggs, butter, milk, meat, or fruit. In Belorussia, within the aegis of Army Group Centre, the ration allocated to Jewish inhabitants of Minsk was no more than 420 calories per day.[19]

The destruction of the urban population of occupied Russia was a task beyond the capability of the Wehrmacht. It did not have the manpower to fight a ferocious foe and at the same time kill all his family and friends. The Germans drew back, reconsidered, and decided to go through the motions of feeding the civilian population of captured territories.

Although the invader had seized vast quantities of grain, livestock and dairy produce, it was still unable to feed as well as had been hoped. That situation required the import of food from Germany, an unexpected logistic task that tied up valuable transport.

Another readily recognised group ripe for 'elimination' were captured Russian soldiers. About 3.35 million had been taken during the initial thrusts of BARBAROSSA. These unfortunates were subject to treatment far beyond the pious aspirations of the Geneva Convention. Instructions were issued that allowed for the isolation and immediate execution of those considered to be 'politically dangerous'. No arrangements were made to house the POWs, and the calorific content of their food was below subsistence level. Many of these prisoners were sick or wounded when taken, there was no medical support, and predictably, their life span was very short in German hands.

Of the 3.35 million Russian POWs in July 1941, only 1.1 million survived until December.[20] Of the 2.24 million killed, about 600,000 were shot in accordance with the *Kommissarbefehl* (Guidelines for the Treatment of Political Commissars) that instructed the Wehrmacht that if a prisoner was identified as a Soviet Political Commissar they were to be summarily executed. In this case, the percentage of prisoners falling into that category (26 per cent) seems to be highly unlikely and does nothing to disguise a heinous war crime. A further 600,000 Russian prisoners died, allegedly of 'natural causes', between December 1941 and February 1942.

Shortcomings in Backe's master plan became evident very soon after the launch of BARBAROSSA. No specific instructions as to the implementation of the Hunger Plan had been issued.[21] Victory in Russia was anticipated to be achieved by about the end of September 1941. It was expected that victory would release troops from action so that they could be redeployed to enforce the starvation arrangements. However, life is a bit like golf; it is just not fair, and what looked viable on paper was not so on the ground. Major General Hans Leykauf, who was expected to be a senior practioner of the Hunger Plan, commented bitterly:

> If we shoot dead all the Jews, allow the prisoners of war to die, dish out famine to the majority of the urban population, and in the coming year lose a proportion of the rural population to hunger, the question remains unanswered: *who will actually produce economic goods?*[22] [Author's emphasis]

The general had a point. There was a rapid reappraisal. The black market was flourishing and orders for the peasants to bring food into towns were ignored. Iron control was needed and quickly imposed; strict dietary rules were applied. Only those who could contribute to the German cause were fed, at subsistence level; all others were denied food. This blanket decree swelled the ranks of the partisans and caused mass movement from towns to the country. Göring was not swayed, and he accepted the fact that there would be a number of deaths to match the Thirty Years War.[23]

Dead and dying peasants on the street in Kharkov, 1933.

General Wagner noted that some German soldiers were 'very kind' to starving civilians and emphasised that 'every gram of bread or food that I give out of generosity to the people of the occupied territories, I take away from the German people, and my family'.[24]

That statement of Wagner's must be seen in the light of the enthusiastic labours of the *Einsatzgruppen*. Kindness was in very short supply in Russia and Ukraine in 1941–2.

The strict regime of the Hunger Plan was slightly relaxed from time to time. By November 1941, those working for the Germans were allocated 1,200 calories per day and their dependants 850. However, those being provided with this largesse were not to exceed 20 per cent of the total population. Children under 14 were granted 420 calories. The result of this dietary regime was entirely predictable, and over the winter of 1941/2, uncounted tens of thousands of men, women and children died of starvation.[25] They were not alone, and at least a million Russian prisoners of war were abandoned to the winter without shelter or food.

*   *   *

The importance of Ukraine as a food producer has been highlighted during the production of this book as Putin wages his barbarous war on his neighbour. The cutting is from the *Daily Telegraph* of 23 May 2022.

Threat of famine

Russia's invasion of Ukraine has had a profound impact on the distribution of foodstuffs, notably grain. The country accounts for 12 per cent of global wheat exports, 16 per cent of corn and 18 per cent of barley.

Even if Ukraine is able to bring in a harvest, its produce would be unable to leave the besieged Black Sea ports, and some 20 million tons from last year is stockpiled and at risk of rotting.

The countries that will be most affected by a shortfall are in the developing world. Many of them will feel the squeeze from higher prices, which can have political consequences for regimes unable to feed their people.

Agriculture experts have told the United Nations that the world has just 10 weeks' worth of wheat stockpiled and inventories of fertiliser, cooking oil and grains have fallen to their lowest level since 2008.

They have called for "substantial, immediate and aggressive coordinated global actions" to counter what will otherwise be a calamity. The world's leaders need to focus on working out how Ukraine's harvestable wheat not needed for domestic consumption and stockpiled produce can be transported by land if the ports remain shut, or provide the necessary naval back up in the Black Sea to ensure they can leave by ship.

In 1948, when the Soviet Union tried to starve West Berlin by blocking road, rail and canal access to the city, the allies organised an air bridge. At its peak it was delivering 13,000 tons of produce a day. Is it beyond the abilities of the West today to organise a road bridge that would transport Ukraine's produce westwards to European ports from where it can be distributed?

*   *   *

The war in the east between Germany and Russia brought into conflict two of the most barbarous regimes to ever walk the Earth. At this stage, the reader will be feeling a degree of sympathy for the Russian people beset by the monstrous Nazi war machine. The Germans were to be paid back in the same merciless coin that demonstrated they did not have the monopoly on inhumanity. The Russian vengeance, when it came, plumbed the very depths of human depravity. It is little remembered that in 1932–3, Ukraine had suffered a famine that killed over 5 million people. That famine was exacerbated by Joseph Stalin as a means of quelling a Ukrainian independence movement. It is now generally considered to be an instance of genocide. This matter is discussed in more detail in Chapter 20.

Military history is repetitive, and different people of different nations constantly repeat the errors of predecessors. At Sandhurst, St-Cyr and probably West Point, the first lesson on day one is (or should be) 'don't march on Moscow'. Hitler was not a product of any of these august establishments and he replayed a scenario from Napoleon Bonaparte's exploits – and eventually with the same result.

The rape of Ukraine in 1941 is now being replayed, as this book is being written, in 2022. The importance of that country in food production terms is of international significance and unchanged over eighty years.

This chapter would be incomplete without reference to Leningrad and the remorseless siege it suffered, not least because it is recognised as being the longest, the most destructive and most brutal in human history. However, it is perhaps unique in that the usual aim of besiegers is to force the capitulation of the besieged. In Leningrad, capitulation was not an option.

This was not a food denial process like Vicksburg and Metz; it was entirely atypical. In practice, it was similar, but the aim was entirely different. At Leningrad, food denial was intended to be a tool for genocide on a vast scale. Food denial was only an element in the full suite of killing tools employed by the besiegers. It is perhaps the very epitome of German inhumanity. Leningrad was an integral element of Operation BARBAROSSA and one of the three strategically important objectives. In this case, Army Group North was charged with the city's reduction. The Russians were loath to give in easily and in their defence, they constructed 190 miles (306km) of timber barricades, 395 miles (635km) of wire entanglements, 435 miles (700km) of anti-tank ditches, 5,000 earth-and-timber emplacements and reinforced concrete weapon emplacements, and 15,534 miles (25,000km) of open trenches were constructed or excavated by civilians.[26]

These defences proved their worth and were vital to the survival of the city and some of its inhabitants. The norms of human behaviour were breached in Leningrad during the 872 days of the siege, during which the casualties caused were astronomic. The Germans suffered 579,985 casualties but Russian losses were far greater, for which David Glantz provides the remarkable precise figure of 3,436,068.[27]

The city was resupplied, spasmodically, across Lake Ladoga – a process that was easier when the lake was frozen; when it was not, food barges made the journey, under shellfire. Some were sunk, along with their priceless cargoes. Divers sought to recover the now damaged and contaminated grain, with modest success.

In the besieged city with a pre-war population of just over 3 million, food was rationed from 2 September 1941. Initially, manual workers were permitted 600 grams (21oz) of bread per day and there was a sliding scale that allowed children 300 grams. The ration for all was reduced just ten days later and at regular intervals thereafter. The city was under a constant bombardment, which took lives but also resulted in the destruction of food storage facilities. The impact of the losses of grain, sugar and flour was catastrophic and heralded the starvation to come. Reagan relates that: 'starvation took hold and it led to increasingly desperate measures. Much as in Paris in 1870, the animals in the public zoo were summarily slaughtered and eaten, as were domestic pets.'[28]

The adhesive used to secure wallpaper was made from potato starch. Seeing this as a food source, desperate people began to strip paper from their walls. They stewed the result to make some form of disgusting but edible soup. Old leather, shoes, boots, belts and bags were boiled in the hope of extracting nutrients; the soft leather was then eaten. Cannibalism was reported and this phenomenon is examined in wider context in Chapter 21. Hitler, ever the optimist, sent out a directive on 29 September 1941 that said:

> After the defeat of Soviet Russia there can be no interest in the continued existence of this large urban centre ... Following the city's encirclement, requests for surrender negotiations shall be denied, since the problem of relocating and feeding the population cannot and should not be solved by us. In this war for our very existence, we can have no interest in maintaining even a part of this very large urban population.[29]

The citizens suffered from extreme food deprivation, which was particularly acute during the first winter of 1941/2. From November 1941 to February 1942, after further reductions in the ration, the only food available to the citizen was 125 grams (4.4oz) of bread per day, of which at least half consisted of sawdust and other inedible fillers to give it bulk. In conditions of extreme temperatures (down to –30°C or –22°F), public transport was unable to function and that exacerbated the problems of food distribution and casualty reclamation. Death was everywhere, corpses laid in the streets and their disposal into frozen ground was a problem for the energy lacking survivors. Bomb craters became mass graves. By February 1942, about 3,000 people were dying *every* day.[30]

Clearly, this was no ordinary siege. The norm is for the besieger to seek to take the territory and capture the defenders. Hitler wanted neither of these; he just wanted all the people to be killed and the city eradicated. This was compatible with, and complementary to, the Hunger Plan. It does not get much more brutal than that. The inhabitants of Leningrad had only one option and that was to fight. It was not until January 1943 that a logistic corridor could be forced through the encircling German Army.

By November 1941, the German Army had not conquered Russia. The resolute resistance of the Red Army, despite vast losses, was unexpected. The Germans were operating on an ever-lengthening front that had reached almost 1,500 miles (2,414km). Its logistic chain extended back about 1,000 miles (1,609km) and was subject to attack from irregular forces over largely unpaved roads. It faced another uncompromising and savage foe – it was winter. The soldiers were not equipped for the rigour of a Russian winter, the logistic system faltered in the extreme conditions, and cold German soldiers went hungry and died. By February 1942, 60 per cent of the 3.35 million Russian prisoners of war were dead. There were two more winters to come, during which tens of thousands of German soldiers froze to death and increasingly, Hitler's grand plan faltered and eventually died. Germans perished on the Russian Steppes outside Leningrad, Stalingrad and in countless anonymous derelict villages unable to provide shelter as they had been destroyed in the early German advance.

The agony of Leningrad dragged on and it was not until 27 January 1944 that the siege was lifted. The employment of food denial as a genocidal weapon in German-occupied territories had worked at little direct cost, and it had caused the deaths of millions.

The weaponisation of food would, to some degree, be a factor in future campaigns of the Second World War and across the world. It was no less brutal, but the immediate death toll was not of the magnitude caused by the Hunger Plan.

Summary

The enormous loss of life among those unfortunate to fall under the aegis of the Nazis during the Second World War needs no further emphasis. For the Germans, starvation was an efficient means of ridding themselves of 'useless eaters'. They applied their starvation measures ruthlessly, which produced the desired outcome.

Notes

1. Tooze, A., *The Wages of Destruction* (London, Allen Lane, 2006) p. 176.
2. Ibid, pp. 176–7.
3. Ibid., p. 179.
4. Ibid., p. 462.
5. Ibid., p. 463.
6. Ibid., pp. 476–85, 538–49.
7. Nbg. Doc. 2718–PS, *Aktennotiz über Ergebnis der heutigen Besprechung mit den Staatssekretären über Barbarossa*, 2 May 1941 (International Military Tribunal, (ed.) *'Der Prozess gegen die Hauptkriegsverbrecher vor dem Internationalen Militärgerichtshof*, Nürnberg, 14 November 1945–1 Oktober 1946, Vol. 31. Sekretariat des Gerichtshofs, Nuremberg, 1948), p. 84.
8. Gerlach, C., *Kalkulierte Morde. Die deutsche Wirtschafts- und Vernichtungspolitik in Weissrussland 1941 bis 1944* (Hamburg, Hamburger Edition, 1998), p. 46.
9. Beaumont, J., 'Starving for Democracy' (Taylor & Francis, *War and Society*, 8 (2), 1990), pp. 58, 78–9.
10. Ibid., pp. 476–85, 538–49.
11. Tooze, p. 477.
12. Kay, A.J., *Exploitation, Resettlement, Mass Murder* (Oxford, Berghahn Books, 2006), pp. 131–2.
13. Ibid.
14. Gerlach, C., *Kalkulierte Morde* (Hamburg, 1999), p. 256.
15. Lehmann, J., *Agrarpolitik und Landwirtschaft in Deutschland* (Ostfildern, Scripta Mercaturae Verlag, 1985) p. 46. Quoted by Collingham, p. 157.
16. Huegel, A., *Kriegsernahrungswirtschaft Deutschlands* (Konstanz, Hartung-Gorre Verlag, 2003), pp. 308–309. Quoted by Collingham, p. 158.
17. Bartov, O., *Hitler's Army. Soldiers Nazis and War in the Third Reich* (Oxford, Oxford University Press, 1991), p. 74.
18. Gerlach, C., *Kalkulierte Morde*, pp. 265–318.
19. Ibid., pp. 668–74.
20. Streit, C., *Keine Kameraden* (Bonn, Dietz, 1997), pp. 228–37.
21. Kay, p. 207.
22. Boog, H.W., et al., *Der Angriff auf die Sowjet Union* (Stuttgart, Deutsche Verlags-Anstalt, 1985), pp. 1010–11.
23. Ibid., p. 1007.
24. Ibid., p. 1009.
25. Tooze, p. 482.
26. Bidlack, R. (2013). *The Leningrad Blockade* (New Haven, Yale University Press, 213), p. 41.
27. Glantz, D.M., *The Battle for Leningrad 1941–1944: 900 days of Terror* (London, Cassell, 2004), p. 179.
28. Reid, A., *Leningrad: Tragedy of a City under Siege* (London, Bloomsbury Publishing, 2011), pp. 134–5.
29. Boog, p. 1000.
30. Ibid., p. 1019.

Chapter Fifteen

The Battle of the Atlantic: Setting the Scene (1939–40)

The Battle of the Atlantic is more accurately described as a campaign – the longest and most complex in the Second World War. It was hugely destructive. About 3,000 Allied merchant ships were sunk, causing the death of approximately 30,000 seamen. The cost to the Axis forces was of the same order; 27,000, or 75 per cent, of those Germans who went down to the sea in submarines died and now lie in unmarked graves. In essence, the Germans sought to blockade the British Isles and the Allies endeavoured to blockade Germany. Both main belligerents were vulnerable as they were not self-sufficient. This campaign had no boundaries and operations in the Mediterranean were, arguably, an extension of the German policy of food denial wherever Allied troops' assets were located.

The effect of these two mutually destructive blockades was not limited to lives lost at sea. Food shortages, exacerbated by military action, and the ruthless application of the Hunger Plan put in place by the Germans caused an astronomic number of deaths in mainland Europe.

Great Britain entered the Second World War as the nation most dependent upon wheat imports and the need for change in domestic agricultural practice was evident. It appeared that some lessons had been learned from the world war only twenty years before. The new priority was the production of wheat and potatoes, and to that end, land not previously used for the growing of crops was ploughed up and utilised. Farmers were the social group that benefited most from the war as farm incomes quadrupled and the wages of farm labourers doubled.[1]

Food production rates increased rapidly. This was more the product of hard work and an expansion of cultivated land than any sort of technological advances. Pre-war, British farmers contributed approximately 33 per cent of the calories in the national diet. This rose to 44 per cent, and the number of days per year when it could feed itself rose from 120 to 160.[2]

Allotments were reintroduced and again, swathes of public land were allocated for the purpose. An example was the utilisation of Barnes Common, in south-west London, which remained as allotments until about 1952.

Grand Admiral Erich Raeder, Commander-in-Chief, the Kriegsmarine 1935–43.

These improvements, although laudable, were not the all-embracing panacea. Britain ceased importing non-essential foodstuffs (and that is why this author did not see his first banana until 1946). Animal feed was one of many non-essentials, and the imports of sugar, fresh fruit and nuts were severely curtailed. By these means food imports fell from 22 million tons per annum to between 11 and 15 million tons. Priority was given to high-energy foods such as meat and dairy products.[3] Nevertheless, there remained a vast gap between the food available and the food needed. From the British perspective, this was what the Battle of the Atlantic was all about.

It was for the very survival of Britain.

*   *   *

Fortunately, before the outbreak of hostilities there were those with sound judgement who had had enough foresight to plan ahead. In 1938, Leslie Hore-Belisha, Secretary of State for War, had recognised the need to make best use of the foodstuffs available and took expert advice from Mr Isidore Salmon, who headed the J. Lyons and Co. Ltd. catering conglomerate.

His report led directly to the formation of the Army Catering Corps in March 1941. On Isadore's death, later that year, Lieutenant Colonel Sir Geoffrey Salmon, CBE, took up the reins when he was appointed as Honorary Catering Adviser to the Army. It was he who suggested that Richard Byford be appointed Inspector of Army Catering. Byford was commissioned and later became the first Director of the Corps (DACC).

A School of Catering was established in Aldershot, Hampshire, where volunteer soldiers trained as cooks. In 1941, by which time the British Army was 2.2 million strong, the Army Catering Corps was formed.[4] During the Second World War, British Army cuisine was … acceptable. The Corps made best use of the food available and strove to produce hot food, anywhere, at any time. From these early beginnings, the Corps flourished and thirty years later, the British Army was the best fed in the world and much admired.[5]

*   *   *

From the outset of the war, the German U-boat campaign sought to sever the logistic link between North America and the British Isles, and later, the supply line to Russia. Britain depended upon imported food from its then empire and from Africa, Asia, South America and the United States. Sir John Keegan wrote of a 'truly Malthusian decline' if the logistic chain was broken.[6] Then:

> mass hunger would have consumed the nation. Not only would it have been physically and spiritually impossible to 'fight on the beaches … on the landing grounds … in the fields … and in the streets', but Churchill, or more probably his successor, would have had little choice but to sue for peace.

It was for this reason that Churchill wrote that, 'the Battle of the Atlantic was the dominating factor all through the war. Never for one moment could we forget that everything happening elsewhere on land, sea or in the air depended ultimately on its outcome, and amid all other cares we viewed its changing fortunes day by day with hope or apprehension.'[7]

Across the globe by 1942, food was being subjected to controls, and rationing systems were introduced. The aim was to prevent hoarding and to ensure an equable distribution of available food but inevitably, a black market developed, much to the benefit of the wealthy of any nation.

The Battle of the Atlantic had its genesis in the earlier Great War when the Royal Navy starved Germany into defeat. It was that painful episode in German history that, in part, shaped Germany's naval strategy from the early 1930s. The ensuing naval campaign covered most of the globe at one time or another and it is argued by this historian and others that the outcome of the Second World War was, in large measure, decided at sea. Britain and Russia were each dependent upon merchant ships of many nations to deliver armaments, raw materials and, not least, food.

From the outbreak of the war, the one constant was the critically important relationship of Churchill and Roosevelt, which waxed and waned. Churchill was First Sea Lord at the outbreak of war, but later, as prime minister, the two men were each determined to do what was best for their country and often their two aims did not coincide. They respected each other, but it was an unequal relationship and Churchill was often cast in the role of supplicant. Initially, Roosevelt was not prepared to commit his country to a war with Germany, and in avoiding that possibility, he proved himself to be a vastly capable, devious and manipulative politician. He served his country very well.

From his appointment in 1935, Grand Admiral Erich Raeder had been planning for war with Britain. He envisaged a surface fleet of 10 battleships, 15 pocket battle ships, 65 cruisers and 8 aircraft carriers. In addition, he wanted 249 submarines. He calculated that by 1948, he would be able to challenge the RN and win. Nevertheless, it was Raeder's intention to fight the Battle of the Atlantic, whenever it happened, on the surface.

Raeder's subordinate, Dönitz, took a different view, and as a submarine officer who had distinguished himself in the Great War, he was intent on creating an undersea armada. It was fortunate for the Allies that Hitler, who had no experience of naval warfare, chose to interfere in the composition of the fleet and even the specifications of individual ships. Predictably, this damaged Hitler's relationship with Raeder, and when war was declared, the admiral did not have the vital support of Hitler. The Führer persistently ignored Raeder's advice and took the direction of naval strategy upon himself, much to the benefit of the Allies.

Grand Admiral Karl Dönitz (1891–1980), Supreme Commander of the Kriegsmarine (September 1943–May 1945), and President of Germany (30 April–23 May 1945).

Churchill was painfully aware that the very survival of his country was dependent on the defeat of the U-boats, whose activities were directed by Grand Admiral Karl Dönitz (sometimes Döenitz). Dönitz was a committed Nazi and virulent anti-Semite. He was also intellectually gifted and a formidable adversary for the British, and later the Americans, to face.

On the outbreak of war, the Kriegsmarine had only forty-six U-boats, rather less than the sixty that British intelligence had calculated. However, only twenty-two of the type VIIs were capable of extended operations, and given the demands of the maintenance programme, only seven could be deployed at any one time.[8] It could be argued that if Dönitz had been given the resources he needed and the freedom to deploy them as he judged best, then the course of the Second World War might have been significantly different. It is perhaps one of the great 'what ifs' of military history.

In Britain in 1930s there was a yawning dietary gap between rich and poor. It was not a situation unique to Britain and the rich ate well, the poor markedly less so. The very poor often did not have the facilities to cook, worked long hours away from home and had insufficient money for anything but a subsistence diet. About 33 per cent of the poor suffered a deficiency in milk, fruit and vegetables and the effect was to distance them from vital sources of vitamins and minerals, prerequisites for good health.[9] The Rowett Institute carried out a survey and when it proposed to publish its findings it ran headlong into the British Government, which did not want the survey results published. However, Harold Macmillan, then a backbench MP and publisher, decided to publish the survey at his own expense as *Food, Health and Income* in 1937. It changed attitudes.

Notes

1. Wilt, A.F., *Food for War: Agriculture and Rearmament in Britain before the Second World War* (Oxford, Oxford University Press, 2001), p. 225.
2. Ibid., p. 224.
3. Vat, D. van der., *The Atlantic Campaign: The Great Struggle at Sea 1939–45* (London, Hodder & Stoughton, 1988), p. 223.
4. Army Order No. 35 of 1941.
5. The professional training of soldier chefs was a national investment. However, in the pursuit of 'savings', in 1991 the Army Board ordered the disbandment of the Corps. A small rump of soldier chefs was absorbed into the Royal Logistic Corps in 1993. The feeding of the army in the field is, today, much as it was in the 1750s. Contract caterers, amply recompensed, do provide freshly cooked food – but nowhere near the front.
6. Keegan, J.D.P., *The Second World War* (London, Arrow Books, 1990), p. 104.
7. Churchill, W.S., *The Second World War, Vol. V: Closing the Ring* (London, Cassell, 1952), p. 6.
8. Dimbleby, J., *The Battle of the Atlantic* (London, Penguin, 2016), p. 23.
9. Burnett, J., *Plenty and Want: A Social History of Diet in England from 1815 to the Present* (London, Routledge, 1966), p. 281.

Chapter Sixteen

Battle is Joined
(1939–41)

Both Germany and Britain were ill prepared for the war that was to follow, and both were deluded. Hitler thought that he could cheat and bluff his way to the conquest of Europe while Chamberlain was hopeful that Hitler would respond positively to his diplomatic overtures.[1] Meanwhile, the heads of the respective navies felt sure that victory was theirs to grasp. Britain had a powerful navy, but it was not one configured to provide anti-submarine escorts for convoys. Similarly, Raeder was building a surface fleet to take on the RN, but the Kriegsmarine needed to expand its submarine force if it was to interdict food convoys from across the world. For Great Britain, the prime source of supply, its very salvation, was the USA. The vast material resources of this country were to make it the Allies' quartermaster throughout the war. Its manpower was to be a further critical factor, albeit not until 1942.

The outbreak of war brought home to the British the scale of their vulnerability. They needed copious resupply of copper, zinc, manganese, tin, bauxite, tungsten, lead, rubber, iron ore, aluminium, nickel, timber, cotton and jute, and of course food, in all its forms. Pre-war, 95 per cent of Britain's oil was imported; it was the lifeblood of industry, fuelled the RN, and it all had to cross a sea. Now a very dangerous sea.

The Ministry of Food was conceived and established in the first week of the war. Its function was to manage food stocks and their distribution in an equable manner. Of course, it was not quite like that, and in the early days, the Ministry and its factotums were vilified. The introduction of ration books, a reasonable measure, to manage sugar, meat, bacon and fats, was the fount of public anger and roundly rejected. However, needs must … and butter, bacon and sugar duly became the first items whose availability was restricted to those with the requisite 'coupons'. Fresh vegetables, bread and potatoes were three staples never rationed. The rationing system was expanded as the war dragged on, and petrol was limited to between 4 and 10 gallons per month. This allowance was strictly for business and not for leisure motoring.

The seamen serving Britain's needs started to take casualties from 3 September 1939. The first ship to fall to a predatory U-boat was the 8,118-ton (net registered) MS *Athenia*, on the day of the declaration of war. She carried

1,103 passengers and 315 crew and was on passage from Liverpool to Montreal. At around 16:30, she was 60 miles (97km) south of Rockall when she was hit by one of the two torpedoes aimed at her.

The sinking was a misjudgement by Oberleutnant Fritz-Julius Lemp, commanding *U-30*, who mistakenly thought that *Athenia* was either a troopship, a Q-ship or an armed merchant cruiser. The German Admiralty quickly realised that the twenty-eight American passengers who were killed could provide a *casus belli* to Roosevelt and bring the USA into the war.[2]

There was frantic backtracking; Lemp was sent for by Raeder to explain himself. The admiral then reported to Hitler, who ruled that the incident should be shrouded in secrecy. The log of *U-30* was altered, and Germany denied any part in the sinking of *Athenia*. Lemp was absolved of committing a war crime.[3] The cover-up was not revealed until the Nuremberg trials, postwar. Then a witness testified and said:

> Oberleutnant Lemp shortly before my disembarkation in Reykjavik, 19th September 1939, visited me in the forenoon in the petty officers' quarters where I was lying severely wounded. Oberleutnant Lemp then had the petty officers' quarters cleared in order to be alone with me. Oberleutnant Lemp then showed me a declaration under oath according to which I had to bind myself to mention nothing concerning the incidents of 3rd September 1939, on board the *U-30*. This declaration under oath had approximately the following wording: 'I, the undersigned, swear hereby that I shall keep secret all happenings of 3rd September 1939, on board the *U-30*, from either foe or friend, and that I shall erase from my memory all happenings of this day.'
>
> I signed this declaration under oath, which was drawn up by the Commandant in his own handwriting, very illegibly with my left hand. Later on, in Iceland, when I heard about the sinking of the *Athenia*, the idea came into my mind that the *U-30* on 3rd September 1939, might have sunk the *Athenia*, especially since the captain caused me to sign the above-mentioned declaration. Up to today I have never spoken to anyone concerning these events. Due to the termination of the war, I consider myself freed from my oath.[4]

German sensitivity to American public opinion was a feature of the early years of the campaign in the Atlantic and every effort was made to avoid any sort of confrontation. It was no mistake when the MS *Bosnia* was sunk on 6 September. She was a small ship of 2,407 tons and was en route to Glasgow, carrying a cargo of sulphur. Günther Prien, commanding *U-47*, found her 120 miles (193km) off the coast of Portugal. He stopped *Bosnia* by gunfire, but not before she had sent out a distress signal. After the crew were evacuated

Günther Prien (1908–1941), who sank over thirty Allied ships.

into lifeboats, Prien sank *Bosnia* with a torpedo. This incident was the first, and thereafter rare, example of courtesy and chivalry during the Battle of the Atlantic. A Norwegian flagged ship, the *Eidanger*, responding to *Bosnia*'s message, arrived and took on survivors, and after civil greetings, watched *U-47* sail away.

Bosnia was one of the 221 merchant ships to be sunk between September and December 1939, of which 110 were sunk by U-boats, 78 by mines, and 10 by aircraft of the *Luftwaffe*. It was but a foretaste of what was to come.

The Merchant Navy was shocked, and things were not going well for the Royal Navy either. HMS *Ark Royal*, an aircraft carrier, had a narrow escape on 14 September when three torpedoes loosed at her by *U-39* exploded prematurely. The submarine was sunk by the escorting destroyers. HMS *Courageous*, another carrier, was torpedoed in the Bristol Channel by *U-29* and 500 men were lost.

In September 1939, Dönitz was looking for a 'spectacular'. He sent for Prien and invited him to consider breaching the defences of Scapa Flow and attacking a major warship at anchor there. Prien accepted the challenge, and in a remarkable demonstration of seamanship, courage and judgement, on 13 October, he penetrated the anchorage and sank the 34,000-ton battleship HMS *Royal Oak* at her moorings; 835 men were killed or died of wounds.

Prien returned to Wilhelmshaven to a hero's welcome. He was met by Dönitz, and then he and his crew were flown to Berlin to be decorated by Hitler himself.

The loss of *Royal Oak* was a psychological blow and Churchill, the First Lord of the Admiralty, and in effect the Minister for the Royal Navy, had to do some fancy political footwork to avoid the blame for the disaster. He shifted responsibility onto his predecessor in the post, Lord Stanhope.[5]

HMS *Royal Oak*, sunk in Scapa Flow by Prien on 13 October 1939, with a loss of 835 lives.

By the spring of 1940, Dönitz and his U-boats had taken the initiative and the Royal Navy was on the back foot. The sinking of merchant ships had produced three U-boat aces. Prien was one and the other two were Otto Kretschmer and Joachim Schepke. They played a significant part in the destruction of fifty-eight ships in June 1940, with a total displacement of 284,113 tons.[6]

The success of the U-boats was in direct relation to the deficiency of RN escort vessels. The need was for small, fast ships to provide a protective hedge around convoys, but they were not available, and a high price was being paid. Much needed food was rotting on the seabed and Britain was hungry.

Operation SEALION, the German invasion of the UK, was a strong possibility. However, to ensure success, control of the air was a first requisite. The Battle of Britain commenced, and never had the UK been more at risk. Britain won the battle and retained command of its skies. The threat of invasion receded.

The losses at sea were so high that new ships could not be built fast enough to replace them. Convoys had to have better protection and a high priority was to obtain, from the USA, fifty destroyers. However, Roosevelt was not amenable. At the end of July, Churchill told him that four British destroyers had been sunk and a further seven damaged. He said:

> If we cannot get substantial reinforcements the whole fate of the war may be decided by this minor and easily remediable factor. I am confident, now that you know exactly how we stand ... Mr President, with great respect I must tell you that in the long history of the world this is a thing to do *now* ... I feel entitled and bound to put the gravity and urgency of the position before you.[7]

Someone once said, 'there is no free lunch'. Whoever he was, he was correct. Fortuitously, there was in the USA an Anglophile and interventionist group, which suggested that obsolescent naval assets could be exchanged for immediate naval and air concessions in British possessions in the Western Hemisphere. Roosevelt, having had Britain's extreme vulnerability pointed out to him, and taking note of Churchill's desperation, decided to exploit his position when he proposed a 'cruelly lopsided deal' to Churchill.[8] He marketed his proposal, domestically, by proclaiming it to be not only a great bargain, but one without risk and of significant strategic value to the USA. He offered fifty ships:

> which are on their last legs anyway ... by the way, the fifty destroyers are of the same type of ship which we have been from time to time striking

from the naval list and selling for scrap for, I think, $4,000 or $5,000 per destroyer.[9]

In exchange for this largesse, Britain was required to grant the USA a ninety-nine-year lease on seven British colonies. These were Newfoundland, Bermuda, the Bahamas, Jamaica, St Lucia, Trinidad, and British Guiana. The situation was desperate, and Churchill had no option but to accept the offer. However, he was aware of the likely anger that the trading away of British possessions would bring, and he and Roosevelt worked together to massage the announcement of the deal to make it more palatable. It was a national humiliation for Britain. The fifty obsolete ships were transferred to the Royal Navy, in September 1940, and they were critical during the ongoing war in the Atlantic. One of them was the USS *Buchanan*. She was renamed *Campbeltown*, and later, filled with explosives, she was expended as the demolition ship in the raid on St Nazaire on 29 March 1942.

Raeder and Dönitz did not share a common philosophy, a fundamental flaw in German naval strategy. Raeder was convinced that the priority was to build a massive surface fleet, 'an oceanic naval power of the first rank'.

USS *Buchanan* (later, HMS *Campbeltown*), 1,260 tons, launched in 1919 and photographed in 1936. The four funnels are an indicator of her age.

He envisaged that he would need 'up to eighty battleships' to meet his aspirations of a fleet able to engage and defeat the Royal Navy.[10] Raeder was anxious to challenge Britain in the Mediterranean.

Dönitz had other plans, which were to sink as much enemy shipping as quickly as he could. He had demonstrated the power of his relatively small submarine force by the slaughter of convoys HX79 and SC7 in October 1940. Eighty-three ships had left Nova Scotia for Liverpool, but more than 30 per cent were sunk on the voyage. The loss of life and materiel was huge. The twelve ships of convoy HX79 that were sunk had carried 37,480 tons of oil and petroleum products, 11,700 tons of steel, 3,000 tons of iron, 1,700 tons of lead and zinc, 8,000 tons of grain, 19,400 tons of timber and 8,333 tons of sugar. Losses of this magnitude could not be borne.

In 1939, total imports of food and raw materials into Britain were about 60 million tons. By December 1940, this had been reduced to 54 million tons. The downward trend had to be checked because any 'further reduction would also threaten the country's ability to prosecute the war ... it was frightening all the time'.[11]

The fall of France gave Germany direct access to the Atlantic Ocean, and it swiftly established a base for its submarine force in Lorient on the Keroman peninsula. At the end of June 1941, the *U-30*, with five recent sinkings to its credit, was the first to dock there for repair and replenishment.[12] She returned to sea on 13 July.

There was an urgent need to build a protected base for U-boats and the Germans with characteristic energy started to construct perhaps the most stoutly built defence structure in the world. This was allowed to proceed without serious interference by the British. Admiral Ernest King, Chief of the US Navy Staff, constantly and correctly berated his opposite numbers for this manifest failing.

Air Marshal Arthur Harris (know always as 'Bomber') commanded the RAF Bomber Command, and like many senior commanders, he believed he had the monopoly of wisdom, and in this respect, he was not unlike Montgomery and MacArthur. Harris was intent on the destruction of German cities, as he had been instructed by Churchill. Famously, he commented:

> The Nazis entered this war under the rather childish delusion that they were going to bomb everyone else, and nobody was going to bomb them. At Rotterdam, London, Warsaw and half a hundred other places, they put their rather naïve theory into operation. They sowed the wind, and now they are going to reap the whirlwind.[13]

Harris would not release aircraft for anti-submarine patrols and the consensus is that his single-minded inflexibility was a weakness. Later, Bomber

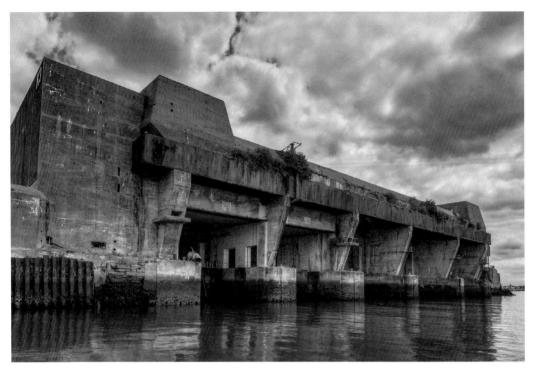

The submarine pens at Keroman, photographed seventy years after they were built. They are so strong that they still defy demolition. (*Adobe Stock*)

Command did engage other targets, but by neglecting the installation at Keroman, until it was completed, Harris made a huge strategic mistake.

When the RAF got round to attacking the installation, the thickness of the concrete was such that the U-boats sheltering in the pens were impervious. They continued to harass the Atlantic convoys and Britain fought on for survival.

The only solution was to isolate the U-boat base and to cut its logistic chain. This was an achievable aim, but at human cost in the city of Lorient. The bombardment started on 14 January 1943 and lasted until mid-February. The population of Lorient was reduced from 46,000 to little more than 500. The protracted bombing killed 206, while many others were wounded. The city was reduced to rubble; the citizens were without shelter and lost all their property. It is suggested that the citizens of Lorient were casualties of the Battle of the Atlantic, just like any of the seamen who went down with their ship.

* * *

One of Roosevelt's most trusted friends and advisors was a wise man called Harry Hopkins. He was an unqualified supporter of Great Britain and had a role as Roosevelt's personal emissary. He became a confident of Churchill and they held each other in high regard.

In January 1941, Hopkins was sent to measure Britain's capability, and not least, its resolve to continue the fight with Nazi Germany. He was given unhindered access to every part of the British state and at the end of his visit, Churchill entertained him to dinner. At that event, Hopkins stood to propose a toast, and he preceded it by saying:

> I suppose you wish to know what I am going to say to President Roosevelt on my return. Well, I am going to quote to you one verse from the Book of Ruth ... 'Whither thou goest, I will go and where thou lodgest I will lodge, thy people shall be my people, and thy God my God.'[14]

Britain had an important friend in this man and in a hand-written letter from Claridge's Hotel in London, he reported to his president in these terms:

> The people here are amazing from Churchill down, and if courage alone can win – the result will be inevitable. But they need our help desperately, and I am sure that you will permit nothing to stand in the way ... Churchill is the govn't in every sense of the word – he controls the grand strategy and ... I cannot emphasize too strongly that he is the one person over here with whom you need to have a full meeting of minds ... This island needs our help now, Mr President, with everything we can give them.[15]

Churchill noted that Hopkins said to him, 'The president is determined that we shall win this war together. Make no mistake about it.'[16] That was very cheering for Churchill, but he needed action, not good wishes. This was the case because although three of the Kriegsmarine's ace U-boat commanders – Prien, Schepke and Kretschmer – had been eliminated by March 1941, Dönitz was not short of courageous and talented men to command his under-sea fleet. It put Britain in continuing great peril, and although Roosevelt held the key to Britain's survival, he needed a compelling reason to commit the USA to war, and as yet, he did not have one – despite Hopkins's advocacy. However, it must be remembered that in 1941 relations between the USA and Japan were worsening and Roosevelt had to manage that very volatile situation too.

Harry L. Hopkins (1890–1946).

In March 1941, Roosevelt made what was to prove to be one of the most important strategic decisions in the war. On 11 March, he signed an 'Act to Promote the Defense of the United States'.[17] By so doing, he committed the USA to supply Great Britain and Russia with food, oil, warships, aeroplanes, ammunition, and other strategically vital materiel, with immediate effect. The implications of Roosevelt's decision were that the balance of the war tilted in favour of Britain and her allies. Roosevelt had warned his countrymen: 'If Britain should go down, all of us in the Americas would be living at the point of a gun … We must be the great arsenal of democracy.'[18]

This new arrangement was known as Lend-Lease, and it functioned until 1945. Roosevelt believed that, by providing comprehensive logistic support to the enemies of the Axis, he was ensuring that the Axis could not impinge on the security of the United States. On that basis his policy, although not entirely altruistic, was nevertheless well judged, timely, strategically vital and of enormous magnitude.

Lend-Lease was, in effect, a political insurance policy but the premium was high. A total of $50.1 billion (equivalent to $690 billion in 2020) worth of supplies was shipped, or 17 per cent of the total war expenditures of the US. In all, $31.4 billion went to the United Kingdom, $11.3 billion to the Soviet Union, $3.2 billion to France, $1.6 billion to China, and the remaining $2.6 billion to the other Allies.[19] Harry Hopkins was deputed to control Lend-Lease.[20]

This was not a one-way street, and a reverse Lend-Lease was instituted. This allowed for the Allies to charge for the use of facilities and totalled $7.8 billion; of this, $6.8 billion came from the British and their empire.

> The terms of the agreement provided that the materiel was to be used until returned or destroyed. In practice, very little equipment was returned, and most was destroyed during the war. Supplies that arrived after the termination date were sold to the United Kingdom at a large discount for £1.075 billion, using long-term loans from the United States.
>
> Canada's Mutual Aid program sent a loan of $1 billion and $3.4 billion in supplies and services [equivalent to $61 billion in 2020] to the United Kingdom and other Allies.[21]

The vast spread of the Battle of the Atlantic was demonstrated on 21 May 1941 when an American flagged freight vessel, the SS *Robin Moor*, was stopped by *U-69*, 700 miles (1,127km) off Freetown in the South Atlantic. The ship was carrying a mixed cargo to the Portuguese colony of Mozambique. This ship had no part to play in the sustenance of the UK but nevertheless, the captain of *U-69* decided that having ordered the crew and passengers – forty-six souls in all – to take to their boats, he would sink *Robin Moor*.

Captain Metzler was perfectly civil; he gave each lifeboat food and water and promised to radio their position to ensure their early recovery. There is no record of his radio message, and it was only thirteen days later that three of the boats were found. The fourth boat was adrift at sea for a further five days.

When the survivors told their story, the press and radio gave it maximum coverage, with a large measure of anger. Many Americans were outraged and felt that this was the *casus belli* that Roosevelt needed, but the President waited, and it was not until September 1941 that events at sea triggered a tacit declaration of war (*see* page 154).

Hitler was without doubt an Allied asset. He launched Operation BARBAROSSA in June 1941, one of the foolhardiest military decisions in history. By attacking Russia, Hitler sealed his fate. Someone once said, 'In WWII Russia supplied the blood, the USA the bullets and Britain the brains.' Certainly, the human sacrifice made by the Russians was vastly greater than all the other Allies combined. It was Hitler's expectation that his population would be fed on Russian grain and that the occupation of Russia would ensure German nutritional autarky. The attack on Russia made that country a participant in the Battle of the Atlantic, if only by proxy.

On 1 September 1941, Roosevelt made another game-changing decision when he announced that in future, not only would US warships escort American ships to Iceland, but he invited ships of all other nations to accept American protection. The signal being sent to Germany was very clear and it became even clearer two days later.

An RAF bomber spotted *U-652* and signalled its position to the destroyer USS *Greer* about 10 miles (16km) away. *Greer* raced to the locality but her captain, Commander Frost, had been given strict terms of engagement. He was limited to tracking, tracing and reporting the submarine's presence; accordingly, he set up a sonar search and the pursuit lasted for three hours. However, by then, the RAF pilot was frustrated at the inaction, and he dropped four depth charges, which, by chance, were close enough to attract the attention of Oberleutnant Georg-Werner Fraatz, the captain of *U-652*. Fraatz assumed, quite reasonably, that the ship above him had made the attack and he reciprocated by directing a torpedo at *Greer*. The torpedo missed and Fraatz counter-attacked with depth charges. A second torpedo also missed and then *Greer* lost contact. This whole incident was something of a military non-event but, politically, it was dynamite.

Ten days later, Roosevelt gave one of his fireside chats to the nation. In this broadcast, he shamelessly distorted the truth and in so doing contrived the *casus belli* he had been seeking. He alleged that the action of *U-652* 'was piracy, legally and morally'. He went on to say, 'The attack was one determined step toward creating a permanent world system based on force and terror and on murder.' Roosevelt, a polished and practised performer, finished his talk by saying, 'If any German or Italian vessels of war enter the waters the protection of which is necessary for American defence, they do so at their own peril.'[22] This was serious – very serious. In effect, it was a declaration of war. The USA had joined the Battle of the Atlantic.

It was not until 8 December 1941 that a state of war was formalised by Germany's declaration. That was another ill-judged decision made by Hitler, who committed Germany to fighting Britain and its empire, the USA, the wealthiest, most powerful country, and Russia, the most obdurate with its almost limitless manpower – all at the same time.

The entry of the USA into the war was welcomed, and from 1942, the bounty of that vast and wealthy land kept Britain and Russia fed and in the fight. A crucial event was the birth of the 'Liberty ship'. Up to late 1941, UK marine losses to U-boats outstripped Britain's capacity to replace them. Then, the British concept of prefabricated ships was seized upon by the United States, and with furious energy thereafter, eighteen shipyards in the USA built 2,710 ships at a cost of $39 million per ship (2022 value).

These ships were welded together, a system far quicker and cheaper than the traditional riveting. Welding was not as strong as riveting and Liberty ships had inbuilt frailties. Nevertheless, these ships went a long way to ensuring the food resupply of the British Isles. The manufacturing and logistic might of the USA was seen in all theatres but perhaps the Liberty ship best epitomised the energy and commitment of the country.

Anti-submarine tactics were developed and polished by the Royal Navy and one of the best exponents was Captain F.J. Walker, DSO***, RN. When the war started this officer had been passed over for promotion to captain. However, he excelled when in command of HMS *Starling*, was promoted and given command of 36 Escort Group, a formation of two sloops and six corvettes. In December 1941, this Escort Group was protecting convoy HG-76. In the course of the

Captain Frederic John Walker, DSO***, RN (1896–1944).

SS *John W. Brown*, one of the last surviving Liberty ships, photographed in 2000.

voyage, Walker's ships sank four U-boats (*U-567*, *U-574*, *U1-31* and *U-434*). He did lose three ships, but this small victory was a portent of things to come.

Thereafter, *Starling* was at the centre of anti-submarine operations. Walker moved on to command 2nd Support Group and in July 1943, his team sank three more U-boats and a month later, three more. Ten further U-boats were destroyed by Walker's Group before they participated in the D-Day landings and thwarted any enemy submarine activity.

The constant pressure had fatigued Walker. Over-strain, overwork and battle fatigue had taken too much toll on him as he rarely lay back and took a rest. He died on 9 July 1944, aged 48. He had played a major role in the winning of the Battle of the Atlantic. The ASDIC system was designed by British engineers to detect underwater targets. It gave the technology to the USA in September 1939 and both countries developed the tool, which proved to be a godsend during the campaign. Sonobuoys were a spin-off device developed by the British in 1944.

The movement of food was still costing many lives and about 1,400 ships traversed the Barents Sea to Russia at the cost of eighty-five merchant ships and sixteen ships of the Royal Navy.[23] The nadir was the voyage of the Anglo/American convoy of thirty-five ships, designated PQ17, which sailed in July 1942 for Murmansk. Admiral Sir Dudley Pound, the First Sea Lord, in the face of an anticipated attack by the battleship *Tirpitz*, withdrew the escorting warships and ordered the merchantmen to 'scatter'. It was a catastrophically bad decision. Only eleven ships reached Russia. Of the 180,000 tons of supplies, carried by PQ17 and intended for Russia, only 64,000 tons were

HMS *Starling*, a Black Swan Class sloop, underway in 1943.

delivered.[24] Admiral of the Fleet Sir Dudley Pound resigned and died of a brain tumour soon after.

* * *

The Battle of the Atlantic extended across the globe as the Axis powers applied their food denial strategy as widely as possible. The Germans and Italians were determined to apply starvation conditions wherever they could, and they focused on the fortress island of Malta, where siege conditions existed between June and November 1942.

The island was not self-sufficient because Maltese agricultural production could only feed about 30 per cent of the 260,000 population. Malta was dependent upon imported food and administrative measures were put in place to ensure supplies were distributed fairly among the inhabitants of the Maltese islands. Ration books were issued, and permits given to grocers to provide the customer with such essential commodities as:

sugar	laundry soap	corned beef
coffee	lard and/or margarine	tomato paste
matches	edible oil	kerosene.

The siege was lengthy, bloody, and eventually unsuccessful. Malta's salvation came, in part, with Operation PEDASTAL, a major relief convoy mounted in August 1942. Arguably, the single most critical cargo in that convoy was the fuel, needed to keep the RAF in the fight. This fuel was concentrated in the American flagged tanker SS *Ohio*, which sailed with a British crew, along with thirteen other ships. The convoy sailed from Britain on 3 August and reached the Strait of Gibraltar on the night of 9/10 August.[25]

Thereafter, the ships of PEDASTAL were subject to the most intense air and submarine attacks and nine of the fourteen ships were sunk. The SS *Ohio* epitomised the courage and determination of the convoy participants.

> On the afternoon of 14 August, *Ohio* was surrounded by ships to nurse the tanker to Grand Harbour and several American volunteers from *Santa Eliza* manned anti-aircraft guns on *Ohio* during the tow.[26]

The weight of the tanker kept breaking the towlines, while constant air attacks were made by twenty bombers, which destroyed the rudder and holed her stern. The damage put *Ohio* in a sinking condition, with her weather deck awash. The stricken tanker was towed in by the destroyers HMS *Ledbury* and *Penn*, secured to her on either side. A third ship, the minesweeper HMS *Rye*, was secured to her stern to stabilise her passage.[27]

Ohio was towed into Grand Harbour at 09:30 on 15 August, to cheering crowds and a band playing 'Rule Britannia'.[28] The crowd fell silent as the

SS *Ohio*, supported by destroyers, makes her way into Valetta Harbour, 15 August 1942.

ships entered harbour, men removed their hats, women crossed themselves, and a bugle sounded *Still*. The tanker discharged oil into two tankers and water was pumped in at the same time, to reduce the chance of structural failure. *Ohio* settled on the bottom just as the last of the fuel was emptied.[29] On 19 September 1942, this remarkable ship, now in two halves, was towed out to sea and sunk.

The Battle of the Atlantic still had over three years to run and the two main protagonists each lived on restricted diets. In Britain, no one was recorded as dying of starvation. In Germany, many starved, but they were not necessarily Germans, much more likely the victims were imported slave labourers who were treated appallingly, not least in the Channel Islands, which were occupied throughout the war. Any death from starvation in Europe from mid-1941 was not an accident.

The USA was a major player in the Battle of the Atlantic but so too were the navies of Britain, Canada, Poland, Norway, Holland and Brazil. It was all of these, in combination, that won the Battle of the Atlantic. The war bankrupted Britain and hastened the end of its empire. However, it proved to be a catalyst for economic recovery and fed the burgeoning wealth for the USA, which emerged from the conflict as one of the two great powers. This all lay ahead, and in 1942, Walker's anti-submarine tactics were still being developed.

Summary

The German aim to starve the United Kingdom into submission failed. The support of the USA and the gallantry of the Royal Navy maintained a sufficient flow of food that although the people of the UK suffered food deprivation, they did not starve. In fact, the Allied blockade of German ports caused food shortages in Germany.

Notes

1. Burnett, J., *Plenty and Want: A Social History of Diet in England from 1815 to the Present* (London, Routledge, 1966), p. 24.
2. Harwood, J., *World War Two at Sea* (Hove, England, Quid Publishing, 2015), p. 20.
3. Lemp was drowned on 9 May 1941 when his boat *U-110* was forced to the surface by HMS *Bulldog*, *Broadway* and *Aubrietia*. A complete Enigma machine was captured with the relevant code books. The course of the war was radically changed. Hollywood made a film of the event, unhindered by the facts.
4. Schmidt, A., Testimony at the Nuremburg Trials, 1946.
5. Churchill, W.S., *The Gathering Storm* (Boston, Houghton Mifflin Co., 1948), p. 385.
6. Dimbleby, J., *The Battle of the Atlantic* (London, Arrow Books, 1990), p. 86.
7. Churchill to Roosevelt, 31 July 1940, *The Finest Hour*, p. 356.
8. Dimbleby, p. 89.
9. Roosevelt, E. (ed.), *The Roosevelt Letters Vol. III, 1928–1945* (London, G. Harrap, 1952), p. 329.
10. Bird, K.W., *Erich Raeder, Admiral of the Reich* (US Naval Institute Press, 2006), p. 159.

11. Defence Committee minutes, 13 October 1940, TNA CAB 66/13/2kl.
12. Blair, C., *Hitler's U-Boat War*: Vol. 1 (London, Cassell, 1996), p. 172.
13. Harris, Marshal of the RAF Sir Arthur, *Bomber Offensive* (London, Greenhill Books, 2005), p. 52. Harris reported that he made the remark, a quotation from the Old Testament (Hosea 8.7), to Marshal of the RAF, Charles Portal, Chief of the Air Staff, as they watched London burning under German bombing.
14. Sherwood, R.E., *The White House Papers of Harry L. Hopkins*, Vol. 1 (London, Eyre & Spottiswoode, 1948), p. 5.
15. Ibid., p. 246.
16. Churchill, Sir W.S., *The Grand Alliance: The Second World War*, Vol. 3 (Boston, Houghton Mifflin, 1950), p. 21.
17. Ebbert, J., Hall, M.-B. & Beach, Capt E.L., *Crossed Currents* (London, Brassey, 1991), p. 28.
18. Raich, B. (ed.), *Franklin D. Roosevelt Selected Speeches* et al. (Eastern Press, 1957), pp. 256–7, quoted by Dimbleby, p. 120.
19. McNeill, W.H., *America, Britain, and Russia: their Co-operation and Conflict, 1941–1946* (London, Oxford University Press, 1953), pp. 772–90.
20. O'Sullivan, C.D., *Harry Hopkins: FDR's Envoy to Churchill and Stalin* (Maryland, Rowman & Littlefield, 2014), p. 53.
21. Crowley, L.T., Lend-Lease. In Walter Yust (ed.), *10 Eventful Years* (Chicago, Encyclopedia Britannica Inc., 1947), 1:520, 2:858–60.
22. Franklin D. Roosevelt, Fireside Chat, 11 September 1941, www.presidency.ucsb.edu/documents/fireside-chat-11.
23. *Artic Convoys* (Imperial War Museum, iwm.org.uk).
24. Churchill, Sir W.S., *The Second World War* Vol. IV (Boston, Houghton Mifflin, 1950), p. 237.
25. Cunningham, Admiral Sir Andrew, *Despatch on Mediterranean Convoy Operations*, 1941 pp. 33–44.
26. Ibid., pp. 183–4.
27. Sadkovich, J., *The Italian Navy in World War II* (Westport, CN, Greenwood Press, 1994), p. 297.
28. Shankland, P., *Malta Convoy* (London, Fontana Press, 1989), p. 200.
29. Ibid., p. 202.

Chapter Seventeen

Japanese Expansion
(1931–45)

In the 1930s, Japan and Germany had a shared philosophy. In both countries, the population was indoctrinated with the belief that they were a superior race, and as such, had complete freedom of action to impose their will on lesser beings. This lay at the very heart of Adolf Hitler's political odyssey. Similarly, that same deluded mindset was to drive the expansion of the Japanese Empire at the cost of tens of millions of lives. In addition, both Germany and Japan adopted and exploited 'victimhood'. The Germans had a point, and they were victims of the merciless Treaty of Versailles, signed in July 1919. On the other hand, Japanese victimhood was based on little more than affronted pride.

The Japanese considered themselves to be ill-used by the other great powers, and in the 1930s, the Japanese press voiced dissatisfaction on the inequalities that permitted the USA to annex the Philippines but the Japanese seizure of Formosa (now Taiwan) as its first colony in 1895 was disapproved. 'Why', it asked, 'was there no opposition to Great Britain's control of India, but Japan's control of Korea (1894–1945) was subject to criticism?'

A feeling of victimhood was generated, and it was fuelled by the press. Clearly, political forces were gathering and Japan's relations with other powers were at risk. Japan noted and envied the USA, which had a record of interfering in the affairs of other sovereign states – evidenced by its occupation of Haiti (1915–34), Nicaragua (1912–33), Cuba (1892–1902 and 1906–9), the Dominican Republic (1916–24) and Columbia (1902). Troops from the USA made incursions into Panama in 1908, 1912 and 1918.[1] Not unreasonably, and understandably, the Japanese view was, 'If they can do it, why can't we?'

The Japanese had established its Kwantung Army on the Liaodong Peninsula since 1905, when it went to war with Russia over their shared designs on Manchuria and Korea. This occupation of the Liaodong Peninsula was on the basis of a lease agreement designed 'to protect Japanese interests'. It was a curious arrangement that only worked because China was not a coherent, organised state. There was no one to oppose the Japanese, who took full advantage of what appeared to be an open goal. In 1931, using their well-established base on the Liaodong Peninsula as a launch pad, the Japanese contrived to fabricate an 'incident', which, they asserted, was a *casus belli* that justified the annexation of the whole of Manchuria.

To the Kwantung Army, Manchuria represented a treasure house. The economic imperative was plain to see, as Japan depended upon Chinese imported raw materials such as 90 per cent of its iron, 75 per cent of its lead, zinc oil, dyes and chemicals, 64 per cent of its coal and 46 per cent of cast iron. It also provided gold, coal, soya beans and livestock. Crucially, and most importantly, it was a source of rice.[2]

The abundant raw materials when sent to Japanese manufacturers could then be marketed back in Manchuria, which they saw as the economic and strategic panacea to Japan's ills.[3] The use of violence to achieve its political and economic aim was readily embraced, and in a bizarre arrangement, the Kwantung Army established itself as an autonomous political entity. It acknowledged Tokyo but ignored its strictures. The conduct of Japanese forces throughout Asia, from 1931, was off the 'depravity scale', and ever since, it has been the subject of extreme revulsion.

The second Sino-Chinese war (1937–45) was as barbaric as war can be. The Japanese employed every device to maim, mutilate and kill its enemies and many others who were no more than bystanders. Starvation was too slow and although prisoners were frequently starved to death, the Japanese did not, specifically, employ food denial as a weapon.

Russia and Japan went to war in 1938 and the latter, although defeated, continued to entertain ambitions for expansion of its empire. This was fuelled by a surfeit of naïve self-assurance. From 1931, Japan's most important trading partner was the USA, which took 40 per cent of its exports and accounted for 34.4 per cent of its imports. The USA provisioned 49.1 per cent of Japan's iron, 53.6 per cent of its machine tools and a highly critical 75.2 per cent of its oil.[4] The availability from US sources of manganese and molybdenum was no less important. Japan was obliged to import aluminium and nickel from elsewhere. By any economic yardstick, Japan, already deeply engaged in a war with China, was in no position to contemplate further military adventures. However, Japan noted the aggressive posture being adopted by Germany in Europe, which gave every indication that Germany shared Japan's intentions to expand its territories.

Britain had an extensive colonial empire in Asia and its writ ran over India, Burma, Malaya, Singapore, Hong Kong and a number of small island groups in the South Pacific. It did not have the military means to defend these assets, and the British knew that the USA would not aid a colonial power.

Despite Roosevelt's strong Anglophobic and anti-colonial views, he and his Secretary of State, Cordell Hull, shared Britain's misgivings and recognised the need to curtail Japan's expansionism. Roosevelt put an oil embargo in place and then faced Japan with impossible and unrealistic demands. It was an ultimatum – and Japan recognised it as such. One of the demands was that Japan withdrew its 1 million soldiers from China immediately. This was patently impossible and gave Japan no room for manoeuvre.

Just as Roosevelt planned, Japan prepared to wage war. Japanese action on 7 December 1941 was not the 'Day of Infamy' as it was labelled in American propaganda. It was, in fact, a superbly planned, well-executed and entirely predictable pre-emptive strike. War is a nasty, brutal business; there are few discernible rules. It is not at all like cricket; a coin is not spun to see who is to bat first. A pre-emptive war is one launched in anticipation of immediate aggression by another party, and in this case, the attack on Pearl Harbor has entered the history books. To this day, it is incorrectly and misleadingly described as 'The Day of Infamy'.[5]

The reality is that it was a very powerful, but not unreasonable response by Japan to the impossible, non-negotiable demands made upon it by the USA. Since then, the USA has, on occasion, employed pre-emptive strikes itself. The pre-emptive strike is an integral part of current US defence strategy.

The Japanese air attack on the US Fleet at Pearl Harbor on 7 December 1941 was only part of a well-composed and coordinated assault on diverse targets across Southeast Asia. The Japanese plan was to take and hold colonial territory, and by so doing, force the Western colonial powers of Britain, Holland, France, and to a lesser extent, the USA to the conference table.

Japanese territorial aspirations were initially satisfied by the skilfully planned, well-coordinated and efficiently executed military operations throughout Asia in December 1941 and early 1942.

However, the capture of vast swathes of colonial countries called for a commensurate logistic plan to feed the all-conquering army. It was food, or the lack of it, that was to prove to be the Japanese Achilles' heel.

Prior to 1941, Japan imported about 20 per cent of its food (Britain imported 50 per cent). This modest 20 per cent was critical because it included all its salt, 92 per cent of its sugar, most of its soya beans and about one third of its rice.[6] The urban population was dependent upon Korean and Formosa for rice (both Japanese colonies). Japan could get by without sugar and it reduced consumption from 800,000 tons per annum to 182,000 tons by 1945. There was a downside: sugar had contributed 7 per cent of the national calorific intake and the reduction in availability reduced energy levels and impacted on the palatability of the diet. It was the provision of salt and rice that was of the highest priority.

In peacetime, the Japanese diet was predominantly fish, and as the Pacific War raged, that fish, increasingly, was squid. This is usually found in coastal waters and an indication that deep-sea fishing had ceased. A combination of the shortage of labour, fuel, and even of cotton and hemp used for the manufacture of fishing nets, was further exacerbated by the increasing American control of the sea. Japan's agricultural economy gave little room for manoeuvre.

> Farming was already predominantly arable and the only way to increase the rice harvest was to extend the cultivated area, but virtually every scrap of flat land and even hillsides were already covered with paddy. Wartime labour shortages and a precipitate decline in fertiliser imports also impacted hard on agricultural productivity ... less food created a greater dependence on imports.[7]

The Japanese Army sprawled across Southeast Asia, and it was left in no doubt that it had to 'live off the land'. This presumed that the indigenous inhabitants had food enough to provide for hundreds of thousands of non-productive and uninvited guests. The Japanese showed particular animosity towards those of Chinese heritage, because Japan was engaged elsewhere, in a brutal war with China.

In Malaya, the majority of rice farmers were hard-working Chinese. The invaders butchered an estimated 50,000 ethnic Chinese, and the production of much needed rice almost ceased.[8] Apart from the unspeakable, criminal brutality, the killing of the rice farmers had no place in a coherent policy.

Japan was a country with over 5 million of its men under arms, deployed over a vast expanse but with neither the ships nor the logistic resources to support them.[9] The USN's submarine blockade was progressively degrading the Japanese merchant fleet and Japanese soldiers were starving to death across the Pacific.

Distribution of Japanese Army personnel, August 1945.

Location	Number
Japanese mainland	2,388,000
Kurile Islands, Sakhalin	88,000
Taiwan, south-west Islands	169,000
Korean peninsula	294,000
Manchukuo	664,000
China and Hong Kong	1,056,000
Southern and mid-Pacific region	744,000
Rabaul region	70,000
Total	5,473,000

Chinese Nationalist soldiers on operations against the Japanese, June 1938. The muddy floodwater concealed areas of deeper water, and in this situation, any soldier who was wounded was likely to drown.

Summary

The core Japanese strategy failed and not least because its expansion across Southeast Asia was logistically flawed, in the longer term. The fallacious policy was that Japanese forces would be fed from the conquered territories. For example, Singapore was itself dependent on food imports, and its conqueror's needs could not be met from local resources after its victory.

The Pacific War was fought primarily by the Americans and Japanese, although British, Australian and Dutch forces played a minor role. This was to be a logistic war between two mismatched opponents in which food denial would be a major factor.

Notes

1. Paine, S.C.M., *The Wars for Asia 1911–1949* (New York, Cambridge University Press, 2012), p. 24.
2. Ibid., p. 28.
3. Nash, N.S., *In the Service of the Emperor* (Barnsley, Pen & Sword, 2022), p. 10.
4. Burkman, T.W., *Japan and the League of Nations* (University of Hawaii, 2008), p. 107.
5. Beres, L.R., 'On Assassination as Anticipatory Self-Defense: The Case of Israel' (*Hofstra Law Review*, 1991), p. 321.
6. Dower, J.W., *Embracing Defeat: Japan in the Aftermath of World War II* (London, Penguin, 2000), p. 91.
7. Collingham, L., *The Taste of War* (London, Penguin Group, 2011), p. 229.
8. Ooi Giok Ling, *Southeast Asian Culture and Heritage in a Globalising World – Diverging Identities in a Dynamic Region* (Farnham, Surrey, Ashgate Publishing Ltd., 2012), p. 97.
9. Trefalt, B., *Japanese Army Stragglers and Memories of the War in Japan, 1950–75* (London, Routledge, 2003), p. 26.

Chapter Eighteen

The War in the Pacific: Guadalcanal to Okinawa (1942–5)

To step back chronologically, in mid-1942, the Japanese Empire had reached its apogee and in the first five months of the year, Japan took over a greater area than any country in history and did not lose a single major ship. The statistics are overwhelming. Japan took 250,000 Allied prisoners, sank 105 Allied ships, and seriously damaged a further 91, while it lost only 7,000 dead, 14,000 wounded, 562 planes and 27 ships, but no cruisers, battle-ships or carriers.[1] The coordination of these widely dispersed operations was an excellent demonstration of high-grade and skilful staff work. The logistic plan to support the differing and widely dispersed operations should invite admiration, and in the short term, it does, but in time, the collapse of the arrangement for the supply of garrisons across the Pacific was to be the Achilles' heel of Hirohito's Empire.

It was an act of indescribably poor judgement for Japan to launch an attack on the USA, the British Empire, and the Dutch while at the same time fighting China. The odds were stacked against Japan because the USA was, by a very large measure, the wealthiest, most powerful, best logistically equipped nation on Earth. It had plenty of everything and an industrial base that was expanding on a daily basis.

From mid-1942, food, its production and distribution were a constant head-ache for the Japanese, and its adversary exploited this vulnerability ruth-lessly. The first instance of food denial was on the island of Guadalcanal, a British possession in the Solomon Islands that had no agricultural base and could not support any invaders. This island had been taken, virtually un-opposed, by the Japanese, who had then toiled to build an airstrip. This airstrip was, briefly, strategically important. The Japanese were dependent on a resupply system that faced American opposition from August 1942, when American Marines invaded Guadalcanal and took the airstrip.

At the initial landing, the Japanese had been massively outnumbered, but Guadalcanal is a large land mass about 140 miles long (225km) and 39 miles (63km) wide. It was densely covered in very thick jungle, with the smell of

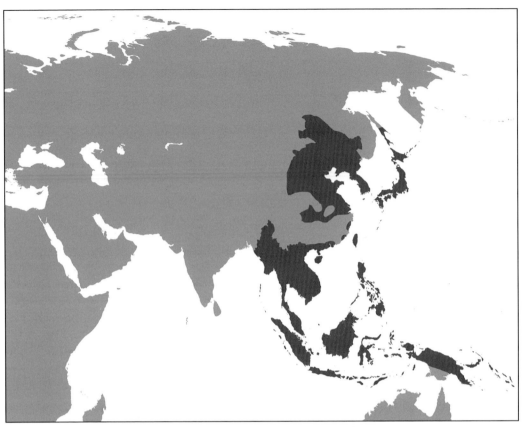

The apogee of the Japanese Empire in April 1942.

decaying vegetation ever-present. For the Japanese, access to its lengthy coastline was easy and rapid reinforcements and supplies were quickly delivered, always at night, by fast ships. This process became known as the Tokyo Express.

The Battle of Savo Bay (just off Guadalcanal) was fought on 8–9 August 1942, when the Japanese inflicted a serious defeat on the US Navy (USN). This encouraged the Japanese to reinforce their garrison on the island, found by the 28th Infantry Regiment, commanded by Colonel Ichiki Kiyonao. On 19 August, a further 917 soldiers of the 28th landed from destroyers at Taivu Point. This was about 9 miles (14km) east of the strategically important airstrip, known as Henderson Field, and well beyond the defended perimeter. The unopposed landing was uneventful but Japanese intelligence had failed to provide Ichiki with an accurate estimate of American strength, and optimistically, he determined to make an attack on the American eastern perimeter during the night of 20/21 August.

The attack on the perimeter was a failure and heavy losses were inflicted on the Japanese around Alligator Creek (later known as the Battle of Tenaru). After dawn, the marines counter-attacked and savaged the demoralised enemy. Ichiki was killed, possibly by his own hand. A total of 789 Japanese corpses were counted and only about 30 of the original 917 reinforcements survived unwounded.

Thereafter, the Americans dominated the island, and they were able to completely disrupt the Japanese supply system to such effect that starvation set in. It became evident to the Japanese high command that the occupation of the island was no longer militarily viable, and on 28 December, Hirohito was advised of the need to withdraw. This was accomplished with considerable skill, on 1 February 1943, when 4,935 men were evacuated.

The death toll, modest by that of the Sino-Japanese conflict, was nevertheless high by the standards set early in this war. The Americans had 1,592 killed and about 8,000 wounded. Eighty-five Australians were killed at the Battle of Savo Island, but the number of Solomon Islanders killed is unknown. For the Japanese, the latter stages of the campaign were notable for the deaths from malnutrition, neglect and disease. They had 19,200 killed, but over half of their fatalities (10,700) were attributed to medical causes and that is, in part, a reflection of the logistic deficiencies in this part of the campaign. This instance of food denial was to be repeated across the Pacific.

Whilst Japanese soldiers starved on Guadalcanal, many of their comrades were engaged in Papua. In January 1942, they had established a strong naval and air base at Rabaul, located on the north-eastern tip of New Britain. The Japanese aspired to extend across the Owen Stanley Mountains to occupy Port Moresby. The Allies, aware of the importance of the Papuan Peninsula and its vulnerability, had plans to reinforce the area and construct an airstrip at Buna, which lay on the coast at one end of the 100-mile (161km) Kokoda Trail. In the meantime, on 10 July, a six-man team was inserted to survey the ground around Buna. The Japanese beat the Allies to the punch, and on 21 July 1942, landed 13,000 men at Gona and Buna. Once again, Japanese intelligence failed the men on the ground, to whom it was suggested that Port Moresby could be attacked from the north-west by way of the Kokoda Trail from Buna. Tomitarō was given the task, and having established beachheads at Gona and Buna, he determined that he would indeed march, by way of the Kokoda Trail, across the Owen Stanley Mountain range and capture Port Moresby. Air cover would be provided by Admiral Mikawa's 11th Air Fleet, based in Rabaul.

That was the plan.

However, Horii was operating under a serious misapprehension, having been assured by his intelligence sources that there was a trafficable road from Buna to Port Moresby. It came as an unwelcome shock to discover that the trail was, in fact, a narrow, very steep, rutted track, unusable by wheeled vehicles, with many steep inclines that ran through rainforest and across a

The inhospitable Kokoda Trail.

formidable mountain range.[2] It was probably terrain as difficult as existed anywhere on Earth.

Food resupply rapidly became the issue. The further the Japanese fought their way across this tortuous terrain, the longer became their logistic chain and the more food that was eaten by the porters to sustain them on their journey to the front. For the front-line Japanese soldiers this was not food denial imposed by an enemy, but increasingly by the environment and the limitations of their domestic logistic system. For the first time in this war, Japanese soldiers fought to take their enemies' food. It became an unlikely and unexpected priority.

The Australian defenders exploited, to full advantage, the Owen Stanley Range. The trail made its way up 10,000-foot mountains, and across cavernous ravines and raging rivers. The jungle was thick, matted, and infested with ticks and mosquitoes. It was very hot and humid, and torrential rain fell every day. Swarms of trillions of flies, ever-present, added to the torment. It was a deeply unpleasant place to be.

On that basis, the defenders could not believe that the Japanese would, from choice, seek to fight in these conditions. However, to the considerable credit of General Horii Tomitarō and his soldiers, they cut their way by hand through the thickest jungle and up the most precipitous of mountainsides. They made slow and hungry progress against resolute Australian delaying tactics. Nevertheless, by mid-August, the Japanese had reached beyond the halfway mark and were at 'The Gap', the steepest part of the trail. Here, 'the thin air and blazing sun increased the misery of the ordeal.'[3] The evacuation of casualties was now a major logistic burden, more so for the Japanese the further up the trail they progressed. On 16 September, advance units of Horii's force had reached Ioribaiwa, from whose heights Port Moresby could be seen in the distance below.[4] Horii realised that he could go no further and was obliged to halt because his supply system had completely broken down. His men were starving, short of ammunition and the porters were struggling to cope with an increasingly lengthy round trip upon which they consumed a high proportion of the food they were carrying.

The Australian 7th Infantry Division had now reached the theatre and it took the fight to Horii. General Horii had anticipated that he could, and would, capture enemy food stocks. But that was no basis for an extended foray into enemy territory, and by this time, Japanese operations were entirely aimed at obtaining food – any food. The Australians were able to observe the Japanese fighting each other: 'In the scramble for punctured tins and mud-stained rice, the warrior spirit evaporated, and the Australian rearguard went unmolested.'[5] The Australians made it a practice to leave damaged or contaminated food behind and their enemy suffered from the consequent gastric complaints.

While Horii's men suffered on the Kokoda Trail, fellow soldiers were starving on Guadalcanal. On 23 September, the Japanese high command realised that it did not have the capacity to provide logistic support to both campaigns, and Horii was ordered to withdraw to Buna. Withdrawal, a euphemism for retreat, is one of the most difficult operations to carry out successfully. Withdrawal can very quickly degenerate into a rout and only well-disciplined troops can succeed.

Horii, to his great credit, executed a textbook withdrawal back down the trail, carrying his wounded. However, on 4–11 November, at the Battle of Oivi-Gorari, Horii's force was routed, and discipline collapsed. This breakdown in good order was accompanied by amoebic dysentery and a powerful strain of malaria, which devastated the undernourished soldiers. It caused the death of many as they sat in their foxholes. In the Buna area, further retreat was inhibited by the flooded Kumusi River. Horii decided to raft down the river with a few of his personal staff. Later he took to a canoe but was swept out to sea and drowned.[6]

The campaign along the Kokoda Trail was a very modest affair when compared to the much greater battles still to be fought by the Americans on and over the Pacific. Kokoda, although involving relatively small forces, was disproportionately important because it was the first time that the Japanese had suffered a defeat on land. They lost 2,050 killed and approximately 4,500 incapacitated by sickness and wounds. The Australians and Papuans had 625 killed, 1,055 wounded and over 4,000 sick.[7] They had demonstrated that, good though the Japanese soldiers were, they were not supermen and could be beaten. Allied morale rose as a result.

The Japanese owed their defeat, in very large measure, to a combination of poor intelligence, logistic naivety and then the inevitable inability to feed their soldiers. The war in the Pacific was unique in many ways, not least in the vast area covered by the operations and the resultant depth and complexity of the logistic arrangements made by both major combatants.

The forces of the USA were the recipients of probably the most sophisticated supply system in the world and that was supported by a powerful navy. The USN submarine fleet was deployed to counter the Japanese surface transport resupplying the garrisons in its captured territories.

The Japanese military strategy was that its forces would subsist on captured food. In 1942, for the most part, this was a practical solution. But the behaviour of the Japanese across Southeast Asia quickly alienated the captive populations and that, in turn, reduced cooperation and depressed the harvest of rice – the staple constituent of the Japanese diet. Famine in Vietnam, China and Bengal all led to a reduction in the availability of rice and contributed to the hunger of Japanese soldiers and that of the indigenous people whose land they had usurped.

This was not the end of operations in Papua New Guinea; attacks on Port Moresby, the only port providing support for operations, continued from the air. However, as part of the strategic plan, the Americans had moved on and

Papua New Guinea became a military backwater. That said, there remained a vast, undefeated Japanese Army, which was never beaten, and the survivors eventually surrendered in September 1945.

MacArthur delegated the containment and destruction of this force to the Australian Army, and over the next three years, starvation killed many more Japs than the Australians. Japanese garrisons were effectively besieged and denied food and medical supplies. David Stevens suggests that 97 per cent of Japanese deaths in this campaign were from non-combat causes.[8] This figure is unsupported by any evidence but there is no doubt that food denial was a major factor in the deaths of an estimated 202,100 Japanese throughout the campaign on New Guinea, Bougainville, New Britain, New Ireland and the Admiralty Islands. Allied killed were Australia 7,000 and USA 4,684.

It was the aim of the USN to blockade Japan, degrade its merchant marine and by so doing destroy the Japanese logistic chain. Food denial was an integral element of that strategy, and eventually, it was highly effective.

In many instances, the Japanese paid a high price for their reliance on locally sourced food. Guadalcanal and the Kokoda Trail are two such instances in which local resources were lacking and Japanese soldiers succumbed to starvation.

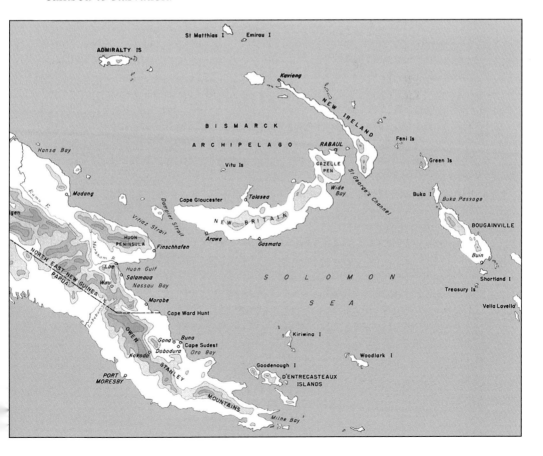

The American blockade got off to a poor start when the torpedoes fired by USN submarines failed to function correctly. American submarine commanders complained bitterly but it was not until 1943 that Lieutenant Commander F.B. Warder, USN, commanding USS *Seawolf*, brought matters to a head. After testing, it was discovered that there were three complementary issues. The first was that the new MK14 torpedo persistently ran about 10 feet deeper than its setting; the second was the premature detonation of the torpedo; and the third was the jamming of the detonators when it did actually strike a target. It had taken nearly two years but, by the close of 1943, the USN was playing a major role in the degradation of the Japanese merchant fleet and food denial was contributing to the starvation of Japanese across Southeast Asia.

American strategy in the Pacific War was to advance on the Japanese home islands by taking islands occupied by the Japanese and to acquire Japanese landing strips or to build new strips. The aim was to establish air bases close enough to Japan to bring it into the range of the new B-29 bomber fleet, but this process would take about eighteen months of hard campaigning and tens of thousands of lives.

Shrewdly, the two senior US commanders, General Douglas McArthur and Admiral Chester Nimitz, realised that it was not necessary to spend American lives by seeking the possession of every coral island and that in some cases these strategically unimportant islands could be bypassed, their garrisons isolated, blockaded and starved. Such places were Truk and the fortress and naval base of Rabaul.

Located in eastern New Britain, Papua New Guinea, Rabaul was chronologically the first major installation to be bypassed. It was a well-defended target and it bristled with anti-aircraft guns and housed a garrison of over 100,000 men. Nevertheless, on 12 October 1943, 349 American aircraft made a first assault on Rabaul. Bad weather delayed a second wave until 18 October. There were further raids on 23 October and 2 November.

Meanwhile, a strong Japanese force sailed from Truk to defend Rabaul. Admiral William Halsey's 3rd Fleet was the major Allied force in the area but had only the two carriers *Saratoga* and *Princeton*, together with their embarked air arms. If Halsey committed his aircraft to an attack on Rabaul, he would be taking a very serious risk. His carriers would be unprotected, and he was courting heavy losses at the hands of Rabaul's formidable defences, which were now supplemented by the cruiser force.

Nevertheless, undaunted, Halsey moved his carriers closer to the target and then, under cover of a weather front, on 4–5 November, he launched all ninety-seven of his available aircraft. Their attack was supplemented by a land-based bomber force of twenty-seven B-24 Liberators, protected by fifty-eight P-38s. This combination overwhelmed Rabaul and caused very serious damage to six of the seven ships in the Japanese cruiser force. Fifty-six Japanese planes were destroyed. Allied losses were seventy-seven, of which only ten were carrier-based. Halsey made a further attack on 11 November, having been reinforced by elements of the 5th Fleet. He now had under command the carriers *Essex, Bunker Hill* and *Independence*.

The Japanese made the fundamental mistake of reinforcing failure and flew in hundreds of aircraft from Truk to Rabaul, most of which were swiftly eliminated. The surviving aircraft flew back to Truk, leaving a destroyed Rabaul, which played no further part in the war. It became a de facto prisoner of war camp. To the credit of the soldiers, abandoned by their government in Rabaul, they turned to and became self-sufficient. They grew their own food and 69,000 survived to surrender on 12 September 1945.[9]

Truk Atoll is in the central Pacific, part of the Caroline Island chain. It is situated about 970 nautical miles (1,800km) north-east of New Guinea, and today is part of the Chuuk State and a constituent of the Federated States of Micronesia (FSM). The lagoon is an enormous natural harbour of 820 square

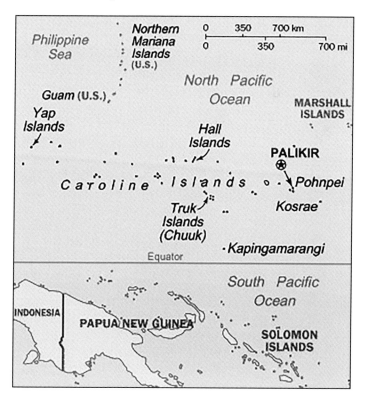

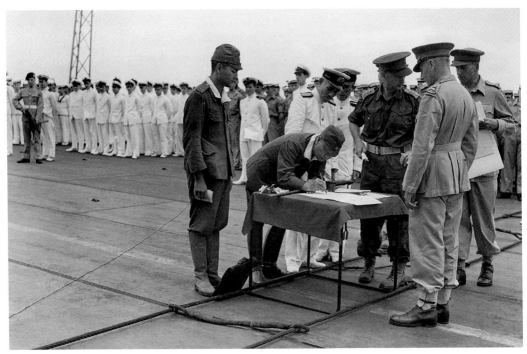

General Imamura signing the official document of surrender of the 139,000 Japanese in New Britain, New Ireland, the Solomons and New Guinea, on the flight deck of HMS *Glory* off Rabaul, 12 September 1945. Lieutenant General Sturdee, GOC First Australian Army, who signed for the Allies, is closely watching the Japanese general from the other side of the table. Vice Admiral Kusaka Jinichi signed the treaty for the Japanese Southeastern naval forces. (*IWM*)

miles (2,124km²), with a perimeter of 140 miles (225km). The Japanese made the lagoon its main naval installation in the South Pacific and built extensive defence works in anticipation of an American invasion.

The island was garrisoned by about 40,000 soldiers of the 31st Army, and as they expected the Americans to invade Truk, they prepared accordingly. As a first measure, prudently, the Imperial Japanese Navy (IJN) moved its Combined Fleet 1,306 miles (2,102km) from Truk to Palau island. Truk island was extensively equipped with concrete fortifications that housed shore batteries and anti-aircraft guns. It was a misnomer, but journalists had christened Truk 'the Gibraltar of the Pacific'. There is no doubt that, in 1944, Truk's position remained strategically significant. It provided a centrally placed shipping and aircraft staging post, for Japanese military assets on passage from the home islands of Japan, through to the multiple islands mandated to Japan after the First World War. It was all the more important after the destruction of Rabaul in late 1943.

However, as the Americans swept through the Pacific, Truk faced the prospect of being isolated by Operation CARTWHEEL and the island-hopping strategy of the USA. The IJN was busily engaged in the movement of its assets; its major ships had left the haven of Truk Lagoon when, on 17 February 1944, the USN launched Operation HAILSTONE. This was an attack by 560 carrier aircraft and the effect was overwhelming. Japanese losses were 2 light cruisers, 4 destroyers, 3 auxiliary cruisers, 6 auxiliary ships, an aircraft ferry, 2 submarine tenders and 3 smaller warships. In the grand order of things, it was the sinking of 32 merchant ships that was a logistic calamity. In addition, 250 Japanese aircraft were destroyed, the majority on the ground. American losses were 25 aircraft and 40 men killed. Over 4,500 Japanese were killed. The remainder stood to repel the invasion.

The Americans never did invade Truk.

The 36,000 soldiers of 31st Army manned their guns, became hungry and they starved. The bypassing of Truk was an astute, no-cost decision by the Americans and one they employed as they gained ascendancy when similarly bypassing Japanese garrisons and unwanted airfields in the Bismarck Archipelago, the Caroline Islands and the Palaus.

American progress across the Pacific had been inexorable and by the end of 1943, the defeat of Japan was assured. The bypassing of some Japanese garrisons was both pragmatic and effective. Japanese garrisons were starving, at minimal cost to the USA. Hunger may have been the outcome of these operations, but food denial had not been a factor.

On Truk, the skeletal survivors surrendered in August 1945, witnesses to the awful impact of food denial. Their number was severely depleted by starvation.

Allied, principally American, progress through the Pacific is shown in the table following:

1943	2 January	Buna, New Guinea
	10 May	Attu, Aleutian Islands
	7 August	Guadalcanal and Tulagi
	25 August	New Georgia
	1 November	Bougainville, Solomon Islands
	15 December	Arawe Peninsula, New Britain, Gilbert Islands
	26 December	New Britain, Cape Gloucester
1944	31 January	Kwajalein, Marshall Islands
	17 February	Truk
	22 April	Aitape and Hollandia, New Guinea
	27 May	Biak Island, New Guinea
	15 June	Saipan
	19 June	Guam
	24 July	Tinian
	15 September	Morotai and Peleliu

The Japanese delegation from Truk boards USS *Portland* to surrender in August 1945.

	11 November	Iwo Jima
	15 December	Mindoro, Philippine Islands
1945	19 February	Iwo Jima
	1 April	Okinawa

The Pacific War was, in logistic terms, without parallel. The manipulation of thousands of ships, their maintenance and resupply of food, fuel and ammunition was masterly. It was also prodigiously expensive. Similarly, the well-being of almost a million men ashore and afloat was an exercise inviting admiration.

The resolute resistance of Japanese garrisons across the Pacific had demonstrated that those who served their emperor would rather die than surrender. The aim was to kill as many Allied soldiers as possible. The planners could see that an invasion of the Japanese home island could cause a death toll running into millions.

In Japan, the food situation was bad and getting worse. Nimitz initiated Operation STARVATION; this was the mining of Japanese coastal waters to augment the submarine blockade and to further degrade Japan's merchant fleet. Major General Curtis LeMay, commanding the US Army Air Force (USAAF), was responsible and he deployed 160 aircraft to place 2,000 mines in April 1945. The operation was carried out at night at relatively low altitudes and with radar-assisted navigation. B-29 aircraft were employed but they had to be adapted to carry the ordnance that varied in size and shape to their usual bombload. Crews were given special training and rehearsed in the role.[10]

The operation commenced on 27 March 1945, when 1,000 parachute-retarded influence mines with magnetic and acoustic detonators were sown.[11] Later, water displacement variants were in the mix. This mining operation was the most efficient means of destroying Japan's shipping throughout the war in terms of risk damage per unit of cost. It was more efficient than either the strategic bombing or submarine campaigns.

Eventually, most of the major ports and straits of Japan were repeatedly mined, severely disrupting Japanese logistics and troop movements for the remainder of the war, with 35 of 47 essential convoy routes having to be abandoned. For instance, shipping through Kobe declined by 85 per cent, from 320,000 tons in March to only 44,000 tons in July.[12]

Operation STARVATION was ruthless, and it sank more ship tonnage in the last six months of the war than the efforts of all other sources combined. The Air Force flew 1,529 sorties and laid 12,135 mines in twenty-six fields on forty-six separate missions. Mining demanded only 5.7 per cent of the XXI Bomber Command's total sorties, and only fifteen B-29s were lost in the effort. In return, mines sank or damaged 670 ships, totalling more than 1,250,000 tons.[13] This was food denial in the grand manner. The blockade of Japan was all enveloping and unrelenting. Japanese civilians were facing imminent starvation. Richard Frank commented:

> Japan's 1945 rice crop was collapsing. About half the population of Japan lived in a dire food deficit area south and west of Tokyo on Honshu. The coastal shipping that normally provided the backbone of Japanese internal transportation had been destroyed. The only alternative to movement of large quantities of rice from surplus to deficit areas was by the limited rail system. If the US knocked out the rail system, Japan would be locked on a course for famine involving about half the 72 million population.
>
>   The Japanese rail system was, by US or European standards, both weak and extremely vulnerable. Combining the rail bombing, blockade and the failure of the 1945 rice crop promised to threaten death by starvation to a large swath of the Japanese population. Even though the war ended before the rail system was devastated, the extremely diminished

rice supply available for the period through to November 1946 generated a massive depopulation of Japan's urban centers.

Tokyo's inhabitants, for example, plunged from about 4.5 million at the end of 1944 to 2.5 million in mid-1946. Famine in 1946 was only forestalled by the infusion of massive amounts of US food that fed 18 million Japanese city dwellers in July, 20 million in August and 15 million in September 1946. Occupation authorities estimated this food saved 11 million Japanese lives.[14]

Summary

The American campaign in the Pacific was, in simple terms, a contest between two badly matched logistic organisations. The forces of the USA were superbly equipped, fed – and led. Their Japanese opponents could only offset the massive logistic deficiency by selling their lives in the defence of small islands of transitory importance.

The Americans set out to starve the Japanese and succeeded to the extent that, post-war, they had to feed their erstwhile enemy.

Notes

1. Paine, S.C.M., *The Wars for Asia 1911–1949* (New York, Cambridge University Press, 2012), p. 188.
2. Nash, N.S., *In the Service of the Emperor*, p. 155.
3. Costello, J., *The Pacific War 1941–45* [1981] (New York, Harper Collins, 2009), p. 317.
4. McAulay, L., *To the Bitter End: The Japanese Defeat at Buna and Gona, 1942–43* (Sydney, Random House, 1992), p. 12.
5. Grey, J., *A Military History of Australia* (Cambridge, Cambridge University Press, 1999), p. 171.
6. Harries, M. & Harries, S., *Soldiers of the Sun* (London, Heinemann, 1991), p. 343.
7. Williams, P., *The Kokoda Campaign 1942* (Melbourne, Victoria, Cambridge University Press, 2012), p. 235.
8. Stevens, D., 'The Naval Campaigns for New Guinea' (*Journal of the Australian War Memorial*, paragraph 30, retrieved March 2016).
9. Keogh, E., *Southwest Pacific 1941–45* (Melbourne, Grayflower Publications, 1965). p. 412.
10. Caldwell, A., Jr., 'Air Force Maritime Missions' (*United States Naval Institute Proceedings*, October 1978), p. 33.
11. Influence mines are triggered by the influence of a ship or submarine, rather than direct contact. Such mines incorporate electronic sensors designed to detect the presence of a vessel and detonate when it comes within the blast range of the warhead. The fuses on such mines may incorporate one or more of the following sensors: magnetic, passive, acoustic, or water pressure displacement caused by the proximity of a vessel. Source: Garrold, T., ' *Mine Warfare Introduction: The Threat*' (*Surface Warfare Officers School Command, U.S. Navy*, 1998).
12. Spector, R.H., *Eagle Against the Sun: The American War with Japan* (Free Press, 1985), p. 505.
13. Caldwell, p. 33.
14. Frank R.B., 'The Horribles: American Strategic Options Against Japan in 1945' (national ww2museum.org 2020).

Chapter Nineteen

The Philippines and Burma (1941–5)

During the war in Southeast Asia there were three major campaigns that contributed little to the final result but which, nevertheless, caused huge loss of life, much of it from starvation. These were in the Philippines (1944–5), Papua New Guinea (1942–5) and Burma (1944–5).

In late 1944, the Japanese High Command had to decide where to centre its forces against the next anticipated American attack. The decision was that the Philippines were the most likely target but their geography presented a problem. The archipelago consisted of 7,100 islands and spread 1,150 miles (1,850km) from Mindanao due north through the central islands of Cebu and Leyte to Luzon, the largest. Only eleven of the islands had an area greater than 1,000 square miles (2,590km^2) and two, Mindanao and Luzon, made up almost 70 per cent of the Philippines' landmass. Where would the Americans land? They were spoilt for choice. In the meantime, a million Japanese soldiers were fighting and dying in the apparently endless and fruitless war with China, now into its eighth year.

* * *

The Philippines

To strengthen its hold on the Philippines, General Yamashita Tomoyuki was moved to take command of the Japanese troops in the islands. Yamashita had an audience with Emperor Hirohito before he left Tokyo, and both understood he was going to his death. In this new post he answered to Field Marshal Terauchi, whose Southern Army was responsible for the defence of a huge area, covering from New Guinea to Burma and included the Philippines. Yamashita was a very capable soldier, probably the best available, but he was also the man responsible for mass murder in Malaya and Singapore in 1942. He was a war criminal and the events that followed during his command in the Philippines did nothing to dissuade his accusers.

The invasion of the Japanese-held Philippines had been the oft-stated ambition of General Douglas MacArthur, who had been ejected from those same islands on 11 March 1942. As a prelude to his triumphant, well-rehearsed and ego-satisfying return, MacArthur decided that the island of Peleliu should be taken as it had an airstrip that the Japanese *might* use. Accordingly, the island redoubt was invaded on 15 September 1944. Later, Vice Admiral J.B. Oldendorf observed sagely:

> If military leaders were gifted with the same accuracy of foresight as they are with hindsight undoubtedly the assault and capture of the Palaus [a group of islands of which Peleliu, was one] would never have been attempted.[1]

In the event, the Japanese made no use of the airstrip on Peleliu, but those who fought for this worthless island claimed that the Japanese 14th Division contributed to the most savage fighting of the Pacific War. It is impossible to measure 'savagery', but:

> this expedition cost the highest casualty rate [almost 40 per cent] of any amphibious attack in American history. The 1st Marine Division lost 6,526 men, of whom 1,252 were killed; the 81st Infantry Division suffered 1,393 casualties, including 208 dead. Japanese casualties, including reinforcements from nearby islands, stood at 13,600 killed and 400 captured.[2]

It could be argued that bypassing unwanted enemy territory was a cost-effect policy; it saved lives and quickened the advance. However, the Philippines and their liberation was a politically sensitive issue. The Philippines were, for practical purposes, American territory, and the defeat of American arms in 1942 had dented national pride – but much more important, it had dented the reputation of Douglas MacArthur. The general's influence on USA defence policy during the Pacific War was disproportionate to his worth and he was absolutely committed to retaking the islands.

The final decision to initiate the liberation of the Philippines through Leyte was taken by MacArthur in conjunction with Admiral Nimitz. It was to prove to be one of the most ill-judged decisions taken during the Pacific War and presented several obstacles to MacArthur's master plan.

There was only one road in Leyte: the circular Route 2. Other routes were narrow, unmade gravelled tracks that were unsuited to the movement of the vehicles that were needed to provide logistic support to the invading army. The general had decided that Leyte's flat, central valley would be ideal for yet another airfield. He chose to ignore the advice of his senior engineer who told him that the site selected was totally unacceptable as it was a swamp.

MacArthur rejected the advice.[3] He also failed to take note of the impending monsoon, which was unfortunate as 24 inches (61cm) of rain fell during the month of November, and the swamps became lakes. The decision-making by MacArthur and his staff, prior to the invasion, was incompetent, and it did not improve once battle was joined. The performance of this celebrated general was mediocre and had serious consequences for the men under his command.

It has been argued by historians that the invasion of the Philippines was unnecessary and merely an indulgence of MacArthur's ego. The assault on and taking of the Philippines was of no strategic importance but the loss of life was huge and 80 per cent of the 420,000 Japanese who died succumbed to starvation or disease.[4] This starvation was less a deliberate strategy but rather the result of the much wider American submarine activity against the rapidly dwindling Japanese merchant marine.

MacArthur's campaign in the Philippines was a lengthy and very bloody affair, lasting from 20 October 1944 until the surrender of Japan on 15 August 1945. During the course of the campaign, the beautiful city of Manila was destroyed; approximately 100,000 of its citizens were killed and 250,000 were casualties.[5]

The paucity of food available to Japanese troops was a significant factor in their defeat at the hands of the superbly well-supplied Americans in the Philippines. As the Pacific War developed, the absence of a reliable logistic

On 20 October 1944, a few hours after his first troops had landed, MacArthur waded ashore onto the Philippine island of Leyte. It was a polished, stage-managed event, and soon after, the general made a radio broadcast in which he declared, 'People of the Philippines, I have returned!'

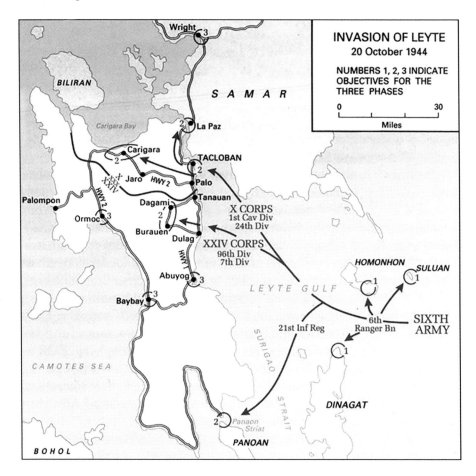

chain combined with an inability to live off the land condemned hundreds of thousands of Japanese to misery and death by starvation. The Americans were able to feed those Filipinos who were in territory they controlled, but those indigenous people under the control of the Japanese shared their invaders' food deprivation and starvation.

Summary

The battle for the Philippines epitomised so much of what went on elsewhere in the Pacific theatre, when ravenous, sickly Japanese soldiers fought more for food than for territory.

The liberation of the Philippines was significant, not only for its impact on American morale, but also because the Japanese Army had been comprehensively defeated in an environment in which they were, allegedly, supermen.

The walled city Intramuros, in the middle of Manila, was destroyed in the bitter fighting during May 1945.

The 'butcher's bill' in the battle for the Philippines was huge. The US Army had 16,233 killed and 47,163 wounded. In operations in Philippine waters the USN suffered 7,270 killed and wounded. The number evacuated to hospital was 'tens of thousands'.

* * *

Burma

The Japanese made their intention towards Burma clear on 15 December 1941, when they made an air raid on Victoria Point (now Kawthaung) at the southernmost tip of Burma on the Kra Isthmus. The attack was ineffective but sufficient to alarm Lieutenant General Thomas Hutton, the GOC-in-C of the Burma Army. His command was a very weak corps of two divisions – 17 Indian Infantry Division and 1 Burma Division. This latter division had been raised as an armed, quasi-police force for internal security duties. It was neither equipped nor trained to meet a modern, fast-moving Japanese army. In fact, 'They proved to be unreliable and even treacherous when subject to the test of battle.'[6]

On 22 January 1942, the Japanese 55 Division invaded Burma by way of Thailand. The British 16 Brigade, in its path, was hopelessly outnumbered and withdrew.

The Japanese swept through thinly defended Burma in the early months of 1942, opposed only by the one effective division, the 17th. This division was then severely damaged, on 23 February 1942, by the blowing of the Sittang

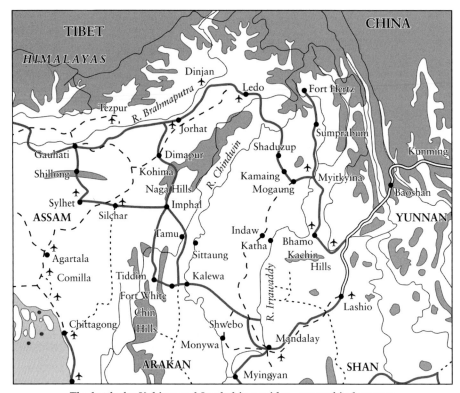

The battle for Kohima and Imphal in a wider, geographical context.

Bridge, with half its number on the wrong side of the river. The GOC, Major General Jackie Smith, was promptly sacked by General Wavell.

The country was firmly in Japanese hands. The invaders, as was their usual practice, sought to feed off the land to the detriment of the Burmese, many of whom had originally greeted the Japanese as liberators. The Japanese offered immediate independence to the Burmese but, by their egregious conduct, quickly lost support and the Burmese judged that British colonial government was a deal less painful than Japanese occupation.

The Allies mounted long-range penetration (LRP) operations, the brainchild of Major General Orde Wingate: in February 1943 (Operation LONG-CLOTH) and March 1944 (Operation THURSDAY). These operations were notable for the fortitude of the participants but, notwithstanding great courage, they were of limited strategic value. Nevertheless, Operation THURSDAY harassed the Japanese logistic chain during the battles for Kohima and Imphal and was successful. However, it did nothing to deter the Japanese from their long-term aim of invading India.

General William (always known as Bill) Slim commanded 14th Army, which was composed predominantly of Indian and other Commonwealth troops. He had positioned his force to defend the key towns of Imphal and Kohima.

From late summer 1942, General Mutaguchi and his XV Army controlled northern Burma and it was Mutaguchi's intention to move against Slim and launch an invasion of India, to be called Operation U-GO. He had ample manpower, ammunition and general supplies but only sufficient rations for three weeks.[7] His solution to that deficiency was to order his men to live on captured British food stocks. The presumption was simplistic in the extreme. Clearly, unless food was captured in the first few days, the capability of his army would be severely degraded.

Mutaguchi's ambition enjoyed the support of Prime Minister Tōjō Hideki and both anticipated that a triumphant march into India would knock Britain out of the war and compel the USA to come to the negotiating table.[8] The

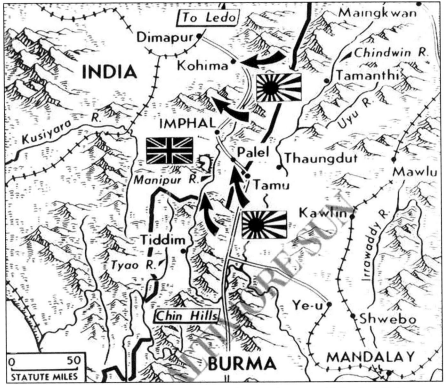

The juxtaposition of the three objectives of General Mutaguchi: Imphal, Kohima and Dimapur.

two prime objectives of Mutaguchi were Imphal, the important British logistic base in Assam, and then to sever the supply line and take Kohima. This would open up a route to Dimapur, another key logistic base in the Brahmaputra River valley. Kohima was strategically important because it was at the head of the mountain pass through which the road to Imphal and Dimapur ran. It was the route into India, and thus of particular interest to Mutaguchi.

On 8 March 1944, three reinforced Japanese divisions and a division of Subhas Chandra Bose's Indian National Army, 155,000 troops in all, crossed the Chindwin River and advanced across the mountain range that separated the two countries.[9]

In 1956, Slim, commenting in *Defeat into Victory* on operations around Imphal, said that they:

> swayed back and forth through great stretches of wild country, one day the focal point was a hill named on no maps, the next a miserable un-pronounceable village a hundred miles away. Columns, brigades, divisions, marched and counter-marched, met in bloody clashes and reeled apart weaving a confused pattern hard to unravel.

If it was confusing to the general soon after the battle, the reader will understand the reluctance of this author to seek to unravel the pattern other than to summarise the result.

The Kohima–Imphal road was overlooked by an attractive ridge that runs north–south. On the ridge, at a sharp bend in the road, was a bungalow, the residence of the local deputy commissioner. The bungalow was surrounded by terraced gardens and with a tennis court. (That area is top right on the map opposite and just above Garrison Hill.) It was to become the site of some of the most ferocious fighting of the Pacific War. The slopes of the ridge were very steep and thickly wooded.[10]

The top of the ridge was arranged as a number of defended areas. North of the ridge, not shown on the map, lay the densely inhabited area of Naga Village, crowned by Treasury Hill, and Church Knoll South. West of Kohima Ridge were GPT ridge and the jungle-covered Aradura Spur. The various British and Indian service troop encampments in the area gave their names to the features that were to be important in the battle. For example, Field Supply Depot became FSD Hill or merely FSD.[11]

General Slim was fortunate to obtain, from a battlefield casualty, an outline of the Japanese plan. This made it clear that Kohima was the focus of Mutaguchi's operation, and that General Satō Kōtoku's 31 Division had been allocated to the task. Nevertheless, there existed the possibility of Dimapur falling to the Japanese, and that had to be confronted. Slim was aware that the

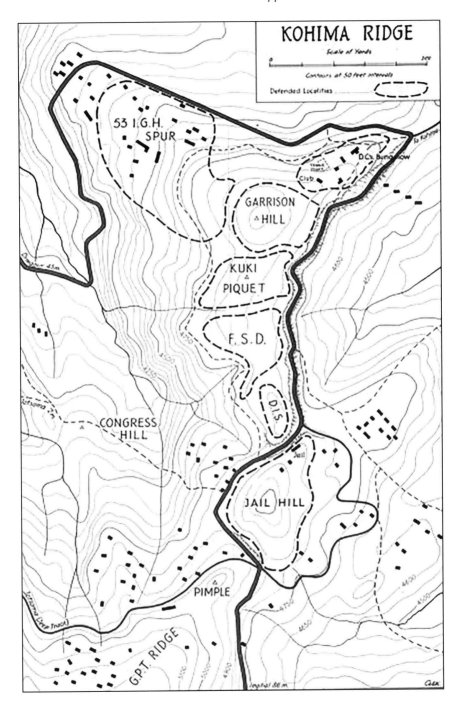

majority of his soldiers available for the defence of his major logistic base were those serving the lines of communication. He was deficient in infantry and artillery and was obliged to ask his superior, General Sir George Gifford, commanding 11 Army Group, for reinforcement so that he could defend the Dimapur logistic base area – 11 miles (18km) long and 1 mile (1.6km) wide.[12]

5th Indian Infantry Division was airlifted from the Arakan, where it had contributed to the successful battle of the Admin Box, in which the opposing Japanese troops had suffered starvation. The bulk of the division was deployed around Imphal but its 161 Brigade with 24 Mountain Artillery Regiment were sent to Dimapur.[13] In addition, the British 2nd Infantry Division and the Indian XXIII Corps were summoned to the ensuing battle.

General Satō's prime objective was Kohima. He was at odds with his commander, Mutaguchi, and resisted his order to send a force directly to Dimapur. He did eventually concur and despatched a battalion. However, Lieutenant General Kawabe Masakazu countermanded the order and the battalion returned to the Kohima front. It did not help Mutaguchi/Satō relations.

The defence of Kohima was in the hands of 4th Battalion, The Queen's Own West Kent Regiment, and a battalion of the Assam Regiment. These 1,200 men faced 15,000 of Satō's. From 3 April 1944, sixty-four days of hand-to-hand fighting followed. Much of the fighting was concentrated on Garrison Hill and the DC's tennis court. However, Satō was running out of time. His soldiers had consumed their rations and there was no likelihood of any resupply. Mutaguchi did not manage Satō very well, and when Satō was deeply committed to taking Kohima, Mutaguchi ordered him to reinforce those attacking Imphal.

The siege of Kohima was lifted with the arrival of 2 Division. The 31st Japanese Division was now in a parlous state. It had been bloodily repelled and it was starving. From 18 April to 13 May, British and Indian soldiers of 14th Army counter-attacked to drive the Japanese from the positions they had captured along the Kohima–Imphal road. They succeeded in dislodging the enemy from the ridge, but the road remained blocked, and it was not until 22 May that British and Indian troops met at Milestone 109 and reopened the road.

The significance of the Battle of Kohima was that it was the first battlefield defeat of the Japanese Army. The impact went far beyond Burma.

On the day that 14th Army linked up, Satō's division was starving; on 25 May, Satō announced that he was going to withdraw unless he was re-supplied. Food was not forthcoming, and Satō was as good as his word. On 31 May, he abandoned his positions in Naga Village and all positions north of the road. Mutaguchi was, predictably, not pleased, and in any army, it is career threatening to give one's commander an ultimatum. However, it was

22 May 1944. Two elements of 14th Indian Army meet at Milestone 109.

not until 7 July that Satō was sacked. As Satō's men struggled south, getting weaker every day, they were pursued by the well-fed XXXIII Corps.

On 9 July, Mutaguchi received orders to suspend his operations and he recognised the need to withdraw 15th Army.

On the long trek back over the mountains in the pounding rain men fought one another for food. Thousands of sick and wounded fell out on the march and killed themselves with grenades. The paths were seas of mud and, when a man stumbled, he became half buried in slime, shoes were stolen from those struggling to extricate themselves. Light machine guns, rifles, helmets, gasmasks – anything useless – littered the trail. Only the will to live propelled the survivors; the men hobbled along with improvised canes and those who lasted out a day's march huddled together for sleep that rarely came because of the constant downpour. Many drowned ... and the Chindwin claimed many lives in its monsoon-swollen waters.[14]

In the rain, with no place to sit, we took short spells of sleep standing on our feet. The bodies of our comrades who had struggled along the track before us, lay all around, rain-sodden and giving off the stench of decomposition. Even with the support of our sticks we fell amongst the corpses again as we stumbled on rocks and tree roots made bare by the rain and attempted one more step, then one more step in our exhaustion.[15]

In addition to the hostile climate and jungle, Slim's 14th Army was in pursuit, and it added to the total destruction of Mutaguchi's army. Japanese losses were (depending on the source) between 53,000 and 65,000 killed or missing. The British/Indian 14th Army lost 4,064 dead, missing and wounded – a modest cost for such a massive victory.

Summary

The campaign in Burma continued for over another year but the outcome was never in doubt after Kohima. The Japanese, always hungry, starved to death in their tens of thousands. Some fought on and gave their lives willingly

This Japanese soldier grasped an artillery shell between his knees and was prepared to detonate it when an Allied vehicle approached. He was killed before he had the chance to do so.

in a hopeless cause that was of no importance in the wider context of the Pacific War.

The image opposite illustrates the commitment of Japanese soldiers. However, regardless of the depth of commitment, the campaign is a compelling example of the criticality of food supply and an illustration of the cataclysmic outcomes that result from failure.

Notes

1. Heinl, R.D., *Soldiers of the Sea: The US Marine Corps, 1775–1962* (Annapolis, USN, 1962), p. 473.
2. Eggenberger, D., 'Peleliu – Angaur', *An Encyclopedia of Battles – Accounts of Over 1,560 Battles from 1479 B.C. to the Present* [1967] (New York: Dover Publications, 1985), pp. 327–8.
3. Hastings, Sir M., *Nemesis: The Battle for Japan 1944–45* [2007] (London, Collins, 2016), p, 201.
4. 'Final report, progress of demobilization of the Japanese Armed Forces, Part III: Overseas Areas', retrieved 10 March 2016. 109,890 Japanese military personnel repatriated immediately after the war; that leaves about 420,000 Japanese dead or missing.
5. Hastings, Sir M., *Nemesis*, p. 174.
6. Thompson, J., *Forgotten Voices of Burma* (London, Ebury Press, 2010), p. 3.
7. 'Burma Operations Record: 15th Japanese Army in the Imphal Area and Withdrawal to Northern Burma' (Office of the Chief of Military History, US Army, 1957), p. 72.
8. Ooka, S., *Fires on the Plain* (trans. Morris, I., Tokyo, Charles F. Tuttle Co., 1957), p. 179.
9. The INA was composed of Indian soldiers captured by the Japanese who were persuaded to fight against their fellow countrymen and the British. It was never a serious military threat to Slim's 14th Army.
10. Allen, L., [1984] *Burma: The Longest War 1941–45* (London, Phoenix Press, 2000), p. 228.
11. Rooney, D., [1992] *Burma Victory: Imphal and Kohima, March 1944 to May 1945* (London, Cassell, 1992), p. 74.
12. Allen, p. 206.
13. Ibid., pp. 229–30.
14. Tolland, J., *The Rising Sun: The Decline and Fall of the Japanese Empire 1936–45* [1970] (New York, Random House, 2003), pp. 614–15.
15. Kazuo Tamayama and John Nunneley, *Tales by Japanese soldiers of the Burma Campaign 1942–5* (London, 2000), p. 178.

PART FIVE

FAMINE

Chapter Twenty

Ukraine, Bengal, Vietnam, and China (1931–46)

The strategy of food denial is a legitimate *ruse de guerre*, which Adam Matuszczyk, the sociologist, defined as being 'acts against one's opponent by creative, clever, unorthodox means, sometimes involving force multipliers or superior knowledge'.[1]

Throughout human history, crops have failed, usually because of adverse climatic conditions but, in several cases, either an aggressive enemy has exploited the weakness and turned it to military advantage, or the government has failed to remedy the situation. The question posed is – 'is it a legitimate *ruse de guerre* to take advantage of a famine for political or military ends?' Whatever the answer, the cruel reality is that famine is often exploited. This chapter will briefly examine four such incidents to illustrate the vulnerability that famine produces.

During the period 1930–3, Ukraine and the grain-producing areas of southeast Russia suffered a protracted drought. The yield of successive harvests was poor, and the situation was exacerbated by the collectivisation of the farming industry. Under this politically inspired system, farmers were stripped of their land, and property that may have been in their family for many years was confiscated. The former owners, *kulaks* (defined as being rich peasants), were obliged to work their land for no reward other than subsistence living. This was an element in an attack on the culture of the *kulaks* and historian Robert Conquest alleged that Stalin had ordered that they were 'to be liquidated as a class'.[2]

There were other political factors that added to the lethality of the famine. Collectivisation was only part of a broader, five-year plan of an economic and social engineering philosophy. This caused a thrust towards greater industrialisation and so reduced the number of individuals available to work the land.

There are two schools of thought. One argues that the disaster in Ukraine was mere ineptitude on Stalin's behalf; the counterview is that the loss of life was a calculated genocide. Historians are divided on the issue, but all agree on the consequences of the famine. Several million people died and estimates of the death toll range from 5.7 million to 8.7 million. Starvation did not account for all deaths as an untold number of *kulaks* were executed and others banished to the far reaches of Russia, where they perished. Stalin and compassion were strangers, and he certainly did nothing to ameliorate the effects of the famine. Standing by and withholding food when people starve makes him complicit in their deaths.

The famine in Ukraine resulted in a weakened country less able to pursue independence from the USSR, and consequently, the winning of national sovereignty was delayed until July 1990.

*   *   *

About ten years after the Ukraine famine, a similar disaster struck the Bengal (now Bangladesh) region of India. In 1942, this was one of the most deprived regions on Earth. It was an agrarian society; the population existed in a situation in which starvation was a constant threat and extreme poverty was the norm. An influential Bengali businessman, Mirza Ahmad Ispahani, testifying in 1945 to the inquiry, commented: 'The Bengal cultivator, [even] before the war, had three months of feasting, five months of subsistence diet and four months of starvation.' After the event, the 'Famine Inquiry Commission' sought to describe the ratio of population in European terms. It commented that:

> The area of the province is 77,442 square miles, rather more than the area of England, Wales, and one-half of Scotland. The population is a little over 60 million, which is well in excess of that of the [entire] United Kingdom, and not much less than the aggregate population of France, Belgium, Holland, and Denmark.

Throughout the British Empire, its territories were expected to be self-sufficient, and that was the case in Bengal, where responsibility for governance was delegated to the governor of Bengal, who answered to the viceroy.

It was against this background that the dominant industry of Bengal, agriculture, was bereft of energy, innovation or investment. The need for food exceeded availability and then, to make a bad situation worse, a combination of climatic vagaries, a rising population supplemented by refugees fleeing from the war in Burma, widely spread, unmanageable debt, and a reduction in rice production all served to trigger social change. All the ingredients for a catastrophe were in place. The famine was an inevitable consequence, and it was, arguably, an avoidable, man-made crisis.[3]

Life in Bengal in 1942 was bleak and it got very much bleaker as the area was ravaged by a series of natural disasters. The first of these was an outbreak of *Cochliobolus miyabeanus*, which is a strong plant pathogen. Usually referred to as 'brown spot disease', it infected the winter rice crop, on which millions were dependent. Predictably, the infestation of this disease had a drastic deleterious effect on rice crop yield. The crop in Bengal was severely reduced by more than 40 per cent, a major accelerant in the starvation conditions and subsequent loss of life. This virus is so deadly that the USA gave thought to deploying it against Japanese garrisons in the Pacific. In the event, it did not do so.

Whilst wrestling with the effects of brown spot disease, on 16–17 October 1942, the low-lying delta of Bengal was hit by a massive cyclone, which caused widespread flooding, and the flood also served to disperse brown spot further. Three storm surges laid waste to 450 square miles (approximately 1,200km[2)], in which people were reduced to refugees. Estimates suggest that 14,500 people and 190,000 cattle were drowned. Stocks of rice, in store, were destroyed.[4] The incidence of malaria rose as the storm damage affected 3,200 square miles (approximately 8,300km^2) of Bengal.[5] The effect of the cyclone was catastrophic, and the arithmetic makes for grim reading. Indian historian Janam Mukherjee estimated that 7,400 villages were devastated and a further 1,600 villages were under water for weeks to follow. He alleged that 527,000 houses and 1,900 schools were lost. Malaria took many more lives as the mosquito bred in the placid floodwater.[6]

The malnutrition in Bengal gave rise to further ill health and loss of life. There was increased pressure on family life. The economy was faced with rising inflation that worsened the debt situation as incomes did not rise to meet it. There were some who exploited the misery of others, particularly those deeply in debt, but in possession of land – they were very vulnerable to 'land grabbing'. This was summarised by David Arnold, who wrote:

> In Bengal ... more serious and intractable [than population growth] was the continuing subdivision of landholdings and the chronic burden of indebtedness on the peasants, which left them by the late 1930s in a permanently 'semi-starved condition', without the resources to endure a major crop failure or survive the drying up of credit that invariably accompanied the prospect of famine in rural India. With no fresh land to bring under cultivation, peasants' holdings shrank as the output of rice *per capita* dwindled.[7]

The British campaign against the Japanese restricted the import of rice to Bengal. It then initiated a scorched-earth policy to deny food to the Japanese. But, by doing so, it exacerbated the situation in its Indian colony. Thereafter, a system was put in place to prioritise the distribution of food, which favoured those employed in government service, the armed forces, civil servants, and those engaged in any occupation in support of the war effort. The aim was to retain these key people in post.[8] However, the result of this policy was to further deny food to those at the bottom of the socio-economic scale. Appeals to the British Government were largely unproductive as Britain was immersed in the Battle of the Atlantic, struggling for survival, and shipping was not available to move grain across the face of the globe.

Ian Stephens, CIE, who was the editor of the British-owned *The Statesman* from 1942 to 1951, publicised the famine. From August 1943, Stephens began a 'relentless battle for eight weeks' to show his urban readers in Kolkata (then Calcutta) that the famine was real.[9] An administrative glitch exempted photographs from Emergency Rules in force, so Stephens sent photographers out to take images of the victims. Their publication was widely regarded as 'a singular act of journalistic courage and conscientiousness' – the Indian historian Janam Mukherjee, writing in 2015 and commenting on Stephens's work, suggested that 'without which many more lives would have surely been lost'.[10] Writing on the topic some twenty-three years later, Stephens commented:

> Death by famine lacks drama. Bloody death, the deaths of many by slaughter as in riots or bombings is in itself blood-stirring; it excites you, prints indelible images in your mind. But death by famine, a vast low dispirited noiseless apathy offers none of that. Horrid though it may be to say, multitudinous death from this cause … regarded without emotion as a spectacle, is until the crows get at it, the rats with kites and dogs and vultures, very dull.[11]

The rural peasants were hit hardest by the famine, and they took despairing measures to survive; they disposed of possessions, stored food and ate the survivable minimum. The disposal of the dead was an expense and so cadavers were abandoned, family structures broke down and they dispersed, and old people were left to their own devices. Some men, of necessity, joined the army.

The famine led to civil unrest, and on 8 August 1942, the Indian National Congress launched the 'Quit India' movement as a nationwide display of non-violent resistance.[12] The British reaction was immediate, and the leaders of the movement were promptly imprisoned. This was counterproductive as the leaderless movement then turned its hand to sabotage and violence. Matters escalated; 66,000 dissidents were taken into custody and 19,000 were convicted of civil offences or transgression of the Defence of India Act. The protests became increasingly violent. Judith Brown, writing in 1991, alleged that the police fired on 2,500 protesters but does not say where or when, or if any were killed.[13]

A group of Bengali children orphaned by the famine and left with nothing – not even clothes. One wonders what became of them. (*Kalyani Bhattacharyee and Manoj Sarbadhikar*)

In the early months of 1943, some food began to trickle into Bengal, but the relief process was poorly managed and largely misdirected to the relatively wealthy.[14] In 1980, Paul Greenough wrote that, in his opinion:

the Provincial Government of Bengal delayed its relief efforts primarily because they had no idea how to deal with a provincial rice market crippled by the interaction of man-made shocks, as opposed to the far more familiar case of localised shortage due to natural disaster.[15]

The expectation of the Bengal Government was that the Government of India would rescue Bengal by bringing food in from outside the province (350,000 tons had been promised but not delivered). Finally, they had long stood by a public propaganda campaign declaring 'sufficiency' in Bengal's rice supply and were afraid that speaking of scarcity rather than sufficiency would lead to increased hoarding and speculation.[16]

It was the appointment of Field Marshal Wavell, as Viceroy, in September 1943 that finally had the desired effect. Within two weeks of his appointment, he directed the military to undertake the transport and distribution of crucial supplies; 15,000 soldiers and RAF personnel delivered relief to the most distant parts of Bengal along with much needed medical support.[17] The situation was much improved when the rice crop in December 1943 exceeded expectations and was the largest ever seen. Wavell was widely praised for his efforts and relief operations ceased in December 1943.

The death toll was vast and the human misery unfathomable. Historians disagree, as they often do, on the ghastly numbers. Estimates vary between

1.7 million and 3 million. This author believes that the number of those who died is close to the upper figure.

The Bengal famine has been the subject of countless books and it has been a political football for eighty years. The key issue is that Bengal, as a part of India, was a British colony. There can be no doubt that, despite the local governance, the viceroy had responsibility for the huge loss of life, but he answered to HMG in London, and that is where the 'buck' stopped.

The governance of Bengal was inept, and as the famine developed, the British response was weak and ineffective. The colonial power was engaged in a European war of survival on the other side of the world, and its immediate priority was feeding its domestic population. However, the UK was morally responsible for the well-being of its 60 million Bengali citizens, and it failed them. It left an eradicable stain on the British Empire's reputation and added to the strength of India's independence movement. It underscores the point that active food denial or, in this case, inadvertent food deprivation, is a catalyst for significant loss of life and domestic and political change.

*   *   *

Famine, almost unknown in the Western world, was a constant in the lives of the Asiatic people, and in 1944–5, Vietnam suffered much as had the people of Bengal. The cause of the Vietnamese famine was, however, somewhat different. Vietnam was part of the French colonial empire and grouped with Cambodia, Laos and Guangzhouwan (an area of China leased to France) to form Indochina. The capital of this empire was Hanoi.

Japan had been at war with China since July 1937, and after the fall of France in 1940, the predatory Japanese invaded Vietnam in September. An agreement was reached on 9 December 1940, in which:

> French sovereignty was confirmed. The French still controlled their own army, and the administration of Indochina. Japanese forces were free to fight the war against the Allies from Indochinese soil.[18]

The Japanese permitted the French to have nominal control and the colony continued to be administered, at long range, by the Vichy government. However, both countries, combined, were at the root of a man-made famine that took about 2 million lives. There were several factors that combined to create a disaster. The USA bombed Japanese targets, and in the process, destroyed dykes, a vital part of the irrigation system, important for rice cultivation. Crop failures in 1943–5 had a cumulative effect and rice stocks were further depleted when both the French and Japanese burnt rice and maize to fuel power stations. The need to burn edible food was because the effective bombing campaign of the USA had cut the supply of coal from the north of the country to Saigon in the south. The result was a case of the law of unexpected consequences. The diplomat Bui Minh Dung observed:

> the Japanese occupation of Vietnam was the direct cause, in the final analysis, of several other factors, in turn affecting the famine, but their military efforts together with their economic policy for the Greater East Asia Co-Prosperity Sphere per se seem to have systematically played a role considerably greater than any other factors in the Vietnamese starvation.[19]

The inept French colonial 'government' failed to take any positive remedial steps and hindered the famine alleviation response.[20] The Japanese, characteristically, were unmoved by the human misery around them. The crop failures were accompanied by a succession of typhoons. Heavy rainfall in August–September 1944 caused extensive flooding and the loss of rice plants.

A Vietnamese appraisal of the disaster was published by Ken Maclean, who quoted three sources that related the famine to the political turmoil that followed. The first of these, Vỹ, pointed out that there were three different but interlinked forms of oppression during the conflict: 'Japanese fascism, French colonialism, and the feudal system of the Vietnamese themselves'. He added, 'It was inevitable that by twisting the worm [by which he meant the suffering brought about by the Great Famine], you would cause [us] to rise up.' The second source, Khoa, another survivor of the famine, explained, 'We could not stand it anymore; we had nothing left to lose, and the famine was simply the drop of water that caused a full glass to over-flow.' A third, Phong, was more succinct. He simply said, 'The famine was part of a long historical process; we had no choice but to rebel.'[21]

From 1945, Vietnam was at war for thirty years. By 1975, the famine was history, but its legacy is still evident today. The loss of life after the famine was enormous and the three distinct wars wrought vast political and social changes over a swathe of Southeast Asia. It also had an impact far away from Vietnamese shores and caused serious political division in the USA.

* * *

Occasionally, someone, somewhere does something that defies rational thought and causes untold loss of life and misery. BARBAROSSA would fall into this category. On a smaller scale, but, in its own way just as devastating, was an extraordinary decision made by Generalissimo Chiang Kai-shek, the leader of Chinese forces opposing the Japanese invasion. Chiang was also the leader of the anti-communist Nationalist Government. In mid-1938, Chiang was on the back foot as successive Japanese victories had given them control over northern China.

He sought to stem the continuing advance of the Japanese Army in western and southern China and decided that one way to achieve that aim would be to deny them access to territory, and the tool for the job was to be water. He had no idea of the power he was about to unleash.

The decision was taken to unleash the waters of the Yellow River by breaching the dikes that channelled it. The first breach was made on 5 June 1938 and a second on 7 June. The effect was instantaneous. The torrent gushed from dikes which had been carefully maintained for centuries, and flooded thousands of square miles, much of it among the most productive farmland in China. The crops were lost, thousands of villages disappeared under the deluge, and that, in turn, created a major refugee crisis as millions of villagers fled from what had once been their home. The death toll has never been accurately determined but an initial loss of 800,000 is suggested by Jay Taylor.[22] There were considerable but uncounted Japanese deaths. The Yellow River was diverted, and its water flowed into smaller rivers that could not contain the volume of water and further flooding was the result. A post-war report suggested that floodwater had inundated 32 per cent of land and 45 per cent of villages in twenty affected counties.[23] Starvation was a natural consequence of the destruction of farmland, and it was Chinese citizens who died at the hand of their leader.

The flood was not a military master-stroke. Most of the million-strong Japanese Army were unaffected and although the attack on Zhengzhou was delayed, Wuhan nevertheless fell to assaults from a different direction. The flooded area was a wasteland, and the effect of the flood was felt for decades after. The fertile farmland was covered in an uncultivable, thick layer of silt. The receding water left structures that were uninhabitable. Chiang's decision has been described as the 'largest act of environmental warfare in history and an example of scorched-earth military strategy'.[24]

The victims of Chiang's folly looked for a scapegoat, but they lived in an unsophisticated society and were subject to propaganda by the Chinese Communist Party, led by Mao Zedong. He

Mao Zedong (1893–1976).

directed the anger of the victims at Chiang, his political rival, and used the disaster as a means of recruiting people to his party. Mao was probably the only person to benefit from Chiang's activity.

Summary

Famine is a natural phenomenon, usually brought about by adverse climatic conditions. There have been times when the famine conditions have been exploited for political reasons. Still so today, and such awful events stir strong emotions.

The Bengal famine, for example, is still being presented as the wanton genocide it most definitely was not. Similarly, the Irish potato famine, awful as it was, is often reported with a strong political bias.

Notes

1. Matuszczyk, A., *Creative Stratagems: Creative and Systems Thinking in Handling Social Conflict* (Kibworth, England, Modern Society Publishing, 2012), p. 21.
2. Conquest, R., *The Harvest of Sorrow: Soviet Collectivisation and the Terror-Famine* (New York, Oxford University Press, 1986), p. 117.
3. Greenough, P.R., 'Indian Famines and Peasant Victims: The Case of Bengal in 1943–44' (*Modern Asian Studies*, 1980), 14 (2), pp. 205–35.
4. Famine Inquiry Commission 1945, pp. 32, 65–6, 236.
5. Greenough, pp. 93–6.
6. Brennan, L., 'Government Famine Relief in Bengal, 1943' (*The Journal of Asian Studies*, 47 (3), 1980), pp. 541–66.
7. Arnold, D., *Famine: Social Crisis and Historical Change* (New York, NY, Wiley-Blackwell, 1991), p. 68.
8. Famine Inquiry Commission 1945, p. 30.
9. Ghosh, S., 'Famine, Food and the Politics of Survival in Calcutta, 1943–50', in Sarkar, T., Bandyopadhyay, S. (eds) (Abingdon, Routledge, *The Stormy Decades*, 2018), pp. 211–12.
10. Mukherjee, J., *Hungry Bengal: War, Famine, and the End of Empire* (New York, NY, Oxford University Press, 2015), p. 125.
11. Stephens, I., *Monsoon Morning* (London, Ernest Benn, 1966), p. 184.
12. Bayly, C. & Harper, T., *Forgotten Armies: Britain's Asian Empire and the War with Japan* (New York, NY, Penguin Books Limited, 2005), p. 247.
13. Brown, J.M., *Gandhi: Prisoner of Hope* (New Haven, CT, Yale University Press, 1991), p. 340.
14. Brennan, L., 'Government Famine Relief in Bengal, 1943' (*The Journal of Asian Studies*, 1988, 47), p. 548.
15. Greenough, P.R., pp. 205–35.
16. Ibid., p. 127.
17. Mukherjee, p. 141.
18. Cooper, N., 'French Indochina' (Academia.edu).
19. Ibid.
20. Huff, G., 'Causes and consequences of the Great Vietnam Famine 1944–45' (*The Economic History Review*, 72, 2018), pp. 286–316.
21. Maclean, M., *Vietnam's Great Famine, 1944–45* (History Reformatted in Archival Form Clark University, 2016), p. 191.

22. Taylor, J., *The Generalissimo Chiang Kai-shek and the Struggle for Modern China* (Cambridge Mass, Belknap Press of Harvard University, 2009), pp. 154–5.
23. Muscolino, M.S., *The Ecology of War in China: Henan Province, the Yellow River, and Beyond, 1938–1950* (Cambridge University Press, 2014), pp. 29–31.
24. Dutch, S.I., 'The Largest Act of Environmental Warfare in History' (*Environmental & Engineering Geoscience*, 2009, 15 (4)), pp. 287–97.

Chapter Twenty-One

Cannibalism

In a book about hunger and starvation, the practice of cannibalism has to be addressed. It is aberrational behaviour, but it is *sometimes* triggered by extreme hunger when it is perceived to be the only alternative to death.

In the Western world, cannibalism is regarded as repugnant and reprehensible but it is not a crime, although it could generate indictment on related issues such as the disposal/desecration of a corpse. However, the eating of human flesh has been practised to some extent since time began.

It is argued that cannibalism can be reasonably split into three main categories. First is the eating of enemies as a cultural norm. It was commonplace in New Guinea, the Solomon Islands and the Amazon basin. Similarly, cannibalism was practised by the Maori of New Zealand until about 1830. Professor Paul Moon, who lectures in New Zealand history at the Auckland University of Technology, wrote:

> Cannibalism was not a food issue, but people were eaten often as part of a post-battle rage. Enemies were often captured and killed later to be eaten or killed because of a minor transgression. Rather than disposing of the body, it was prepared to be eaten. Part of the practice was also to send a warning to other tribes. One of the arguments is really if you want to punish your enemy, killing them is not enough. If you can chop them up and eat them and turn them into excrement, that is the greatest humiliation you can impose on them.[1]

The second form of cannibalism is the consumption of a person from within the same community and it is termed endocannibalism, which is a form of ritual cannibalism in which the body is consumed as part of the grieving process. There is a belief that by eating a human's flesh, the attributes of that body will be transferred to the eater.[2] Andrew Woznicki explored this culture in an Amazonian tribe and wrote of his experience in an Indian newspaper.

A third form of cannibalism of relevance to this text is that which is hunger driven. This form of cannibalism subdivides into two. The first is the eating of a dead person. The second is the *killing of an individual in order to eat them*. This is patently not only repugnant but also criminal.

Cannibalism is so rare in the modern Western world that instances are painfully documented. Cannibalism had been given wide publicity when

The Raft of the Medusa, **painted in 1818–19 by Théodore Géricault, depicting events following the loss of the French frigate** *Medusa* **in July 1816.**

Géricault's painting *The Raft of the Medusa* was exhibited in 1819. He depicted an event of three years earlier.

The story of the Donner Party, a group of American pioneers who were trapped in deep snow in the Sierra Nevada mountains in the winter of 1846/7, attracted a great deal of attention. There were forty-eight survivors, who had eaten the bodies of the thirty-nine who had died.

The second Sino-Japanese War (1937–45) was every bit as bloody as the Burma campaign and the Pacific campaign. Here, two Asiatic nations fought without quarter for eight years. The Japanese presence in China was, in part, to meet its aspiration to support the home islands with Manchurian food. The Chinese matched the Japanese in the brutal and merciless treatment they both inflicted on the Chinese population. Theodore White, an American journalist, visited the war zone in 1943. He commented upon ever-present death, with corpses on roadsides. The desperate peasants ate leaves, peanut husks and drank the green slime from pools of water. He reported: 'A doctor told us a woman was caught boiling her baby. She was not molested because, she insisted that the child had died before she started to cook it.'[3]

During the Second World War, there were frequent incidences of hunger-driven cannibalism, perhaps an unhappy endorsement of the efficacy of food denial. In Leningrad, the death toll was vast, and food was very scarce.[4] The people trapped in the city starved and the bleak winter of 1941/2 produced reports of cannibalism that were recorded by the NKVD,[5] whose files reported the first use of human meat as food on 13 December 1941. The report outlined thirteen cases ranging from a mother smothering her 18-month-old to feed her three older children to a plumber killing his wife to feed his sons and nieces.[6]

The NKVD was meticulous, and by December 1941, when winter had only just started to bite, they had arrested 2,105 individuals. They made the distinction between the eating of the dead and those who accelerated a death in order to devour the body. The latter group were summarily shot, and the others imprisoned.

The Soviet Criminal Code had no provision for cannibalism, so all convictions were carried out under Code Article 59–3, 'special category banditry'. Instances of person-eating were significantly lower than that of corpse-eating; of the 300 people arrested in April 1942 for cannibalism, only forty-four were murderers; 64 per cent of cannibals were female, 44 per cent were unemployed, 90 per cent were illiterate or with only basic education, 15 per cent were rooted inhabitants, and only 2 per cent had any criminal records. More cases occurred in the outlying districts than in the city itself. Cannibals were often unsupported women with dependent children and no previous convictions, which allowed for a certain level of clemency in legal proceedings.[7]

A feature of life in besieged Leningrad was that given the dreadful conditions, the majority of the population did seek to maintain their social norms.[8] Although murder of a neighbour in order to eat them was unusual, murder to obtain a ration card was much more prevalent; 1,206 such murders were recorded. This figure should be viewed in the context of the massive and recurring loss of life. For example, in January and February 1942, 100,000 citizens died each month.[9]

The Pacific War, largely fought between Japan and the USA, induced the Japanese to commit cannibalism throughout the theatre. On 10 December 1944, Lieutenant General Adachi Hatazō, the Japanese commander of

Lieutenant General Adachi Hatazō (1890–1945). He committed suicide while awaiting trial for war crimes, not cannibalism.

18th Army in New Guinea, issued an order that 'while troops were permitted to eat the flesh of Allied dead, they must not eat their own'.[10] The evidence of widespread Japanese cannibalism is overwhelming. Much of it was less for the food and more to demonstrate a contempt for the enemy by first mutilating and then killing and eating the victim. The ghastly results of cannibalism were recorded by an Australian soldier, who recovered the body of a comrade from his battalion:

> He had been stripped and both of his arms were cut off at the shoulder. The stomach had been cut out and the heart, liver and other entrails had been removed, all fleshy parts of the body had been cut away ... a Japanese mess tin appeared to contain human flesh was lying four to five yards away ... between two dead Japanese soldiers.[11]

In this case, clearly the soldier had been the victim of cannibals, and although the nature of his death is unknown, the barbarity of cannibalism for whatever reason is difficult to understand or condone – easily said when one is not hungry to the point of madness. Hatam Ali, an Indian soldier taken prisoner and sent to New Guinea to help build an airfield in 1943, recorded that when the Japanese ran out of food, the guards would select one prisoner each day who was taken out, killed, and eaten. He said, 'I personally saw this happen.'[12] Lord Russell records, in ghastly and graphic detail, examples of Japanese cannibalism, which were often accompanied by the most extreme torture – such as the extraction of organs from a living victim.[13] This is human behaviour that simply beggars belief.

Cannibalism as a sign of contempt for an enemy is exemplified by what is now known as the Chichi-Jima Incident. In 1944, the island of that name, 700 miles (1,126km) south of Tokyo, was a key part of the Japanese communication system, and a supply base that housed a garrison of 25,000 men. The very effective American blockade had caused one of the commanders, Lieutenant General Tachibana Yoshio, to reduce the daily ration for his men from 400g (14oz) of rice per day to 250g (9oz). Despite that, in September 1944, neither Tachibana nor his troops were on the edge of starvation.

The importance of the island made it a regular target for the US Army Air Force, and in September 1944, nine American aviators survived the shooting down of their planes and were taken prisoner. One of these survivors was the future President of the USA, George H.W. Bush, and it was only he who lived to tell the tale. His companions, Lloyd Woellhof, Grady York, James Dye, Glenn Frazier Jr., Marvell Mershon, Floyd Hall, Warren Earl Vaughn and Warren Hindenlang, were subjected to extreme physical abuse and protracted torture over several months and then they were decapitated. The bodies of the airmen were butchered, by medically trained individuals, and their livers and other organs were eaten by Japanese officers. This barbarism was not hunger related.

When the US captured Chichi-Jima, the fate of the airmen was investigated, and Tachibana and eleven others were tried for war crimes. They were not tried for cannibalism because, horrible though it is, it is not a crime. The indicted group were, however, tried for murder and 'prevention of an honourable burial'. Four officers were found guilty and duly hanged. The remainder served less than eight years in prison.[14]

Vice Admiral Kunizo Mori was Tachibana's co-commander and the overall commander of the Chichi-Jima air base at the time of the incident. Apparently, Kunizo believed that the consumption of human liver had medical benefits. He embraced endocannibalism, and on that basis, was a participant in the Chichi-Jima Incident. He was tried and found guilty, but avoided the death penalty. However, sometime later, he was re-tried by the Dutch and hanged.

During the life of the brief and bloody Japanese Empire (1931–45), all normal humanity was set aside by the Japanese. Across Southeast Asia, its soldiers murdered spontaneously for entertainment and cannibalism was just one example of commonplace aberrational behaviour.

Finally, and the Japanese Empire apart, it should be acknowledged that not all cannibals are psychopathic animals and most of those driven to eat human flesh only did so because there was absolutely no alternative other than death. The reader might ponder, briefly, how he/she would respond in such a situation.

*   *   *

Within living memory and the most recent incidence of reported cannibalism occurred soon after 22 December 1972, when an aircraft carrying a rugby team from Uruguay hit an Andean mountain. Of the forty-five passengers, twelve were killed outright. The survivors were confronted with a dreadful scene. They were at 11,710 feet (3,569m) and above the snow line. It was chaotic, people were trapped and in shock. Some died soon thereafter and a further eight were suffocated two weeks later, when an avalanche engulfed the wrecked plane.

Carlitos Páez, one of the survivors, remarked wistfully, 'If we'd had mobile phones, it would have been a different story.' But in 1972, mobile phones were just a distant technical ambition. Páez added, 'Eating human flesh wasn't that difficult; there was nothing else to be had. In the mountains it was just snow, rock and ice.' He recalled that 'human flesh doesn't taste of anything really'.[15]

Robert Canessa, a medical student, was the first to raise the matter of eating the bodies lying frozen in the snow. He was one of the only sixteen surviving passengers. He commented:

> we would have starved to death otherwise. My only trouble was that these were the bodies of my friends … it was of course the only solution, but we didn't have their permission to eat them. So, we promised each other that that if one of us died the others were obliged to eat their bodies.

Paul Read wrote a bestselling book, which sold 5 million copies. It was entitled *Alive* and in it he chronicled the details. Soon after, Hollywood made a film with the same name.[16] Fifty years later, the survivors still meet each year to mark the grisly event in which, in desperation, they shared the bodies of the dead. The meeting is not without a degree of irony as they usually barbeque beef and sausages – very different to their earlier diet.

> Of course, the idea of eating human flesh was terrible, repugnant. It was hard to put it in your mouth. But we got used to it. In a sense, our friends were some of the first organ donors in the world, they helped to nourish us and kept us alive.[17]

Read spared his readers none of the stomach-turning details and speaking of the survivors, he said, 'they started eating out of skulls making a cuisine out of flesh.' Not unreasonably, the subjects of his book were appalled by the original manuscript but Read judged correctly that people 'would understand' – and they did. Canessa and another passenger, Fernando Parrado, made a heroic foray to get help, and against all the odds, they succeeded.

Today, Canessa is a distinguished paediatric cardiologist, who won a scholarship to study at Guy's Hospital in London. He said reflectively, 'God has been very nice to me.' He went on to say that he sees in his patients the same fierce will to live that he experienced in the mountains. He told Campbell, 'I tell them we have to climb mountains and I will be your guide.'

Notes

1. Moon, P., *This Horrid Practice* (Penguin Books, 2008).
2. Woznicki, A.N., 'Endocannibalism of the Yanomami' (*The Summit Times*, 1998, 6), pp. 18–19.
3. White, T.H. & Jacoby, A., *Thunder out of China* (London, Victor Gollancz, 1947), pp. 166–7.
4. Salisbury, H.E., *The 900 Days: The Siege of Leningrad* (Da Capo Press, 1969), p. 590.
5. NKVD – People's Commissariat of Internal Affairs: The Soviet police and secret police from 1934 to 1943.
6. Reid, A., *Leningrad: Tragedy of a City under Siege, 1941–44* (London, Bloomsbury Publishing, 2011) p. 287.
7. Ibid., pp. 288–92.

8. Kirschenbaum, L., *The Legacy of the Siege of Leningrad, 1941–1995: Myth, Memories, and Monuments* (New York, Cambridge University Press, 2006), pp. 231–63.

9. Reid, p. 284.

10. Richmond, K., *The Japanese Forces in New Guinea* (Monograph, Australian War Memorial, awm.gov.au., 2003), pp. 185–6.

11. Tanaka, K., *Hidden Horrors: Japanese War Crimes in World War II* (Oxford, Westview Press, 1996), p. 115.

12. Ibid., 115–16.

13. Russell, Lord of Liverpool, *The Knights of Bushido* (London, Cassell, 1958), pp. 233–40.

14. Welch, J.M., 'Without a Hangman, Without a Rope' (*International Journal of Naval History*, 1 (1), 2002).

15. In a phone call interview with Mathew Campbell, *The Sunday Times*, 16 October 2022.

16. Read, P.P., *Alive: The Story of the Andes Survivors* (Philadelphia, Lippincott, 1974).

17. Ramon Sabella, telephone interview with Matthew Campbell.

PART SIX

COUNTER-REVOLUTIONARY WAR

Chapter Twenty-Two

The Franco-Vietnam War
(1946–54)

Food denial tactics discussed so far have all dealt with 'conventional war' in which the aim was to seize territory, cut the logistic supply chain, subjugate the inhabitants both military and civilian and push them into starvation conditions leading to surrender.

It was different in Vietnam, post-Second World War, when the French fought the so-called 'Dirty War'. The background to that war dates back to the Japanese invasion of the country in September 1940. The defeated French were permitted to operate a nominal government, as the Japanese used Vietnam as a staging post for its conquest of Thailand and Burma. American attitudes changed after the Japanese invasion, and in 1944, the USA recognised the volatility of the situation in Vietnam and opened a headquarters for its 'Office of Strategic Services' (forerunner of the CIA) in Kuomintang in southern China. By 1943, Roosevelt was speaking about the merits of Vietnamese independence.

Roosevelt was deeply opposed to colonialism in any form, and constantly voiced concern about the iniquity of brown people being governed by white people. However, his concerns for 'brown people' did not extend to those of his own country, in which 'African-Americans' (in today's parlance) were subject to extreme discrimination. Roosevelt raised the issue of independence for India constantly with Churchill, advocating immediate action, despite the impracticability of such a measure in the middle of a war. His son Elliot reported the president as saying:

> When we've won the war, I will work with all my might and main to see to it that the United States is not wheedled into the position of accepting any plan that will further France's imperialistic ambitions or will aid and abet the British Empire it *its* imperial ambitions.[1]

American agents worked closely with Vietnamese groups fighting the Japanese and specifically with Hồ Chí Minh, the acknowledged leader of the Vietnamese resistance movement. Known as the 'Vietminh', Hồ's acolytes furnished the Americans with intelligence in an informal relationship, and in return, Hồ Chí Minh welcomed the tacit support being offered for an independent Vietnam.

From October 1944, Vietnam was hit by a devastating famine (*see* pages 200–201) but despite the misery abroad in the land, Võ Nguyên Giáp was conducting low-level guerrilla activity, against the Japanese. Hồ Chí Minh selected him to command the Vietnam Propaganda and Liberation Front. Initially, the National Army of Vietnam (NVA), this was to be the forerunner of the People's Army of Vietnam (PAVN). It began as a very small force, only thirty-four strong.

Giáp was not a soldier, and he never had any military training. He was a teacher by profession, but he was quick-witted, efficient and utterly ruthless. He and Hồ Chí Minh perfected a 'hearts and minds' policy in which they inculcated in their adherents a sacrificial courage and commitment to the cause that matched that of the Japanese. In 1946, Giáp was leading only a small group. He was a student of Revolutionary War, and although not yet a capable practitioner, he was learning on the job.

He was to prove to be, perhaps, the most capable logistician of the twentieth century. Giáp is the only self-taught, top-level general and he was a

Hồ Chí Minh (1890–1969), photographed
at the age of 56.

General Võ Nguyên Giáp (1911–2013),
pictured in 1957, aged 46.

very serious player in regional affairs for the next thirty tempestuous and bloody years.

At the end of the Second World War, there was a power vacuum in Vietnam and Hồ Chí Minh swiftly filled it. Hồ persuaded Emperor Bảo Đại to abdicate and then Hồ led his supporters into Hanoi. In a form of words borrowed from the American declaration of independence, and with visible OSS support, he proclaimed independence for North Vietnam.

In the south, the Communist Party under Trần Văn Giàu was taking an aggressive posture. The defeated Japanese were loath to lay down their arms and into this social, political and military maelstrom, Major General Douglas Gracey and his 20th Indian Division, 20,000 strong, arrived to restore stability. Gracey declared martial law but depended on the assistance of armed Japanese to help maintain civil order.

Officers of the OSS, although having no responsibility, interfered in the political mélange and one officer, Lieutenant Colonel A.P. Dewey, angered Gracey sufficiently that he was expelled. Dewey was assassinated on his way to the airport. He was the first American to be killed in Vietnam. The assassins thought that Dewey was French. It was a portent of things to come.

During the period November 1945 to April 1946, the British troops were replaced by French soldiers, many of whom were of colonial heritage. By May 1946, the French Army in Vietnam was 46,513 strong and well prepared to fight a conventional war. Unfortunately, the Vietminh were not prepared to accommodate the French in the manner of their engagement. It is germane to consider the view of T.E. Lawrence, who opined:

> Guerrilla war must have a friendly population, not actively friendly, but sympathetic to the point of not betraying rebel movements to the enemy. Rebellions can be made with 2 percent in a striking force and 98 percent passively sympathetic.[2]

The political wing of the Vietminh engaged in negotiations with the French whilst at the same time killing French soldiers as they traversed the rough tracks that passed for roads in the Vietnam of the 1940s. It was similar to representatives of the IRA proclaiming a desire for peace whilst killing British soldiers and Protestant civilians, some thirty years later.

War finally broke out on 20 December 1946, when French and Vietminh forces clashed in Hanoi. The exchange of fire escalated when the three French ships, *Chevreuil* (Chamois-class, minesweeping sloop), *Savorgnan de Brazza* and *Dumont d'Urville* opened fire on the Chinese and Vietnamese quarters of the port of Haiphong. The cruiser *Suffren* was present but did not add its guns to the bombardment. Nevertheless, the consensus is that about 6,000 civilians were killed. Not the least of the results was that the 2 per cent advocated by Lawrence was quickly exceeded.

There followed eight years of savage enmity in which the French were quite unable to cope with the flexible, sporadic, widely spaced attacks of the Vietminh. Although the French recognised the need to control the sources from which the Vietminh would obtain its food, it went about the searches for food stocks in a heavy-handed, brutal manner. The killing of unarmed civilians became commonplace and by its conduct the French completely alienated the population.

The Vietminh was being supplied by China and in order to disrupt that logistic flow the French established a number of forts in northern North Vietnam along the Chinese border. These forts, which were not mutually supporting, became a burden. They had to be resupplied with food and ammunition, and initially, aerial resupply met the need. However, access to these forts through the rainforest was a different matter. Any ground-based approach was subject to ambush and the evacuation of wounded was difficult, bordering impossible. The French Army was road bound; its artillery was similarly road bound and its operations were inevitably restricted and predictable.

The French played into the hands of the Vietminh. They adopted tactics appropriate for war in Europe but useless in a jungle setting. To compound the problem, they appointed a series of second-rate generals who clung to the border forts that were like tethered goats, awaiting the pleasure of the neighbourhood tiger.

T.E. Lawrence had been quoted some years earlier when he said shrewdly that 'guerrilla war is more intelligent than a bayonet charge'.[3] This was being borne out daily as the French flayed unsuccessfully to pin down its adversary.

Successive commanders seemed to be content to serve out their tour and then leave Vietnam much as they found it. In the meantime, French losses mounted, the searches for food were insufficiently productive to swing the balance and the Vietminh, now commanded with great élan by Giáp, increased in capability and confidence. The exception to the mediocre generals was General Jean de Lattre de Tassigny, who decided to build a defensive belt around Hanoi and the Red River delta. He was energetic and resourceful, and he assumed command in 1951 but died in office in 1952. With him died any hope the French had of retaining its grip on Indochina.

Successive French Governments were worn down by the war, and public opinion became increasingly unenthusiastic. During the early 1950s doubts grew about how long its stresses and costs could be sustained.

The mood in Paris began to shift towards accepting the need for a negotiated settlement.[4]

This was revolutionary war, but whatever it was called, the French were incapable of dealing with an enemy who invariably initiated the battle but would not then stay and fight. The French sought to find and destroy any food stocks, and in the process, committed needless and unproductive atrocities. The French did not have any truck with a 'hearts and minds' policy.

There were no front lines in this war, and the acquisition of territory was never an object of the Vietminh. Its aim was to kill French troops, destroy the credibility of the colonial government, and to sap the French Government's resolve.

The USA, always strongly and vociferously anti-colonial, had a rethink. It decided that colonialism was to be preferred to the communism on offer from the Hồ Chí Minh and his Vietminh. The USA changed tack and threw its weight behind the French, and thereafter, provided political and logistic support.

However, with the untimely death of de Lattre, command eventually devolved onto General Henri Navarre, who was described as being 'brilliant, authoritative, decisive, exacting but trusting, expecting his orders to be obeyed'.[5]

Time magazine published an article about him and used the phrases 'icy reserve, cold and aloof, attractive to women and having an 18th-century fragrance about him, clever and ruthless'.[6]

It appears that Navarre had hit upon a master plan.

Notwithstanding all of his personal qualities, this general gave every impression of being logistically illiterate. He decided that he would establish a major base, deep in the jungle, and from here he would launch armoured thrusts into Vietminh country – this, despite having only ten tanks, and the country being totally unsuited for armoured vehicles. Navarre was clearly delusional.

Navarre also intended to lure the Vietminh into a major, set-piece battle in which he would destroy it. With those two aims in mind, he created the defended area of Điện Biên Phủ (DBP) – a series of reinforced hilltops that were mutually supporting. Logistic support would be delivered to the airstrip in the centre of DBP and redistributed from there. Navarre assumed that he would have complete command of the air and was assured that his artillery was sufficient to crush any assault on the perimeters of the fortress. By now, French efforts to disrupt Vietminh food supplies had, in effect, ceased and Navarre wanted only to focus on his set-piece battle that he was confident he would win.

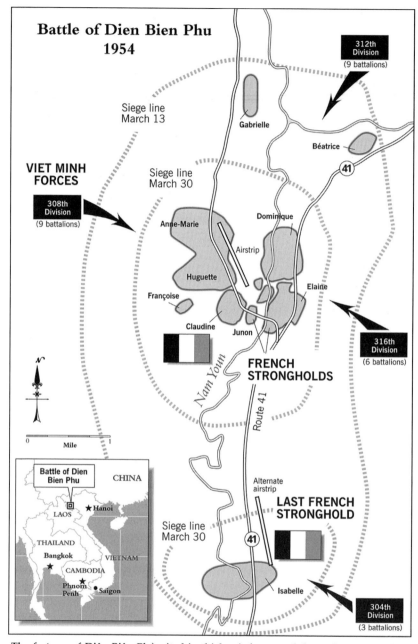

The fortress of Điện Biên Phủ, sited in thick rainforest and dependent upon aerial resupply. The various strongpoints were allegedly named after the mistresses of the commander, Colonel Christian de Castries.

Lieutenant General Henri Navarre (1898–1983).

However, Navarre started to entertain doubt and he alerted Marc Jacquet, Secretary of State for Associated States, and his civilian superior, saying:

Two weeks ago, I would have put the chances of victory at 100 percent – Điện Biên Phủ is in a very good position … I have assembled there a strong force of infantry and artillery, equivalent to a heavy division. I have given command to a senior officer of whose energy I am certain … Battle has been accepted on terrain of our choosing and under the best conditions against an enemy of whose resources we were unaware up to about 15 December. But, during the last two weeks serious intelligence informs us of the arrival of new resources (37mm AA guns, perhaps heavy artillery and motorised equipment); and if these really exist, and the enemy succeeds in getting them into action, then I can no longer guarantee success with certainty.[7]

The soldiers manning the fortress were not all Frenchmen, quite the opposite. Many were Vietnamese; others hailed from Morocco, Syria, Chad, Guadeloupe, Lebanon and Madagascar.[8]

History shows that Navarre's plan was hopelessly flawed. He underestimated his enemy very badly and the logistic genius General Giáp not only marshalled a major army around DBP, but he put in place a system to keep it fed. Giáp's artillery, its magnitude, and its ability nonplussed the French and French counter-battery fire failed.

Giáp had a force of about 60,000 soldiers and supporting porters in the jungle surrounding Điện Biên Phủ. The logistic effort to maintain and feed a force of this size in a hostile environment set a new logistic benchmark and Giáp, quite rightly, is recognised as being a logistician of the very highest order.

With DBP surrounded and under siege, Navarre inexplicably launched Operation ATLANTE, about 400 miles (644km) to the south. This divided his available aircraft and reduced his logistic capability. ATLANTE did not achieve its aim and it was terminated as the situation in DBP became critical. Navarre considered evacuating the fortress but realised the impracticability of that option and recognised that the battle he had initiated would have to be fought to a conclusion. From 1946, the French had focused on cutting off the food supply to the Vietminh and had failed. Post-war, Vietminh Colonel Bùi Tín made the following extraordinary statement:

> We took what precautions we could. General Giáp issued special orders on hygiene ... Drinking water was to be boiled. The troops were to use clean socks after washing their feet in warm water and salt. They should have hot rice with adequate meat and vegetables at least once day and sleep for at least six hours every night ... uniforms were to be changed every two or three days.[9]

Whilst conceding Giáp's logistic skills, this statement defies belief. Propaganda needs to be credible if it is to be believed and this statement, by Colonel Bùi Tín, is absurdly incredible. 'Uniform changes every two or three days' – for 60,000 men? That is quite a task for any laundry, especially for one serving customers located in the midst of a rainforest.

Navarre's plan for aerial resupply and casualty evacuation came to naught in the face of Giáp's anti-aircraft artillery – manhandled for miles through the jungle. Resupply of the fortress became problematic and although food was an issue, it was not critical when 7,000 French troops surrendered on 7 May 1954.

The French were defeated, humiliated, and left Vietnam soon after. Their legacy was the hatred of the inhabitants, a country in ruins and a triumphant communist government in North Vietnam. In 1954, at Geneva, the great powers agreed to divide Vietnam at the seventeenth parallel. The object was not to create two Vietnams, but to establish the conditions that would lead, peacefully, to the reunification of the nation after elections planned for 1956. However, those elections were vetoed by the USA on the basis that the 'wrong side' would win. This was not a ringing endorsement of the American claim to be the 'home of the free and the cradle of democracy'.

The Americans then moved to establish what it anticipated would be a permanent, non-communist South Vietnam. That was at odds with the North Vietnamese aspiration, which was reunification of the country as a communist state.

Summary

Food denial as practised by the French had failed in Vietnam. The brutality of the food denial operations was such that they exacerbated the poor relations with the civilian population and promoted Vietminh recruitment.

The USA had been able to observe French mistakes and had the opportunity to learn from them. Giáp had demonstrated the efficiency of revolutionary war, and from 1948, revolutionary war was testing another empire not so very far away.

Notes

1. Roosevelt, E., *As He Saw It* (New York, Duell, Sloan and Pearce, 1946). pp. 114–16, quoted in 'The Anti-Colonial Policies of Franklin D. Roosevelt', Foster Rhea Dulles and Gerald E. Ridinger (*Political Science Quarterly*, Vol. 70, No. 1, Mar 1955), pp. 1–18.
2. Lawrence, T.E., 'The Science of Guerrilla Warfare', *Encyclopedia Britannica*, 1929.
3. Ibid.
4. Freedman, L., *Command: The Politics of Military Operations* (London, Allen Lane, 2022), p. 37.
5. Ibid., p. 38.
6. The Battle of Indochina (*Time* magazine, 28 September 1953).
7. Fall, B.B., *Hell in a Very Small Place: The Siege of Dien Bien Phu* [1966] (New York, Da Capo Press, 2002), quoted by Freedman, p. 43.
8. Cincinnatus (C.B. Currey), *Self-Destruction: The Disintegration and Decay of the United States Army During the Vietnam Era* (New York, W.W. Norton, 1981), p. 10.
9. Simpson, H.R., *Dien Bien Phu: The Epic Battle America Forgot* (London, Brassey's, 1994), p. 33.

Chapter Twenty-Three

The Malayan Emergency
(1948–60)

The Malayan 'Emergency,' the latest manifestation of revolutionary war, was always referred to as the 'Emergency' and so called because, if it were termed a war, London-based insurers would have judged it to be a 'civil war' and would not have met any claims.[1]

The Emergency had at its heart social issues. After the Second World War, the Malayan economy was weak; there was widespread unemployment and a burgeoning trade union movement, which fermented unrest by exploiting the generally poor pay levels, food costs and high inflation. The Malayan Communist Party (MCP) found these conditions well suited for recruitment to the party. Strike action was regularly taken between 1946 and 1948. Malaya was not a happy country as it recovered from Japanese occupation.

Four-fifths of its 50,850 square miles (131,700km^2) were covered in dense rainforest, home to bears, elephants, tigers and deer among many more species. The forest was: 'Harsh and elemental, implacable to all who dared to trifle with its suffocating heat or hissing rains, the jungle ... has remained untamed and unchanged.'[2] It was in the jungle that the emergency was most manifest.

The population of 5.3 million was a mélange of Mohammedan Malay, ethnic Chinese, Indians, about 75,000 Aborigines and a small but hugely disproportional and influential European element, perhaps 12,000 strong. These were colonial days, and the convoluted federal government was composed of nine Malay states, each, nominally, the preserve of a sultan. The British Governor General, Sir Edward Gent, sat atop the colonial bureaucracy.

The response to the social unrest by the British colonial government was unsophisticated, bordering brutal. The Colonial Police Force, assisted by British and Commonwealth soldiers, was employed to break strikes in support of employers who used all legal means to quell the workforce. Then there was a serious escalation when strikebreakers were killed by Communist militants. The colonial government caused the arrest of identified left-wing activists, and on 12 June 1948, the largest and most influential trade union organisation, the Pan Malayan Federation of Trade Unions (PMFTU), was banned.[3]

Malaya was the producer of half the world's rubber and about a third of its tin. It was also a source of coal and timber. All in all, Malaya was of significant importance to the British economy. These natural resources were exported to the USA and helped to pay the massive debt owed to America by Britain for the logistic support given in the Second World War. To put that into context, Malayan rubber exports to the USA were of greater value than all the domestic exports from Britain to America.

In 1948, the British Empire was being dismembered; India had already departed, the Palestine Mandate had ended, and plans were afoot to give independence to Malaya, among many other territories. However, on 16 June that year, three days after the banning of the PMFTU, the Emergency was launched when three Chinese assassins killed, sequentially, the British managers of three rubber plantations. The colonial government promptly outlawed the Malayan Communist Party (MCP) and arrested known dissidents.

Chin Peng (1924–2013), pictured in 1947.

The leader of the MCP, Chin Peng, OBE, had fought against the Japanese occupiers during the war and been decorated for his endeavours. However, now he and his followers formed the Malayan National Liberation Army (MNLA), with the aim of overthrowing the colonial government and installing one more suited to his communist taste. Chin Peng was supported by former members of the Malayan Peoples' Anti-Japanese Army (MPAJA). These were seasoned, well-trained soldiers and predominantly of Chinese ethnicity. They enjoyed the tacit support of many in the Chinese community.[4] Chin Peng deployed his supporters in bases deep in the rainforest. These groups started to assault police stations and military installations.[5] Secondary targets were the tin mines and rubber plantations – the long-term aim was to bankrupt Britain.

To achieve his aim, Chin Peng matched his 5,000 MNLA full-time troops against strong Malayan Government forces composed of 250,000 Malayan Home Guard, 40,000 regular Commonwealth soldiers, several battalions of the King's African Rifles, Gurkha battalions, 37,000 special constables and 24,000 Federation police. Chin Peng had hosts of sympathisers, many drawn from 500,000 of the 3.12 million ethnic Chinese then living in Malaya. His troops were named as Communist terrorists (CT).

There was a particular component of the Chinese community referred to as 'squatters' – 600,000 people who scraped an existence living on the edge of the jungles where the MNLA were based. This allowed the MNLA to coerce them into providing money but, more importantly and critically, food. It also provided a dribble of new recruits.[6]

The British were as innovative and ruthless in their defence as always, but in Malaya, not always well disciplined. Although war crimes are unusual in British military history, they are not unknown. In Malaya, there were instances of the murder of suspected CTs. One notorious incident, for which there can be no forgiveness, was the murder of twenty-four civilians near Batang Kali in December 1948. The perpetrators were soldiers of the 2nd Battalion, Scots Guards.[7] No one was ever brought to book for the crime, which is a stain on the usually enviable record of the British Army. For decades after, the families of those murdered sought recompense from the British Government, which proved to be obdurate on the matter.

The Emergency quickly took on all the characteristics of a full-on war, but Sir Edward Gent dismissed the concerns of his advisors, one of whom was the vastly experienced and capable Robert (Bob) Thompson.[8] Gent grossly underestimated the dangers posed by the MCP. He was unsupportive of military operations but despite him, the British Army did not cede the jungle to the CTs and pursued them relentlessly.

Patrolling in the jungle was exhausting, contacts with CTs were few but violent. Initially, dead CTs were photographed, and the bodies buried. Later, when it became necessary to prove to the local population that a bandit had been killed, all bodies were brought out for positive identification by the police. It sometimes required the exhumation of dead CTs.

The mainly young national servicemen patrolled, set ambushes, and suffered the privation of living in the jungle, but took the fight to the CT. The most successful British unit was the 1st Battalion, The Suffolk Regiment, which eliminated 200 CTs in their three-and-a-half-year tour. It could be argued that this was a small return for so many millions of man-hours spent slogging through the rainforest, but that is the nature of revolutionary war.

The inertia of Gent could not go on and he was sacked and replaced by Sir Henry Gurney, a thrusting and innovative administrator who, although in office for only two years, laid the foundations for the defeat of Chin Peng.

> Gurney made two profoundly historic decisions, one military, one social, that were to change not only the conduct of the war but the world's thinking on policies when faced with Communist insurgency.[9]

Soldiers of 7 Platoon, 1st Battalion, The Suffolk Regiment exhume three CTs. Grisly work.
(*From Mark Forsdike*, The Malayan Emergency)

Gurney's first decision was that control of the war would rest in civilian hands. He believed it was a war of political ideologies and what was required was armed support for a political war and not political support for an army war. Thompson supported Gurney and argued that only a minute fraction of the population were active members of the MCP. In a war of this nature, one stray bomb that killed an innocent child would make a thousand enemies. He urged that it was better to police villages than to destroy them. In essence, victory lay in the hearts and minds of the people.

Gurney made his second major decision when he conceived the policy of moving and resettling the 600,000 Chinese squatters from the land for which they had no title, to 400 New Villages with a grant of land. The New Villages were fenced; entry and exit were to be controlled. This plan did not win universal international approval, but it was part of a comprehensive food denial policy. The people relocated were provided with a stake in the country's future, and at a stroke, eliminated Chin Peng's major food source. The inhabitants of the New Villages were perhaps homesick but the land upon which they now lived was *theirs*. They subscribed to the Chinese proverb, 'A land title is the hoop that holds the barrel together.'

This policy became known as the 'Briggs Plan', after General Sir Harold Briggs. He was appointed Director of Operations in 1950 and implemented the New Village policy. Briggs believed, correctly, he could defeat the MNLA by isolating it from its food source – the civilian population. Briggs said, 'The people matter – they are vital – but you can't expect any support from people you can't protect.'[10]

In tandem, Gurney set up a system of rewards for information that led to the killing or capture of CTs, and he put $80,000 on the head of Chin Peng (later raised to $250,000). The practical effect was to persuade captured CTs to lead the security forces to their earlier hideout or sell out their erstwhile comrades for ready cash, on the nail, with anonymity guaranteed.

This policy proved to be highly successful. Surrendered CTs were offered half-rate of the standard reward and many previously dedicated communists took the money, ran, and established themselves in business. Years later, some died as successful capitalists.

Gurney was not yet finished, and his next step was to introduce nationwide registration. Everyone over 12 was to have an identity card. The communists took reprisals on the officials administering the system and the photographers taking the ID photos were at extreme risk. Not least of the benefits of the system was that, in effect, it conducted a census and was a valuable tool when the time came to grant citizenship to resident aliens.

A motivator 'to continue the movement' occurred on 6 October 1951, when the MNLA ambushed and killed Sir Henry Gurney as he made his way to Fraser's Hill in Pahang, at 4,777 feet (1,456m), a hill station much cooler than

Food denial in operation. This rubber tapper has been stopped. He will be searched, as will his possessions, even the frame of his bicycle.

The guarded gate at a New Village.

sea level. The killing has been described as a major factor in causing the Malayan population to roundly reject the MNLA campaign, and also as leading to widespread fear due to the perception that 'if even the High Commissioner was no longer safe, there was little hope of protection and safety for the man-in-the-street in Malaya'.[11]

Operations in the jungle were exhausting work and returns were often meagre. Food denial was a weapon, and a scorched-earth policy was initiated. Food was rationed, livestock either killed or confiscated, and in a first example of the use of herbicides, enemy crops discovered in jungle clearings were sprayed. Aircraft were of limited availability and the use of herbicides was only one constituent of the food denial activity. The movement of food was strictly controlled, random searches of all transport including bicycles were instituted and village houses were subject to constant search.

Ten thousand Chinese who were suspected of being communist sympathisers were detained and deported to China.[12] The food denial strategy was working, and it was later complemented by the Briggs Plan.

The tenor of operations in Malaya changed on the appointment of Lieutenant General Sir Gerald Templer (later Field Marshal Sir Gerald Templer, KG, GCB, GCMG, KBE, DSO) as High Commissioner in January 1952. He, and

The face of anti-guerrilla operations. Young British soldiers, probably national servicemen, seeking the CT.

Robert Thompson, the Permanent Secretary of Defence, made a very strong and proactive team. Together they ran what was described as 'one of the most successful of the British Army's counterintelligence campaigns'.[13]

Templer had no doubts of his priorities and he remarked, 'The answer [to the Emergency] lies not in pouring more troops into the jungle, but in the hearts and minds of the people.'[14] Templer was a hard taskmaster; he was energetic, demanding and innovative. He introduced stringent and effective food controls, encouraged CTs to surrender by offering cash payments, and he supported the use of defoliants to kill crops being grown by the CTs in the midst of the jungle. He defended the practice of decapitating dead CTs for the purposes of identification.

Templer's reputation earned him the soubrette 'Tiger of Malay'. His leadership did not go uncriticised. His enthusiastic embrace of the New Villages policy and the compulsory relocation of ethnic minorities with its attendant social disruption, his application of collective punishment, and his killing of livestock available to the CTs have all attracted the attention of latter-day historians. However, Templer was a soldier fighting a ruthless, murderous enemy. He expected no quarter, and he gave none.

In the meantime, the MNLA conducted guerrilla war against public installations and infrastructure. Rubber plantations and their management were

Sir Gerald Templer inspecting the members of Kinta Valley Home Guard (KVHG) in Perak, _c._1952.

prime targets. They murdered clinically, frequently, ruthlessly, to intimidate the civilian population, and they had succeeded until the New Villages were up and running. Nevertheless, defensive measures had to be taken across the country. Planters and miners were all armed and military and police assets were distributed to key locations.

The MNLA hideouts were concealed deep in the rainforest. They had a very strong political ethos, and the CT were subject to political indoctrination aimed at strengthening their communist adherence. The MNLA had an effective intelligence system, the Min Yuen (Peoples' Movement), which also had a food procurement role – where possible.[15] The British intelligence system was the driving force behind military operations and by isolating this population in the New Villages, the British were able to stem the critical flow of food material, information and recruits from peasant sympathisers to the guerrillas. The new camps were guarded by soldiers and police, and were partially fortified to stop people from escaping. This served the twofold purpose of preventing those who were so inclined from sneaking out and voluntarily aiding the guerrillas, and of preventing the guerrillas from sneaking in and extracting aid via persuasion or brute force.

Upon completion of the resettlement programme, the British initiated a starvation campaign, rationing food supplies within the camps and torching rural farmlands to starve out the Communist guerrillas.[16]

The planters stuck to their jobs, and as a group, displayed great courage as they lived in isolated houses, ever at risk of attack. The Emergency dragged on and the military response became more sophisticated. Increasingly, long-range patrols were resupplied by air and greater use was made of the Iban trackers. These very skilled men were eventually grouped in the reformed Sarawak Rangers. In 1951, the Malayan Scouts were formed to conduct operations in the manner of the Special Air Service Regiment, which had been disbanded after the war. In 1952, they were renamed 22 SAS.

This time was one of the most complex in the post-war period for the SAS. Not only was the SAS reformed but it was the longest time that it had been involved in a conflict, as well as involving the largest number of SAS troops deployed in one campaign since 1945. At one stage between 1950 and 1958, the SAS had five squadrons deployed – A, B, D, the Independent Parachute Regiment Squadron (1955–7), and the New Zealand SAS Squadron (1955–7). C (Rhodesia) Squadron had operated with the SAS from 1951 to 1953. Britain's other Special Force unit in existence at the time, the SBS, did not carry out any independent operations in Malaya during the Emergency.[17]

The Emergency was conducted in an environment well suited to 'Special Forces' and organisations were formed to meet the unique circumstances. For example, in mid-1953, the Special Operations Volunteer Force (SOVF) was

A New Village in the mid-1950s, not smart but safe.

Two of the highly effective Iban trackers and members of the Malayan Scouts.

created. This organisation was made up of surrendered enemy personnel (SEP) and other volunteers.

Its 180 ex-communists were split into twelve platoons, each of fifteen men. These men were contracted to serve for eighteen months and were paid at the lowest police rate. They were housed in police barracks, and after training they were sent back into the jungle to persuade their former comrades to surrender. If this persuasion failed, they were to kill. 'By 1954 progress was being made. 723 terrorists had been killed from a remaining enemy force of about 3,000 and by April 1955 large arears of Malaya mostly in the east in Pahang.'[18]

Preparations for Malayan independence had been mooted back in 1944 and Chin Peng's crusade lost its *raison d'être* when, in August 1957, Malaya became the sovereign state of Malaysia and a member of the Commonwealth. Although there was now no discernible political purpose, the diminishing number of CTs continued their insurgency, which finally expired in 1960.

Summary

Approximately 12,000 men and women had passed through the ranks of Chin Peng's army. Of these, 6,698 had been killed, 2,696 surrendered, 2,819 were wounded, and 1,286 were captured. About 1,000 had died, deserted or been liquidated by their commanders.

The cost in lives had been heavy. The Security Force had lost 1,865 killed and 2,560 wounded. A total of 2,473 civilians had been murdered, 1,382 wounded, and 810 were missing (probably dead).[19]

However, 'the ultimate – and very expensive – success of that campaign rested on the hard-won lesson that civilians are best insulated from insurgency wars and not included in them.'[20] Food denial did not alone defeat the insurgency, but it was one of a number of very effective and complementary measures.

Notes

1. Burleigh, M., *Small Wars, Faraway Places: Global Insurrection and the Making of the Modern World 1945–1965* (New York, Viking – Penguin Group, 2013), p. 164.
2. Barber, N., *The War of the Running Dogs: Malaya 1948–1960* [1971] (London, Arrow Books, 1989), p. 13.
3. Newsinger, J., *The Blood Never Dried: A People's History of the British Empire* (2nd ed.) (London, Bookmarks Publications, 2013), p. 42.
4. 'The Malayan Emergency: A long Cold War conflict seen through the eyes of the Chinese community in Malaya', 11 November 2021 (*The Forum*, BBC World Service).
5. Rashid, Rehman, *A Malaysian Journey* (published by Rashid, 1993), p. 27.
6. Tilman, R.O., 'The Non-lessons of the Malayan Emergency (*Asian Survey*, 1966, 6 (8)), pp. 407–19.
7. Hack, K., 'Devils that Suck the Blood of the Malayan people' (*War in History*, Sage Journals, 2018), p. 210.
8. Later, Sir Robert Thompson.
9. Barber, p. 72.
10. Ibid., p. 115.
11. Ongkili, J.P., *Nation-building in Malaysia 1946–1974* (Oxford University Press, 1985), p. 79.
12. Newsinger, J., p. 218.
13. Heathcote, A., *The British Field Marshals 1736–1997* (Barnsley, Pen & Sword, 1999), p. 276.
14. Lapping, B., *End of Empire* (London, St Martin's Press, 1985), p. 224.
15. Christopher, P., 'Malaya, 1948–55: Case Outcome: COIN win' (*Paths to Victory: Detailed Insurgency Case Studies*, 2013), pp. 51–63.
16. Burleigh, M., *Small Wars, Faraway Places: Global Insurrection and the Making of the Modern World 1945–1965* (New York, Viking-Penguin Group, 2013), p. 178.
17. Mackenzie, A., 'The Rebirth of the SAS: The Malayan Emergency' (St Martin's Publishing Group, 2012).
18. Forsdike, M., *The Malayan Emergency* (Barnsley, Pen & Sword, 2022), p. 243.
19. Barber, pp. 320–1.
20. Clarke, M., Professor of War Studies, King's College, London, *The Sunday Times*, 23 October 2022.

Chapter Twenty-Four

The USA-Vietnam War
(1955–73)

By 1954, the French had been soundly defeated by the North Vietnamese, despite the generous logistic help given by the USA. In the Pentagon, analysts were in no doubt as to the reasons for the French defeat, and the expectation was that the USA would turn that analysis to good use, if and when it was to become embroiled in a revolutionary war.

The great von Clausewitz had given the matter some thought, and nearly 200 years before, he mused:

> The first, the supreme, the most far-reaching act of judgement that the statesman and commander have to make is to establish … the kind of war on which they are embarking: neither mistaking it for, nor trying to turn it into, something alien to its true nature. This is the first of all strategic questions and the most comprehensive.[1]

That example of common sense, well known to scholars of military history, was readily available in the Pentagon library but rarely referred to. In the immediate post-Second World War period, the Government of the United States of America was exercised by the apparent rapid spread of communism across the globe, and it believed itself to be responsible for curtailing that ideology. However, the USA was inhibited by a longstanding strategic injunction against committing US military power to a large-scale war on the mainland of Asia. The view was that 'US naval and air power's effectiveness would be diluted, and Asian foes could exploit their great superiority in manpower and bog the United States down in a protracted conflict.'[2]

Despite that well-established injunction, in 1950, the USA had been drawn into a major war in Korea, where it fought Chinese 'volunteers'. The topography of the Korean peninsula was such that, although the USA was able to deploy its Second World War-designed forces to good effect, it and its allies could not prevail. In 1953, a ceasefire was agreed, and Korea was divided at the 38th parallel. During this time, the French were toiling in Vietnam, also fighting communists with American logistic support, but by 1954, the north of that country had fallen to communism.

Successive American presidents from 1953, namely Eisenhower, Kennedy, Johnson and Nixon, were all scarred by the events of the next twenty years when the USA undertook the role of the world's policeman and became increasingly involved in a counter-revolutionary war in Vietnam. American activity was inhibited by the possibility that it could inadvertently trigger active Chinese or Russian support for an insurgent group called the Viet Cong (VC) and that the Third World War would be the result. Thus, the most powerful military power on Earth pulled its punches and did not fully employ its overwhelming air power.

It would be simplistic to see a comparison in the campaigns in Malaya and Vietnam. There are similarities, but they are superficial. Both were conducted in Asian rainforests and the enemy were communist guerrillas, and there was a need to win the battle for hearts and minds. However, the magnitudes of the two conflicts are at opposite ends of the scale. In Malaya, the CTs numbered about 10,000 at any one time. In Vietnam, the VC, and later the North Vietnamese Army (NVA), were hundreds of thousands strong. In Malaya, air power was scarce, in Vietnam, it was limitless. In Malaya, the battle for hearts and minds was won. In Vietnam, it was not only lost, but also needless killing boosted recruitment to the VC. In Malaya, the rehousing of landless Chinese was successful. In Vietnam, the unsympathetic uprooting of villagers from a place their family had occupied for generations bred deep anger.

The American military build-up in South Vietnam started in 1955 (after the partition of the country at the 17th parallel in July 1954), when 760 officers were sent to be 'military advisors' to the South Vietnamese Army in its campaign against the VC. The Government of South Vietnam and indeed every aspect of public life in that country was riddled with corruption and the Americans found themselves dealing with individuals who just wanted to get rich – at American expense. It was a poor foundation upon which to build a military strategy.

The VC were skilful and courageous soldiers. They were well trained and fully committed to the independence of their country and its amalgamation with North Vietnam. They were supported logistically by both China and Russia, and that resupply was channelled down what came to be called the Hồ Chí Minh Trail (HCMT).

This was not a simple, single path; rather it was an assortment of tracks and paths that had been used as trade routes for centuries. In total, it covered about 9,500 miles (15,300km) and was, in places, 50 miles (80km) wide. North to south, as an energetic crow might fly, it was 620 miles (1,000km). However, the route was very much longer as the paths and tracks took the easiest route over some of the most hostile country in Asia. It wended its way through the thinly populated border areas of Laos and Cambodia, over mountains that ranged in height from 1,500 feet to 8,000 feet (460–2,450m) and across count-less rivers and ravines. Passage along the HCMT was very hard physical work. In 1956, it took months to traverse the trail but, by 1970, a fit soldier could make the journey in six weeks.

The development of the Hồ Chí Minh Trail was something of an engi-neering masterpiece. It was less the production of an innovative, efficient machine and much more a memorial to human determination, perseverance and commitment. The people who worked to keep the trail open were un-skilled men, women and children, of whom Vu Thi Vinh was one. In an inter-view with Christian Appy, she recalled volunteering at age 15:

> Sometimes we had to stand forever in water up to our chests. During the rainy season it was almost impossible to get dry ... Anytime bombs hit the trail we had to rush out and fill in the craters immediately.

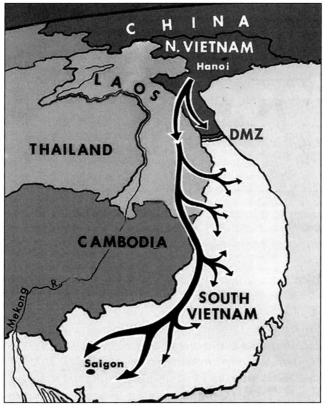

This oversimplified map shows the reach of the HCMT. It had a breadth of 20–50 miles (32–80km) in places and it was about 9,500 miles (15,300km) long.

Porters, supporting the Viet Cong, using bicycles as load-carrying vehicles and travelling through typical trail country. (*Stewart, R.W.*, Deepening Involvement, 1945–1965)

Needless to say, life in the jungle was extremely hard. When we weren't supplied with rice, we ate whatever we could find. We searched for crabs under rocks in the streams and occasionally we were lucky enough to come up with some cassava. Sometimes we had to scrape fungus and moss off rocks, 'aircraft vegetables' we called them because they were the only edible things left after the bombing.

We were so hungry that everything tasted good. The mountain streams were filled with red ginseng trees, we'd boil the leaves and stems and then throw them away and drink the broth.[3]

General Dang Vu Hiep, recollecting his wartime experiences, commented:

In the central highlands there was so little rice we used to say that 'cassava carried rice on its back'. Wherever possible we caught fish and killed animals including tigers, monkeys, and bears, but every soldier had to care for 500 cassava plants so we could continue fighting, even when we could not kill enough game or didn't get rice from the north. From command down to ordinary soldiers, we all grew cassava. Every year we grew close to our objective.[4]

Some explanation is necessary of the importance of cassava. *Manihot esculenta* is commonly called 'cassava'; it is a woody shrub and is a valuable source of carbohydrates. Cassava is the third largest source of food carbohydrates in the tropics after rice and maize. It must be prepared correctly because it contains cyanide. Unsurprisingly, when badly prepared, it can cause partial paralysis and death.

It is evident from the quotes above that food deprivation was a major issue for the VC and it is evident that the American Army was unaware of the opportunities that were open to it.

Le Cao Dai was a Vietnamese VC doctor who had directed the largest jungle hospital in the Central Highlands. He supervised 400 medical staff and usually had 1,000 patients. He had to improvise his equipment and electric power was provided by the energetic peddling of a bicycle power generator. He recalls:

> In addition to malaria, we saw all kinds of diseases – diabetes, lung cancer, tuberculosis, a very high rate of dysentery. Many people died of acute diarrhoea. It was terrible. We did autopsies on them, I found their intestines were as thin as paper. We also had patients with basic nutritional problems; they simply were not getting enough food.[5]

The United States was able to use the war in Vietnam as a vast laboratory in which it was able to test a wide range of innovative weapons. It devised a system that could detect urine but it could not discriminate between a human and animal source. The VC responded to this device by moving buckets of urine around in the jungle, and obligingly, the Americans bombed and strafed empty rainforest. It produced a chemical that prevented mud from drying and its use impeded traffic along the HCMT. The VC had developed a vast network of underground tunnels and they could only be attacked by the few, but very courageous, American soldiers who were prepared to fight in the stygian darkness. Notwithstanding the vast, largely misplaced American expenditure on the development of specialist weapons, when underground it was man on man. American weapons were refined, but the new M-16 rifle was not a success, and when first introduced, American soldiers armed themselves with the AK-47. The Vietnamese General Dong Van Khuyen commented that, during the Tet Offensive (January 1968), the crisp, rattling sounds of AK-47s echoing in Saigon seemed to make a mockery of the weaker, single-shot Garands and carbines fired by stupefied, friendly troops.

The HCMT stayed within the tree line and the canopy provided cover from sight, shade and a modicum of protection for foot traffic from the fire of marauding aircraft. However, by 1961, trucks were being employed on stretches of the Trail and way stations for truck drivers, porters and soldiers were constructed. The HCMT became increasingly sophisticated and five large Base Areas (BAs) were built and concealed. BA 604 was the principal BA, and it was from here that the traffic was coordinated. BA607, BA609, BA611 and BA612 all had different geographic areas of responsibility. The 559th Transport Group, composed of 24,000 men and women, was commanded by General Phan Trọng Tuệ. His organisation was divided into six transport battalions, two bicycle transport battalions, a river transport element, eight engineer battalions and forty-five communication liaison stations. The importance of the 559th to the forces directed by Hanoi needs no emphasis.

For the US, there was a clear need to eradicate not only the cover provided to traffic and personnel on the HCMT but also the adjoining VC cassava fields. To this end, and as early as 1962, the American Joint Chiefs of Staff (JCS), taking the British use of herbicides in Malaya as a precedent, considered that defoliation was a legal military tactic.

Operation RANCH HAND was the name given to the defoliation activity that commenced on a very modest scale. However, in January 1965, 36,000 gallons of a chemical named Agent Orange were sprayed and the effect was an asset to Westmoreland's Search and Destroy operations. The rate of defoliant use accelerated, and later that month, 78,800 gallons were spread across the Boi Loi Forest.

> The plan was to wipe out the enemy's food supply. Agent Orange was an incredibly potent herbicide made even stronger in the hands of the US and South Vietnamese Air Forces, who mixed it to thirteen times its usual strength. It could obliterate whole farms and wipe out entire forests with nothing more than a gentle mist. Their plan was to leave the Viet Cong exposed and hungry – but they could not have imagined the full impact that this plan would ultimately have.
>
> The plan worked, in a sense. From 1961 to 1971, 5 million acres of forests and millions more of farmland were destroyed by Agent Orange. These were farms that the US and South Vietnamese thought were being used to feed the Viet Cong's guerrilla army – but in reality, most were feeding civilians. People across the country starved.
>
> The real impact of Agent Orange, though, took years to come out: 4 million people had been exposed to a chemical that could wipe out any form of plant life it touched. Despite what the chemical's producers had promised, it was not harmless.[6]

In 1970, Dr Cao Dai was given leave to attend a medical meeting in Hanoi. While there, he was briefed on the American use of a new dioxin. He was aware of the spraying of some substance and had noted that soon thereafter

The result of Agent Orange as a herbicide. It was devastating to human beings and its effects are still felt today.

all the foliage died. He was asked if he had treated cancer patients and he confirmed that he had. This was Agent Orange at work, and in 1973, Harvard University conducted a study to measure the levels of dioxin levels in the food being consumed in South Vietnam. Fifty parts per trillion is considered to be the maximum permissible. However, the study found levels of 800 parts per trillion and a mean of 200. The legacy of Agent Orange remains with the Vietnamese and over thirty years later, in 2003, 'one million people still suffered from cancers linked to Agent Orange and about 100,000 people are still alive with birth defects believed to have been caused by dioxin poisoning'.[7]

Food was one of the most important materials carried down the trail and the Viet Cong, always short of food, were dependent on the thousands of porters who laboured to deliver sustenance. In the early days, bicycles were used as transport and they were wheeled for miles through difficult conditions like those in the image on page 238. Over time and in the face of persistent bombing, the HCMT developed from a series of rutted tracks to a road capable of taking large, laden trucks. Vu Hy Thieu, when interviewed by Christian Appy, spoke about the journey south on the HCMT.

> We began the trip south in trucks, there were ten of us in the back of every truck that were all covered in tarps so that from the outside they just looked like ordinary supply vehicles. Resting by day, we travelled at night in small convoys of two or three trucks. We camouflaged the trucks with tree branches which made it harder for the American bombers to detect us. In Thanh Hoa Province the road became so bumpy we had to stand and hold onto the overhead rack. We were not permitted to talk because we might bite off our tongues, the bumps were that bad. We stood all night ... I remember one station that had been repeatedly bombed by B-52s. The trees were completely destroyed, it was like travelling through a desert. The earth was like powder ... We learned to cook without producing smoke. First we dug a big hole for the stove and then a long trench leading away from the hole. In the trench we put a pipe that carried the smoke away from the fire. If you covered the end of the pipe with leaves the smoke would filter through it very slowly. It was called a Hoang Cam cooker and for all of us northern soldiers who had to carry parts of it, it was our closest companion.[8]

The American opposition to the Viet Cong was led by President Lyndon Johnson, who unfortunately held his military in contempt and chose to micromanage the American military response – this to the extent that he took pride in selecting bombing targets. He was responsible for the appointment of Robert McNamara as Secretary of Defence and General William Westmoreland as the Commander of the US Military Assistance Command, Vietnam

Robert McNamara (1916–2009), US Secretary of Defence 1961–8.

(COMUSMACV). This was a toxic combination, as the latter two men believed that conducting war operations were an exercise in 'management'. McNamara was described as:

> the insufferably arrogant auto executive upon whom it never dawned – until it was too late – that managing a large bureaucracy, be it Ford or the Pentagon, had little to do with forging success in a shooting war ... The most disastrous American public servant of the twentieth century, he combined a know-it-all assertiveness with a capacity for monumental misjudgements and a dearth of moral courage worthy of Albert Speer.[9]

Westmoreland's appointment, in January 1964, was not greeted with unanimous approval. An appeal to Cyrus Vance, Secretary of the Army, was made by Brigadier General Amos Jordan, who asserted: 'It would be a grave mistake to appoint him. He is spit and polish, two up and one back. This is a counter-insurgency war, and he would have no idea how to deal with it.'[10] The brigadier was to prove to be correct in his judgement.

In the event, the American war in Vietnam was a protracted demonstration of how not to fight a war. The courage and commitment of a generation of young Americans and limitless logistic strength were not enough to counter inept and dishonest political direction compounded by misguided military tactics.

Revolutionary war came as an unwelcome shock to American soldiers. This is perhaps epitomised in a letter written by Captain Chuck Reindenlaugh about his enemy:

> Our weakness is rooted in our inability to garrison every village, hamlet or settlement. They attack where our forces are not stationed ... imagine a football game in which one of the teams is conventionally uniformed, observes the rules of play. The opposing team, however, wears no uniform and in fact has been deliberately clothed to resemble spectators. This team plays by no rules, refuses to recognize the boundary markers or the Ref's whistle and, when hard pressed by their own goal, the team's quarter back will hide the ball under his shirt and run into the spectator boxes and defy you to find him.[11]

He had summarised revolutionary war, which as he observed, had no structure, no rules, no referee and is frustrating and unfair. Notwithstanding the reality of revolutionary war, McNamara and Westmoreland decided that the war should be viewed in arithmetic terms. To that end, success was expressed in statistics such as 'enemy killed, bombs dropped and vehicles destroyed'. Westmoreland imposed on his soldiers a need for 'body count'. He sought the 'crossover point', which was when enemy dead could no longer be replaced. Officers were evaluated on the body count of their platoon, company or battalion. The system was very quickly corrupted. False and inflated figures were reported, and non-combatant civilians were murdered to inflate the body count. The pursuit of the elusive crossover point was perhaps Westmorland's greatest folly.

Westmoreland also introduced a policy limiting the length of tours in Vietnam. Officers in command had only three months in that appointment. Not long enough for them to get to know their soldiers, not long enough for the soldiers to gain confidence in their officer. Thus, Westmoreland chose to fight a war with an army 'learning on the job'. It was military nonsense. Colonel David Hackworth, a noted warrior, summarised the policy as 'in and out like clockwork ... just long enough to figure out what they didn't know'.

General William Westmoreland (1914–2005), COMUSMACV 1964–8.

American operations during the critical 1964–8 timeframe were encapsulated in the phrase 'Search and Destroy'. This was the first 'helicopter war' and the USA, with its great wealth, was able to deploy 12,000 helicopters. Of these, 10,500 were the Bell Hu-1 (known as the Huey). These aircraft cost $250,000 in 1964, or $2,393,612 at 2022 prices. The cost of training pilots and maintenance crews, petrol, oil and lubricants pushed the cost of this element of Westmoreland's campaign into the financial stratosphere. Over 5,000 helicopters were either shot down or crashed.[12]

The 'search' part of this tactic was to find the VC food, arms and ammunition. Large sweeps were conducted from a secure Landing Zone (LZ) that had been sanitised prior to the assault with an artillery strike. This bombardment warned the VC where the Americans would land, and they reacted accordingly. The search troops would ransack Vietnamese villages, seeking evidence of VC activity – perhaps a store of rice that exceeded the requirements of the individual householder. At that point, the 'destroy' part of the operation was implemented. Frequently, villages were torched, the inhabitants made homeless and some of their number murdered. Those murdered were added to the body count. The VC were obliged to develop tactics to counter the American aerial superiority and fluidity of movement. Lieutenant General Dang Vu Hiep conceded:

> fighting the US wasn't easy. We had to rely on our creativity ... we found a way to deal with their airborne units. In order to engage us, they had to find landing zones (LZ) for their helicopters, so we began to set ambushes where we guessed they would land ... We also learned that, wherever we attacked the enemy their airborne units would bring in more troops at our back, a tactic they called 'leapfrogging'. We figured that out and we began to lay ambushes to our rear to hit the American reinforcements. We began to see the advantage of stretching the enemy forces by luring them away from their large bases. Once their troops were all strung out, we could attack where they were least powerful.[13]

The food denial policy was neither coordinated nor pursued vigorously by the US Army. Nevertheless, its adversary suffered from constant, unremitting hunger. Vu My Thieu said that in his experience, he and his comrades bartered for food with ethnic minority people who lived in the mountains. He gave his trousers for chicken eggs. He said that the most valuable commodity was a pair of sandals made from old tyres – the tribesmen would give a whole pig in exchange. On that basis, sandals were so valuable that at night they were tied to the body. He went on to say that on his journey south and when he entered Quang Tri Province, the road had been almost totally destroyed and food was scarce:

> because so many of our rice sheds had been blasted. What rice we did have was mostly stale or rotten, thanks to jungle dampness and humidity. The guides in that region suffered the most. Their bodies were swollen from beriberi ... we had a better chance of finding food and we shared our meagre supplies with them.[14]

American soldiers and marines deployed into the jungle found it to be stressing, arduous and frustrating. They were invariably soaked to the skin with either rain or their own sweat – usually a combination of the two. They were burdened. They carried ammunition, entrenching tools, medical dressings, morphine, rations, and a great deal of water. Every step they took exposed them to mines or the dreaded punji traps in which a sharpened bamboo spike, covered in excrement, would drive deep into a leg or foot. In due course, when it was time for a meal break, the first priority was the digging of defensive shallow shell scrapes. The jungle floor was a mass of entwined roots, and the creation of the scrape was hard work.

Then the patrol would stop work to eat their C-rations. This was highly nutritious and did not need to be cooked. However, heating the food made it more palatable. The soldiers bartered foodstuff among themselves to compose a meal of choice. They boiled water and made instant coffee and cocoa and accompanied it with dry biscuits spread with melted cheese, a shake of tarragon leaves and dried onion.[15]

When the meal was concluded, there was always unconsumed food, which was left behind as rubbish. As the Americans departed, so the VC swooped on the 'rubbish' and dined on the contents. The Americans regularly and inadvertently partially fed their enemy throughout the war. The VC also obtained food filched from army kitchens and stolen from the quayside. The conclusion has to be that the food denial programme was not a 'joined up' operation. Similarly, the air campaign was muddled, because:

> the USAF never devised a clear strategic bombing policy during the Vietnam War, but still managed to send B-52 bombers to carpet bomb both North and South Vietnam. They delivered the biggest bombardment in military history – 4.6 million tonnes of bombs, estimated to have killed perhaps 2 million Vietnamese. But the terror the US generated with its bombs proved to be no greater than the terror the communist government in Hanoi generated among its own people.
>
> US 'strategic bombing' in Vietnam turned into an even more strategically significant own goal – marginally effective at best, and reprehensible in the eyes of the world.[16]

Lê Duẩn (1907–86), General Secretary of the Communist Party of Vietnam.

The vulnerability of the VC to food shortages is illustrated by the Tet Offensive, which was launched by the North Vietnamese Army (NVA) and the VC on 30 January 1968 – the master plan of Lê Duẩn, who had followed Hồ Chí Minh. It was to be a massive operation in which large numbers of communist troops were able to gather, with their arms and rations outside of every significant South Vietnamese town or city. The intelligence available to the VC and NVA was gathered by the innumerable informants employed by the Americans in their well-resourced bases, in which all the clubs and facilities were staffed by locally employed civilians, of whom, some were active VC.

The optimistic and erroneous assumption in Hanoi was that the invaders would be viewed as liberators by the South Vietnamese and the population would rise up in support. General Giáp, who had been sidelined, warned Lê Duẩn against the offensive, but his advice was ignored. The fact that soldiers of South Vietnam (ARVN) would be allowed to go home to their family village to celebrate the Tet holiday was viewed in Hanoi as a considerable military bonus. All the indications pointed to a crashing defeat for the US and South Vietnam.

Assassination squads were given specific targets, others were directed to key installations and one group was tasked with taking the US Embassy in Saigon. This coordinated multi-pronged attack across the entire country was extraordinary. Westmoreland later claimed that he expected some sort of military operation at Tet, but he had made no contingency arrangements.

The onslaught, when it came, was devastating and the communist forces made swift inroads. The communists had provided their soldiers with rations for a few days assuming that food would be forthcoming but significantly, the civilian population did not support the invaders and did not feed them. Food deprivation was a factor in the subsequent withdrawal.

The US Embassy was breached but the whole attack squad was killed. The ARVN and American forces exacted heavy punishment and by mid-February, the first surge of the offensive terminated. Casualty estimates vary but it is not disputed that the communist forces had lost up to 45,000 killed. ARVN losses were 2,788, and the US, 1,536. In addition, about 14,000 civilians were killed.

By any yardstick, this was a crushing military victory for the USA. However, the battle had been viewed live on American TV and the impact on public opinion was more than Hanoi could possibly have hoped for. The anti-war movement in the USA gained momentum, there was serious social disorder, and the media took up arms against the war.

> Over time, however, ever more Americans came to believe their leaders had misled and even lied to them about the realities of the war. Many concluded that South Vietnam was neither a democratic nor an independent nation, but a corrupt and unpopular regime entirely dependent on US support; that preserving it was not vital to national security and that the USA was itself acting as an aggressor.[17]

When President Nixon took office a year later, he tacitly acknowledged that the war was lost by declaring that his aim was to bring US troops home and that the war against communism would be fought by South Vietnam. Morale in the US forces, still fighting and dying, sank to an unprecedented level but it would be four years before the USA could distance itself from the ongoing war.

Summary

The USA lost a war in Vietnam in which it had control of the air and an overwhelming logistic strength. However, despite having the capability to starve the opposition, its food denial operations were uncoordinated and ineffective.

The iron determination of the Vietnamese to drive the USA from the country, at whatever cost, overwhelmed a mainly conscript US Army.

Throughout the war, USA military operations were adversely affected because they did not control the government of South Vietnam, and in addition, its own government imposed limitations on US forces. There was serious domestic, social disorder when a significant proportion of the population of the USA lost faith in its government and the rationale under which the war was being fought.

The combination of President Johnson, General Westmoreland and Robert McNamara was unfortunate. They were the wrong men, in the wrong jobs, at the wrong time. When replaced by Nixon and Kissinger, defeat was already knocking at the door.

Notes

1. von Clausewitz, C., *On War*, 1832 (trans. by J.J. Graham, revised by F.N. Maude).
2. Record, J., *The Wrong War: Why We Lost in Vietnam* (Annapolis, Maryland, Naval Institute Press, 1998), p. 1.
3. Vu Thi Vinh, quoted by Appy, C.G. [2003], *Vietnam: The Definitive Oral History Told from All Sides* (London, Ebury Press, 2006), pp. 103–104.
4. Dang Vu Hiep, quoted by Appy, p. 11.
5. Le Cao Dai, quoted by Appy, p. 139.
6. Oliver, M., 2017, *Agent Orange: 24 Haunting Photos of The War Crime The U.S. Got Away With* (https://allthatsinteresting.com/agent-orange-victims).
7. Le Cao Dai, quoted by Appy, p. 139.
8. Vu Hy Thieu, quoted by Appy, p. 191.
9. Record, p. 51.
10. Sorley, L., *Westmoreland: The General who Lost Vietnam* (Boston, Mariner Books, 2012), p. 67.
11. West, R., *War and Peace in Vietnam* (London, Sinclair Stevenson, 1995), p. 31.
12. Roush, G., Vietnam Helicopter Pilots' Association, 2018.
13. Dang Vu Hiep, General, quoted by Appy, pp. 10–11.
14. Vu My Thieu, quoted by Appy, p. 92.
15. Finlayson, A.R., *Killer Kane* (Jefferson, South Carolina, MacFarland, 2013).
16. Clarke, M., *The Sunday Times*, 23 October 2022.
17. Appy, p. xxi.

PART SEVEN

THE COLD WAR

Chapter Twenty-Five

Berlin and its Governance
(1945–8)

The seeds of the Berlin crisis of 1948–9 were planted three years earlier at Yalta, a seaside resort on the Black Sea, between 4 and 11 February 1945. The 'Big Three', Churchill, Stalin and an ailing Roosevelt, met there to discuss the new global order that they would put in place, just as soon as Germany finally succumbed to the retribution currently being exacted on its dwindling forces.

Stalin, the host, was determined to provide a scale of hospitality that bordered on the obscene, but reports of the primitive conditions, including bed bugs, that awaited them caused both the visitors to make additional logistic arrangements. The British contingent included in its baggage 1,000 bottles of whisky and gin. 'Churchill recommended whisky as a salve for everything, alleging that it was good for typhus and deadly on lice.'[1] More apposite, he commented that 'the immense task that awaited them was the organisation of world'.[2]

The three politicians came to the conference table with undeclared aims. Stalin aspired to retain the territorial gains his forces had made in the last two years – namely, Czechoslovakia, Romania, Bulgaria, Hungry, Ukraine and Poland – and to install pro-Soviet governments in all of them.

Roosevelt had three aims. The first was to persuade Stalin to join the war against Japan, the second to enlist the support of his two counterparts to support his proposals for an organisation to be called the 'United Nations'. His third, covert, aim was the destruction of the British Empire – an aim he had shared with the Japanese.

Churchill's objectives were to recover and then preserve the integrity and status of both his country and its empire. Secondly, he sought to prevent the Soviet Union dominating post-war Europe.

Stalin invited Roosevelt, as a head of state, to chair the meetings. The latter accepted gracefully and asked for an up-to-date briefing of the current military situation. This revealed the extraordinary advance of Soviet forces over the previous month, in which they had advanced 300 miles (483km) and taken 100,000 prisoners. Soviet soldiers were within 60 miles (97km) of Berlin. General George Marshall briefed on the Western Allies' bombing campaign.

The 'Big Three' at Yalta, and behind them, some of the men who had fought the war.

When he had finished, Churchill suggest dryly that 'the next day's agenda should address the future of Germany, if she has any'.[3]

It was agreed that the city of Berlin would be taken by the Soviets and then partitioned among the Allies – USA, Great Britain, France and Russia. The Soviet forces were to meet up with the Western Allies about 110 miles (177km) west of Berlin. In effect, Berlin would be an island surrounded by the Soviet Army and accessible down agreed road and rail routes.

During the Yalta Conference, the Soviet forces continued their advance towards Berlin, with ghastly consequences for the German population living in their path. At least 2 million German women were thought to have been raped – 1.4 million in East Prussia, Pomerania, and Silesia, and 100,000 in the later battles and occupation of Berlin. Many suffered multiple rapes and some 10,000 died as a consequence, either from injury or suicide.[4] How many civilians were shot out of hand has not been calculated.

The last days of the Third Reich, still some two months ahead, were the epitome of chaos and savagery. When the dust had settled, a team would have to apply a measure of stability. The first member of the team to be selected was a relatively junior American, Colonel Frank Howley. He was a man brimming with aggression and self-confidence, with a powerful ego. He was to be the American representative on the joint British/American Military Government of Berlin, whose role was to administer the western sectors of the divided German capital city – ruined though it was. Howley would also serve on the four-power Kommandatura, whose task was to deal with issues that concerned the whole city and thus would have to have daily dealings with his Russian and British counterparts.

In 1945, the situation in Berlin was unique. The Yalta Conference had arbitrarily divided the city into:

> three sectors and this process produced a logistic nightmare. The city's gas, water sewage and electricity networks did not respect sector boundaries. If supplies were to be restored, it would require the British and Americans to work closely with their Soviet allies.[5]

Although Howley was a dominating personality, he was not the fount of all authority. During the war his function was 'civil affairs' and he had excelled at bringing order to towns liberated by the Allies. His British counterpart was a man at the other end of the spectrum in almost all aspects – Acting Brigadier Robert Hinde (known as Looney). Howley was a brash, extroverted, energetic showman. Hinde was a stiff, Indian Army, Urdu and Pashtu-speaking cavalry officer who had served with distinction in 15/19 King's Hussars in

Brigadier General Frank Howley (1903–93), photographed in March 1949, after his promotion.

Brigadier Robert Hinde (1900–81), later, Major General Sir Robert Hinde, KBE, CB, DSO**.

North Africa, with three DSOs to prove it. Hinde was offered the job in Berlin because the War Office determined that he had the qualities required. He was said to display 'dash, decisiveness, wisdom, supreme courage and [had a deep sense of] responsibility'.[6]

Chemistry is baffling. These two men had nothing in common; they were from vastly different backgrounds and culture. They met and became the firmest of friends from day one. Each admired in the other the qualities they lacked. Nevertheless, Howley did resent that he was junior to Hinde, and quite why he was not made at least an acting brigadier general has never been explained. They would make a powerful team when Berlin fell, and they could take up their responsibilities.

In the meantime, during March and April 1945, both men busied themselves assembling their teams. However, there was a major culture gap and a lack of mutual regard. A series of bonding experiences were created, beer was taken in quantity, and over time, a feeling of team spirit resulted.

The final battle for Berlin was a bloodbath. The Russian General Grigoriy Krivoshein, writing after the war, was very precise on the subject of casualties, asserting that the Soviets lost 81,116 killed in the operations leading to the capture of Berlin. In addition, 280,251 were wounded. Materiel losses included 1,997 tanks and self-propelled guns.[7]

The Soviets claimed to have captured nearly 480,000 German soldiers, while German research put the number of their dead at between 92,000 and

The Brandenburg Gate in the centre of Berlin, June 1945.

100,000.[8] Some 125,000 civilians are estimated to have died during the entire operation.

Little wonder then that, after Hitler committed suicide, the population of Berlin was completely cowed yet had to live with the rapacious Red Army. Immediately post-war, Berlin was a highly disagreeable place, Germans were starving, and hope was in very short supply. The victorious powers established themselves, and with singular lack of empathy for the miserable inhabitants of this devastated city, they lived in bacchanalian splendour.

On 29 June 1945, it was agreed between the four powers (France had been allocated part of what had been the British zone) that each could station 25,000 troops in the city. However, in a sign of things to come, the Russians refused the request that multiple rail lines could be used to access Berlin and insisted on restricting entry to and exit from Berlin to one main road, two air corridors and one rail line.

The Allied powers were anxious to cooperate with the Russians, and at the senior level, General Lucius Clay, the American general, and General Sir Brian Robertson, his British equal, had no doubts as to their political priorities. However, without free access across Soviet–controlled Germany, Berlin 'was an island surrounded by a Red Sea'.[9]

The division of Berlin from 1945. (*Milton, G.,* Checkmate in Berlin)

The early months of the four-power governance (Kommandatura) of the city was marked by distrust, violence and a rapidly expanding black market. The entire city had been pillaged by the Russians, who had removed anything they deemed to be of value; everything else they destroyed. The city was in ruins and the provision of all services – gas, electricity and water – were problematic. Normal social norms were abandoned as Western soldiers took full advantage of the available German women who sold themselves for a bar of chocolate or a pack of cigarettes.

Howley and Hinde had inherited a nightmare and it took firm and capable leadership to instil a modicum of order. The Russians were, at best, difficult, and at worst, truculent and violent. Over the following three years, relations between the Allies and the Soviets were conducted at two levels. The hands-on management of the city and the welfare of its citizens rested at about mid-military level, namely Brigadier Hinde, Colonel Howley and Major General Alexander Gorbatov. Above them were the commandants, Lieutenant General Lucius Clay, Lieutenant General Sir Brian Robertson and General Vasily Sokolovsky. After three months, a French sector of Berlin was carved out of the British sector and a French representative joined the Kommandatura.

It is unnecessary to rehearse the activities of the Kommandatura other than to say that, by early 1948, the rubble had been cleared, and in the western half of Berlin, rebuilding was well advanced and commerce was flourishing. The denizens of East Berlin lived under a repressive Russian regime, and their visits to the West to shop only served to highlight the stark differences.

Relations between the national representatives had been robust but generally positive although the three Western representatives invariably took a different line to that of the Russian. For three years, all the meetings were followed by a social event, when whisky and vodka were taken in heroic measures.

However, from the spring of 1947, the Russian attitude had hardened and the atmosphere at the meetings cooled. One issue upon which agreement could not be reached concerned the Fourteen Points. These regarded the legal and material position of the workers of Berlin. The matter had been under discussion for months without any progress but then, arbitrarily, the Soviet administration issued an order creating a new law to which the Fourteen Points applied. It all came to a head at the meeting on 16 June 1947. The discussion dragged on for thirteen hours, at which Howley asked to be excused as he had a busy day ahead of him on the morrow. The French chairman, General Ganeval, acceded to Howley's request and the colonel left the room.

The Russians claimed to be insulted by Howley's departure and after a display of histrionics, they left in the highest dudgeon. At this distance, one might speculate that there was an element of opportunism in their actions. In the event, this spat was the first incident that led to the eventual breakdown of the Kommandatura in August 1947, when the Russians took down their flag, moved out of their offices and with all their files left, never to return.

The winter of 1947/8 was particularly bleak and although Berliners suffered and starved, the occupying forces did not. The city had run out of coal, firewood and power. People made forays into the Grunewald Forest, 'equipped with knapsacks, baskets and shopping bags . . . jammed together in an overcrowded train and wasting hour upon hour searching for one day's worth of firewood'.[10] Some of the Western occupiers recognised the vast gap between them, the 'haves', and the Berliners, who were most emphatically the 'have-nots'.

In early 1948, Brigadier Hinde was replaced, to general dismay, as he had made a significant contribution to the rehabilitation of Berlin. 'He had worked long and tirelessly for the cause of unity,' and it was felt that without his calm, diplomatic presence the Kommandatura would certainly have broken up.[11] On his departure he was promoted to substantive brigadier (to this point he held only acting rank). Hinde's replacement was Brigadier Edward Benson, who would answer to the new commandant, Major General Otway Herbert. Herbert announced that it was his intention to take an active role in the function of the Kommandatura. 'Herbert was woefully ill-equipped for the momentous events about to hit Berlin.'[12]

Notes

1. Harriman, W.A. & Abel, E., *Special Envoy to Churchill and Stalin 1941–46* (London, Random House, 1975), p. 390.
2. *Foreign Relations of the United States: Diplomatic papers, Conferences at Malta and Yalta 1945* (United States Government Printing Office, 1955), p. 715.
3. Terkel, S., *The Good War: An Oral History of World War Two* (London, Hamish Hamilton, 1985), p. 331.
4. Beevor, A., *Berlin: The Downfall 1945* (London, Penguin, 2002), p. 410.
5. Milton, G., *Checkmate in Berlin: The First Battle of the Cold War* (London, John Murray, 2022), p. 19.
6. Ibid., p. 20.
7. Krivosheyev, G.F. (ed.), *Russia and the USSR in the Wars of the Twentieth Century: Losses of the Armed Forces, A Statistical Study* (Moscow, OLMA-Press, 2001).
8. Glantz, D.M., *When Titans Clashed: How the Red Army Stopped Hitler* (University Press of Kansas, 1998).
9. Hays papers, IWM 20927, quoted by Milton, p. 83.
10. Andreas-Friedrich, R., *Battleground Berlin* (London, Paragon House, 1990), p. 150.
11. Hays papers, IWM 20927, quoted by Milton, p. 239.
12. Milton, p. 239.

Chapter Twenty-Six

The Blockade of Berlin
(June 1948–May 1949)

Stalin aspired to create a unified Germany under Russian control when he had outlined his plans at a meeting with German Communists as early as June 1945.[1] Then he made it clear that the occupied zones would be his focus, and on the British in particular. The breakdown of the Kommandatura in June 1947 was, arguably, a first step in that process.

The Western powers were in Berlin courtesy of the Russians because, back in the heady days of 1945, there was no perceived need for formal agreements on access routes through Soviet-controlled territory, and accordingly, the Western Allies were dependent on Russian goodwill.[2] It was assumed, naïvely, that restrictions to one rail line was just a temporary measure – it was not. The Russians were only prepared to permit three air corridors and then they discontinued the delivery of foodstuffs from East Germany into West Berlin. The Americans and British retaliated by stopping the movement of industrial equipment to the East.

After a period of unsatisfactory political duelling, on 25 March 1948, the Russians imposed travel restrictions on passenger traffic to and from Berlin.[3] Only one week's notice was given, and the restrictions implemented on 1 April were draconian. The Russians demanded the authority to search every truck or train. General Lucius Clay, the American senior officer in Berlin, responded by ordering that all materiel in or out would be transported by air. This became known as the 'little lift'. Aerial supply continued but only in the face of dangerous harassment by the Russian air force. Its aircraft habitually buzzed incoming flights by flying close and across their flight path.

This was an accident waiting to happen, and on 5 April 1948, the predicted accident did happen. A Yak-3 collided with a British European Airways Viking 1-B airliner. All those aboard both aircraft were killed. This was later termed the Gatow Air Disaster. This incident raised the temperature all round and added to the mounting ill feeling between the Allied nations and Russia.[4]

The 'little lift' was only necessary for ten days because, on 10 April, the restrictions on surface traffic were relaxed, although the Russians continued to disrupt movement. From mid-April, stocks of food were accumulated, and by 1 August, there was approximately eighteen days' worth of supplies in Berlin warehouses.

Tension continued to rise as the Russians took a hard line with the Western Allies and they rather complacently concluded: 'Our control and restrictive measures have dealt a strong blow to the prestige of the Americans and British in Germany and that the Americans have "admitted" that the idea of an airlift would be too expensive.'[5]

The Russians continued to apply political pressure wherever possible, and during April 1948, they insisted that Americans working on communication systems in the Eastern zone be withdrawn and then, furthermore, that all barge traffic must, with effect from 20 April, obtain Russian clearance before entering Berlin. However, the trigger for a full-on blockade of Berlin was the introduction by the Allies of the new Deutsche Mark, on 18 June 1948, for use throughout the city. Relations already fraught now broke down as the Russians progressively halted all surface communication. The Allies responded where they could, but the Russians had a much stronger hand. The lack of any formal treaty as to access routes into Berlin was keenly felt, but it was now a non-negotiable issue. However, Colonel Howley observed shrewdly: 'Although the Reds had succeeded in cutting us off completely by land depriving us of the autobahn, the railroad and the canals, the blockade has one flaw. Moscow does not control the skies.'[6]

In mid-1948, the Allied situation in Berlin was fragile, particularly so as the Russians had always insisted that the feeding of the troops and the citizens of the Western zones were solely a matter for the Allies. It would only take one false step to ignite the Third World War and all the participants knew that. Britain was in bad order. It was effectively bankrupt, and food was still rationed (and would remain so until 1954). It was responding to guerrilla war in Malaya, its armed forces had been run down and it was in no position to embark on another European war, and it had large external debts, much of which was in dollars, which had to be earned. To top it all, the United Kingdom was hosting the Olympic Games!

> Her wealth creating ability had declined significantly. She had expenditure related to her inherited position as head of a large empire; to still perceiving herself to be a world power, including occupation responsibilities, and the social and nationalisation programmes of her Labour Government. Unforeseen expenditure would have not been welcomed but the sums involved with the Airlift were not overwhelming. What is likely to be more significant was that impoverished Britain lacked the hardware assets necessary to play the major role she aspired to in the Berlin Airlift.[7]

But then neither was the USA prepared for this eventuality. It had reduced its vast army and dispensed with much of its equipment. It had troops stationed in West Germany, but their function was solely defensive.

It was calculated that West Berlin had sufficient food stockpiled to feed the military for about thirty-seven days. However, feeding the 2.4 million Berliners was another matter, and for them, there was only food for twenty-seven days. Petrol stocks would last for ten weeks, but only if used in the most frugal manner.[8]

The provision of electricity was dependent upon coal and there was about forty-five days' worth of that. Militarily, the Western Allies were no match for the Russians. Although the treaty allowed for each nation to keep 25,000 soldiers in post, in practice, the garrisons were very much smaller. The Americans numbered 8,973, the French, 6,100, and the British, 7,606. General Herbert reported to London saying that if the Russians maintained siege conditions for more than a few weeks, 'the German population will suffer considerable hardship'. He was massively understating the case; the reality was that the Germans would starve to death.

One of the most forceful Allied politicians was Ernest Bevin, the recently appointed British Foreign Secretary. He was uncompromising and concluded that 'the abandonment of Berlin would have serious if not disastrous consequences in Western Germany and throughout Western Europe'.[9] His view was shared by President Truman.

Berlin was indefensible; the Russians had 300,000 soldiers within striking distance of the city. Notwithstanding the huge imbalance in the military assets of the two sides, General Lucius Clay favoured an armoured thrust through the Soviet zone with a 6,000-strong force. He code-named his plan as Operation TRUCULENT. Perhaps it was as well that Clay had not commanded troops in action during the recent war. His plan was patently asinine and General Robertson told him so, adding, 'In such an event I'm afraid my government could offer you no support.'[10]

Bevin hosted a meeting in London with a group of senior American officers, one of whom was Lieutenant General Albert Wedemeyer, whose task was to convince Bevin that air resupply for a beleaguered city was impossible. However, Bevin took the initiative and at the start of the meeting, he declared: 'I have news I believe you will find extremely interesting. I have just come from a meeting of the full cabinet at which it was agreed that under no circumstances will we leave Berlin.'[11]

This was a very significant political statement, particularly as military action is always the result of a political decision. It is the politicians who set the goals and it is the function of the military to achieve those goals. Wedemeyer was shocked, but he repeated that extended aerial air resupply was impossible. Bevin would have none of this and his riposte was crushing. He said: 'I never thought that I'd live to see the day when the head of the American Air Force explained to me that his Air Force cannot do what the Royal Air Force is going to do.'[12]

These were brave words from Bevin, and they changed the face of history, but in fact the RAF was not equipped to undertake the resupply of Berlin unaided. However, Bevin's statement had kicked the ball into play and as Wedemeyer left the meeting, he said to his aide, Frank Roberts, 'I suppose we're meant to do it.' Roberts nodded, and agreed, 'That was the message.'[13]

Bevin did not stop there, and through the American ambassador, he suggested that the USA might send two squadrons of B-29 Superfortresses to Britain to help persuade the Russians that the Allies meant business. He got his wish and sixty of the giant aircraft were redeployed to Britain. The British Government, impoverished as it was, nevertheless endorsed the idea of an airlift and prepared to play a part.

In Berlin, morale was very low and a sense of impending doom was prevalent. On 24 June, land and water connections between East and West Berlin were severed. The following day, the Russians ceased supplying food to the Western zones. Traffic between the East and West zones was subject to interruption, and more importantly, electricity was cut off – the generating plants were all in the Eastern zone. The only way in and out of Berlin was by air. By June 1948, everyone on the Allied side was singing from the same song sheet, if not necessarily to the same music.

The scale of the operation was such that it had to be managed by the USA. In Howley, they had a man well known and respected in Berlin and his assurance, on the radio, that 'We shall not let the people of Berlin starve' was a great aid to civilian morale. Another key player was Ernst Reuter, who had been elected mayor of Berlin but whose appointment was vetoed by the Russians. Nevertheless, he enjoyed support across the political spectrum and was viewed by the Russians with the very deepest suspicion.

General Curtis Le May was a positive commander of the US Air Force dedicated to the airlift. When asked if his aircraft could deliver coal, he said, 'We can haul anything.' However, before he was prepared to commit himself and his men, he needed an assurance that the people of Berlin would see through the difficult times ahead. Ernst Reuter gave him that assurance and Le May was impressed. The RAF was first in the field and was already supplying the British garrison – a tiny dependency compared to the size of the needs of the city and its denizens.

The airlift was in essence a logistic exercise and some measurement had to be made that would ensure that adequate resources were allocated to it. The Americans based their operation on a minimum daily ration for Berliners of

1,990 calories per day. This translated to 646 tons of flour and wheat, 125 tons of cereal, 64 tons of fat, 109 tons of meat and fish, 180 tons of dehydrated potatoes, 11 tons of coffee, 180 tons of sugar, 19 tons of powdered milk, 5 tons of whole milk (for children), 3 tons of fresh yeast, 144 tons of dehydrated vegetables, 38 tons of salt and 10 tons of cheese – a formidable shopping list, but that was the *daily* requirement. It added up to 1,534 tons if the 2.4 million people in Berlin were to survive. In addition, 3,475 tons of coal, diesel and petrol were required – also on a daily basis.[14]

A vast air armada was going to be required to move the 5,000 tons of mixed supplies. The British had been quick off the mark, and they were able to put together a force of 150 Dakota and forty Avro York with a capacity to move about 750 tons per day. It was simply just not enough, and the balance would have to be provided by the other Allies – thus the weight of the operation fell on the USA. Canada declined to be involved on the basis that the airlift could lead to war – and that it was not consulted.

The American aircraft that would have to do most of the heavy lifting was the C-54 Skymaster, of which they had 565 in their inventory. The calculation was that 447 of these aircraft could be dedicated to any airlift, as and when it might be implemented.

There was a consensus among the Allies that an airlift was desirable but there was considerable doubt about the mechanics. The management of a large air fleet operating from many airfields, the air traffic control over the destination and the turnaround of unloaded aircraft posed a unique combination of problems.

It was at this stage that Air Commodore Reginald Waite, CB, CBE, RAF (known as Rex) addressed the matter. Waite had worked on the D-Day planning team and was a skilled logistician. He was a very intelligent, capable and experienced officer, and in 1948, he served on the staff of General Herbert and headed what he called 'The Berlin Air Ministry'.[15] Waite was observed at work by journalist Edwin Tetlow, who wrote:

> His head was bowed over a tiny pocketbook, and he was making drawings and calculations with the stub of a pencil. He was devoting his technical brain shaped by a long service career in every branch of flying, to the problem of Berlin.[16]

Waite was seeking a mathematic solution to resolve the logistic conundrums he faced. In the process, he identified eight airfields in Western Germany from which resupply could be based. There were, however, only two airfields in Berlin, at Gatow and Tempelhof, but these needed to be upgraded to cope with the intense level of traffic. The runways would have to be extended and

A perceptive illustration of how the world viewed Berlin in 1948. (*Milton*)

re-engineered. This work would have to be accomplished within days. Waite explained that the runways would be covered in burning oil and then hard core and tarmac, recovered from Berlin streets, laid on top.[17]

Waite calculated that an enhanced Gatow could receive and process the cargo of 288 inbound flights a day and he allowed two and a half minutes for each aircraft. He commented that that 'included taxiing out, getting on the runway, taking off and getting a safe distance clear at the far end of the runway so that another one could be told to come in'.[18]

The unloading of each aircraft and the distribution of that cargo would require the creation of a labour and transport organisation. Trucks would be waiting, engines running. If the cargo was fuel, it would be driven to a waiting barge that was to be filled from six chutes.

Waite covered all the eventualities but his plan was dependent upon every element working with precision. He took his work to General Herbert, who dismissed it out of hand, as did General Robertson. Waite was not to be thwarted and ignoring the chain of command and service protocol, he took his plan to General Clay, of armoured thrust fame. Clay took time to digest Waite's detailed plan and then pronounced, 'OK, I'm with you.'[19] From that moment, the Berlin Airlift became a reality, and the citizens of that city were given a new lease of life.

From 24 June 1948, what followed was one of the most exemplary logistic operations in military history. There were teething troubles initially, not least in air traffic control. It was found to be inefficient if an aircraft missed its 'slot' on arrival in Berlin airspace to cause it to adopt a holding pattern with other delayed traffic. Filling the skies with circling planes in daylight was dangerous and at night, possibly lethal.

Across the Western world, aviators, mechanics, truck drivers, forklift operators and many more were being reassigned to unexpected places. Waite's selected eight airbases in Western Germany were situated in an arc between Lübeck and Wiesbaden. These bases were to be the giant supermarkets serving Belin with all its needs.

The airmen of all the participating nations worked sixteen-hour days, seven days a week – far in excess of the workload permitted for civilian aviators. In addition to the stress of constant landings and take-offs, they had to contend with the harassment of Russian fighter aircraft that swooped and dived at them as they made their approach. One pilot counted twenty-two Yaks performing acrobatics around him as he landed. General Kotikov arranged for tracer bullets to be fired between incoming planes and had searchlights placed to dazzle pilots.

This airlift was no walk in the park; it was extremely hazardous for the airmen, and on landing, they had not a second to spare as they unloaded, took off and started on another round trip. The Tempelhof airstrip was dominated at one end by a number of five-storey apartment blocks only 400 yards (366m) from the threshold of the runway. It made every landing there 'interesting' and called for skilful airmanship every two and a half minutes.

Despite the initial success of the airlift, which by now was an American-led operation, it did not enjoy the support of the senior echelons of the American military structure. When General Clay went to Washington on 22 July to plead for more aircraft, he was opposed by all of the Joint Chiefs of Staff

(JCOS). He made his case in front of President Truman and presumed he had failed. In the event, Truman overruled the JCOS and additional aircraft were made available.

It was interesting that those who had most opposed the whole principle of the airlift suddenly became its greatest supporters. Wedemeyer, for example, had recently expended time and effort in explaining to an unbelieving Bevin why an airlift could not work. Wedemeyer, now a convinced disciple of airlift, made a very shrewd suggestion to General Vandenberg, the Chief of Air Staff. The suggestion was that Major General William Tunner, an officer who had supervised the airlift across the Himalayas – 'the Hump' – from autumn 1944 until the winter of 1945, be assigned to Berlin. In his previous role, he had supplied the forces of Chiang Kai-shek. Tunner's 20,000 men and 300 planes delivered 650,000 tons of munitions, fuel and food and had to combat some of the most difficult conditions on Earth.

An American aircraft landing at Tempelhof, watched by grateful Berliners.

With this exemplary background, Tunner was the right man in the right place and he rose to the challenge. His appointment ruffled the feathers of Le May, and predictably, those of his subordinate, Brigadier General Joseph Smith, who was currently running the operation.

Tunner was described as 'proud and often cantankerous, efficient to an almost inhuman degree'.[20] He took up his post on 28 July and three weeks later, he had added seventy-two C-54s to the air fleet. He employed 66 per cent of all USAF C-54 aircrews. If any one person deserves credit for the success of the airlift, then Tunner must be considered. He created a level of organisation that allowed the air fleet to exceed the tonnage that had previously been delivered by surface routes. He simplified passage along the air corridors, insisted on adherence to the strictest timetables and abandoned the use of holding patterns for aircraft above the city.

The airlift was working smoothly, all the Allies were cooperating, and Air Commander Waite resolved the issue of salt delivery. This corrosive material could, and did, damage the wiring on the air fleet and Waite suggested the use of Sunderland flying boats because their wiring was in the wings. Later, Halifax bombers with external panniers were used for the same purpose.

The success of the airlift infuriated the Russians, and the French added to their angst. It was decided to improve the airstrip at Tegel, in the French zone. Rubble was crushed into hard core and paving was used instead of tarmac. However, at one end of the airstrip was a 200-foot (61m) radio tower, owned and operated by Soviet Radio Berlin. It was an obvious hazard to aircraft, and French General Ganeval asked General Kotikov to dismantle the tower, for which the French would pay compensation. No one was surprised when Kotikov refused point-blank.

Ganeval was something of a showman and when the strip was completed, he held a celebratory drinks party. All were invited and while the guests were busily refreshing themselves, there was suddenly a mighty explosion. Through the windows, a cloud of dust and smoke rose from the site of the radio tower. Ganeval beamed at Tunner; a problem had been eliminated but the Russians were inflamed. General Kotikov was bedside himself with anger and he arrived, puce with rage. 'How could you do that?' he screamed. Ganeval smiled, 'From the base, with dynamite.'[21]

The winter in Germany is always hard and 1948/49 was to be no different. In late October, thick, impenetrable fog descended on Berlin and the flight pattern was severely disrupted. When that dispersed, thick, low-lying cloud 1,000 feet (305m) thick replaced it. On 3 November, all operations ceased, and in the fog, visibility was down to 20 yards (18m). The airmen tried manfully to fly but, on 15 November, an American Skymaster crashed at Tempelhof when it missed the runway. An RAF Dakota, lost in the fog, crashed in East

Berlin and all five of the crew were killed, then a Lancaster making the return journey crashed into a fog-bound Wiltshire wood – again, all on board were killed. The fog persisted and by the end of November, Berlin was facing a crisis. Food stocks were rapidly reducing, and at best, only ten days' worth remained.

Coal was also running short and in the bitter weather, the electric power was only available for four hours a day. Berliners were used to hunger, and food denial was a weapon with which they were familiar. They thought those days had gone. Once again, the shops were empty and the sick and frail started to die. General starvation was just around the corner. In a brief window of better conditions, the British evacuated 17,000 malnourished children.[22]

The weather did not loosen its grip and Kotikov exploited the situation by encouraging Berliners to register for the abundant fresh food available in the east of the city. Some citizens, driven by cold and hunger, took him up on his offer. For those who remained in the West, the prognosis was dire. Christmas came and went with precious little cheer. It appeared that the hunger afflicting over 2 million people could be decisive in determining Berlin's future.

Then, as the new year of 1948/9 commenced, there was change in the weather. The planes flew again, and the crisis evaporated. Spirits rose and the airlift fell back into its punishing routine. On 4 May, a bright spring day, a message was received in Berlin saying that 'agreement has been reached between the three Western powers and the Soviets regarding the raising of the Berlin blockade'. The effective date was to be 12 May. This was unexpected as any negotiations between East and West Berlin had been conducted in conditions of the greatest secrecy.

The breakthrough had come when Stalin had let it be known that he was no longer troubled by the East Berlin Deutsche Mark. When told of this change of stance, Ernest Bevin said, 'Watch this, Stalin my now raise the blockade.'[23] He was right.

On the night that the blockade ended, many of the people of West Berlin assembled at the checkpoint where the autobahn enters the city. At midnight, the power was restored by the Russians, lights came on and the party started. The first Allied convoy arrived at 01.46 to a tumultuous welcome.[24]

In the weeks that followed there was a vast influx of food and consumer goods, the shops were fully stocked and the lifestyle gap between East and West was emphatically demonstrated.

The Berlin Airlift was the first battle of what became the Cold War. This bloodless encounter was to last until 1991, by which time many of the key players were dead. Aerial resupply continued until 18 August, when the final

RAF flight left Berlin. It was piloted by Flight Lieutenant Roy Mather, DFC, AFC, who had completed 404 flights – the most by any pilot of any nation.

The magnitude of the airlift is contained in the statistics. The USAF delivered 1,783,573 tons in a fifteen-month period; the RAF, 541,937 tons; the RAAF, 7,968 tons. Of that total, about two-thirds was coal. The USAF C-47s and C-54s flew 92 million miles, 'almost the distance from Earth to the Sun'.[25] General Tunner, writing after the event, said that, at the height of the airlift, 'an aircraft reached Berlin every thirty seconds'.[26]

There were costs and 101 died; of these, forty were British and thirty-one were American; in most cases, they died in non-flying accidents.[27] However, seventeen USAF and eight RAF aircraft crashed. The financial cost was shared between the USA, UK and Western Germany.

Summary

In Berlin, the weapon of food denial was employed by the Russians, but it failed in the face of the overwhelming logistic strength and political resolve of its adversaries – principally, the USA.

The Berlin Airlift demonstrated that food denial is not assured of success unless all logistic routes are blocked. Kut and Metz are examples of when it was. Partial blocking leads to partial success and the U-boat campaign in the Atlantic during the Second World War failed because Britain was never exposed to starvation conditions.

Erwin Rommel said, 'Before the fighting proper, the battle is fought and decided by the quartermasters.'[28] Rommel did not specifically mention food, but he did highlight the criticality of logistic strength. To reiterate the thought expressed on page 1, it is suggested that although the logistics of warfare are all about 'bullets, bandages and bread', often the most important of these is 'bread'.

Notes

1. Miller, R.G., *To Save a City: The Berlin Airlift, 1948–1949* (Texas, A&M University Press), p. 11.
2. Larson, D.W., 'The Origins of Commitment: Truman and West Berlin' (*Journal of Cold War Studies*, 13, No. 1, Winter 2011), pp. 180–212.
3. Miller, p. 20.
4. Clarks, D., 'Soviet-British Plane Collision Kills 15; Russian Apologizes' (*The New York Times*, 6 April 1948), p. 1.
5. Miller, p. 23.
6. Howley, F., *Berlin Command* (New York, G.P. Putnam's Sons, 1950), p. 205.
7. Keen, R.D., doctorate thesis, *Half a Million Tons and a Goat: A Study of British Participation in the Berlin Airlift June 1948 – May 1949* (University of Buckingham, 2013), p. 60.
8. Milton, p. 255.
9. Bullock, A., *The Life and Times of Ernest Bevin* (London, William Heinemann, 1960–83), p. 576, quoted by Milton, p. 256.

10. Collier, R., *Bridge across the Sky* (London, Macmillan, 1978), p. 55.
11. Ibid., p. 65.
12. Milton, p. 261, quoting Frank Roberts interview, transcript https://nsarchives2.gwu.edu/cold war/interviews/episode 1/roberts6.hmtl.
13. Ibid.
14. Miller, pp. 20–30.
15. Milton, p. 266.
16. Tetlow, E., 'Russia had Planned to Get Us out of Berlin by 1 August (*Daily Telegraph*, 9 July 1948).
17. Reginald Waite papers, KCLMA, quoted by Milton, p. 267.
18. Ibid.
19. Ibid., Milton, p. 268.
20. Reeves, R., *Daring Young Men* (New York, Simon & Schuster, 2011), p. 65.
21. Tunner, W.H., *Over the Hump* (New York, Duell, Sloan & Pearse, 1964), p. 212. Collier, p. 146.
22. Milton, p. 299.
23. Bevin in a memorandum. Foreign Office, TNA FO371/76549, quoted by Milton, p. 313.
24. Milton, p. 316.
25. Major, G.C., *Berlin Airlift: Logistics, Humanitarian Aid and Strategic Success*, archived 16 January 2007 at the Wayback Machine.
26. Tunner, p. 218.
27. Turner, H.A., *The Two Germanies Since 1945: East and West* (Yale University Press, 1987), p. 27.
28. Quoted by FM Lord Wavell in *Soldiers and Soldiering* (London, Jonathan Cape, 1953).

Conclusions

This text has trawled over warfare conducted worldwide for the last 150 years or so and has demonstrated that food denial is, without question, an effective weapon, and further, that it is relatively risk free for the initiator. However, it is not always successfully implemented and there have been several large-scale failures, as the last chapter demonstrated.

The Federal states in North America were able to harness their logistic superiority over the Southern States. The blockade they mounted was sufficiently effective to make the provision of food a major issue for General Lee and his army. It inhibited his movement and was a considerable factor in his defeat.

The militarily illiterate decision by Louis Napoleon III to declare war on Prussia in 1870 was compounded by the inability of the French Army to maintain an effective logistic system in its own territory. Food supply was an issue and especially so during the siege of Metz, and to a lesser extent, that of Paris.

The capitulation of the fortress of Metz was unquestionably the result of inept leadership, which, when supplemented by the food denial strategy of the Prussians, proved to be irresistible. Although the denial of food to the 2 million residents of Paris did not generate starvation, it did breed acute social discontent and eventually, a violent revolution was the result. Food deprivation in Paris was the trigger for major social, political and diplomatic changes that extended far beyond Paris, and which are still evident today.

The British surrender at Kut in April 1916 was an entirely predictable disaster and the consequence of having the wrong people in the wrong appointments at the wrong time. On that basis, perhaps Hardinge, Nixon and Duff might reasonably be described as 'The Toxic Trio'. Notwithstanding the inept command chain, it was food denial, ruthlessly applied by Generals von der Goltz and Nureddin, who cut the British logistic chain that depended entirely on free navigation of the Tigris. The starvation of the Kut garrison and capitulation was the result.

In the First World War, the Germans and the British each sought to blockade the other. The German campaign was conducted under the sea and while the British controlled the surface. In both countries, the population suffered from malnutrition. However, the power of the Royal Navy prevailed, and Germany suffered protracted food deprivation. That, in turn, led to defeat, civil disorder and ultimately, to revolution.

In that case, food denial had very serious, unexpected, long-term consequences. The privations of Germany in the period 1914–19 was the motivator that drove the political and military ambition of Adolph Hitler. His espousal of victimhood, quest for living space, and the autarky it promised, eventually cost tens of millions of lives, only twenty or so years later.

The blockades of the First World War were reprised in the Second, and on much the same terms. The Germans attacked, with great success, ships supplying the UK. The U-boats of Dönitz were a war-winning force, and they came very close to success. This view is robustly challenged by Clay Blair, the American historian, who judged that 'at no time did the German U-boat force ever come close to winning the Battle of the Atlantic or bringing on the collapse of Great Britain'.[1] Churchill, who was somewhat closer to the event, and arguably better equipped to comment, famously declared that 'the only thing that ever really frightened me during the war was the U-boat peril'.[2]

During the campaign in the Atlantic (1940–5), the British were dependent on imported food from North America and its empire. The survival of the UK owed everything to a combination of American logistic support, Liberty ship construction, fifty overpriced, obsolete destroyers, the Royal Navy, Ultra intelligence, and the unbreakable resolve of the 'man on the Clapham omnibus'. Hastings concluded that the 'mobilization of the best civilian brains, and their integration into the war effort at the highest levels, was an outstanding British success story'.[3]

The food denial aspiration of Germany in which it attempted to starve the UK into submission failed. The Allied winning of the campaign reset the future of much of the world, and the results are reflected in the current juxtaposition of political and military power. That is an impermanent situation, and as American power and influence wains, so the ascendency of India and China is progressively supplanting it.

It could be argued that the food denial strategy of the USA during the Pacific War of 1942–5 was one of the most effective in military history. The supremacy of the USA at sea was the main factor in its winning of that campaign. Thousands, probably hundreds of thousands of Japanese soldiers and the indigenous people amongst whom they lived starved as a result of a very weak Japanese logistic supply system that was systematically destroyed by a highly efficient submarine blockade of the home islands.

Technology moved on, and in Malaya and later in Vietnam, chemical means were employed to deny food to guerrilla forces waging revolutionary warfare. In Malaya, defoliation was inexpertly and sparsely applied and proved to be of limited value. Nevertheless, the strict control of food and its distribution was a factor in the defeat of Chin Peng and his acolytes.

The French, when fighting the first Vietnam War (1945–54), attempted to cut the food supply to their guerrilla enemy, the Vietminh, but with limited success. However, when the USA took up the anti-communist cause in Vietnam, it introduced 'Agent Orange', which was widely employed from 1961. This chemical was highly effective, but it had frightful, unforeseen consequences, and today, fifty years after that war, people are still suffering the effects. 'Agent Orange' has been responsible for far more deaths and human misery after the war (1955–75) than it caused during the war. The war in Vietnam was a disaster from an American standpoint. It cost the country 58,000 lives, caused international abhorrence and major domestic turbulence. Food denial failed in Vietnam.

The Russian attempt to starve Berlin into submission failed in the face of Allied resolve backed by vast American logistic resources. The world teetered on the edge of the Third World War, just as it would in Vietnam and in the Cuban Missile Crisis.

Food and its availability are now, and will always be, significant factors in any war. Indeed, food is already and increasingly a factor in countries **not** at war. It is predicted that one of the effects of climate change, a world population of 8 billion and rising, will be the forced migration of millions to more benign climes. Water will become a valuable and diminishing resource, a rising world population will exacerbate the nutritional health of the entire population and the future is bleak.

Food and its provision will be an increasingly critical factor in the maintenance of world peace.

Notes

1. Blair, C., *Hitler's U-Boat War: The Hunted 1942–1945*, Vol. II (London, Cassell, 1996), p. xii.
2. Churchill, Sir W.S., *The Second World War Vol 2: Their Finest Hour* (London, Cassell, 1946).
3. Hastings, Sir M., *All Hell let Loose: The World at War 1939–45* (London, Harper Press, 2011), pp. 275–7.

Research on the Effects of Extreme Hunger and Starvation

by Dr H.L. Meiselman

Introduction

My training was in Research Psychology, with primary interest in foods and other consumer products. I have researched how people make food choices and food rejections. I studied soldiers working in training out of doors for extended periods of time – interestingly, the soldiers struggled to eat enough to maintain body weight (whilst the rest of us struggle to lose weight). But I have never studied extreme hunger and starvation, which is why I was interested in Tank Nash's latest book examining these issues within wars. My goal in this commentary is to provide some research context for the understanding of extreme hunger and starvation from the limited research on that topic.

* * *

Hunger and starvation are very interesting topics in the sciences dealing with eating and drinking. Of course, most of this area deals with normal eating and drinking and with the common pathologies associated with eating and drinking, including anorexia, bulimia, binge eating, and various addictions. But surprisingly, we know very little about extreme hunger and especially starvation, even though hunger and starvation continue to plague human-kind. Here I am not referring to the form of hunger that we encounter in our normal lives, nor even the hunger that we experience in extended under-eating, but rather extreme hunger, when the body is seriously threatened.

Some of the reasons we know so little about extreme hunger and starvation are the challenges in conducting this type of research. Extreme hunger and starvation are life-threatening conditions, and therefore not amenable to traditional methods of research involving human subjects. Most professionals in contact with people who are starving are there to provide aid and comfort, and research is not their priority (or their skill) and would probably be rejected based on ethical grounds.

So, what do we know about extreme hunger and starvation? One can begin by looking up these words in Wikipedia, which gives an overview of the topic. And right there we see the classical reference to research done during the Second World War in the United States at the University of Minnesota by Dr Ancel Keys, physiologist, and Dr Josef Brožek, psychologist.[1] The research lasted about one year (November 1944 to December 1945). The study was conducted with thirty-six conscientious objectors who refused to fight as soldiers but were willing to undergo the rigours of a prolonged hunger study. In fact, hundreds of conscientious objectors volunteered for the study. The study was aimed at determining the challenges of starvation as Europe approached the end of the war, with millions starving.

The Minnesota Starvation Experiment included four phases:

(1) twelve-week baseline control;
(2) 24-week starvation, causing each participant to lose an average of 25 per cent of his pre-starvation body weight, and two recovery phases, in which various rehabilitative diets were tried;
(3) first rehabilitative stage restricted by eating 2,000–3,000 calories a day; and
(4) second rehab phase, unrestricted, letting the subjects eat as much food as they would like.

This classical study, which is still heavily referenced today when one searches for starvation research, studied people in demanding and long-term condi-tions, but not the conditions of actual starvation. The diet fed during the starvation phase was 1,570 calories, which was enough to cause weight loss but today is recommended to some dieters. Redman et al. reviewed improved health statistics in starvation studies (called caloric restriction), including when participants were fed 1,500 calories per day for three years.[2]

Perhaps most important, the Minnesota study participants knew that the researchers would not kill them, whereas people starving in real life are afraid for their lives. Further, the starvation phase lasted twenty-four weeks, rather than the many months and longer reported in Nash's history of starvation as a weapon of war. The blockade of the Southern Confederate ports by the North in the US Civil War lasted from 1861 to 1865 (*see* Chapter 3), the British blockade of German ports in the First World War lasted 1914–19 (*see* Chapter 12), and the Hunger plan within Germany during the Second World War lasted multiple years (*see* Chapter 14).

Keeping these limitations in mind, what happened to the starving volunteers? Major changes were observed in physical, psychological, behavioural and social variables.[3]

(1) Preoccupation with food; food and eating were focal points in conversations, reading, dreams, and daydreams.

(2) During mealtimes, participants were possessive over their food.

(3) During the rehabilitative phase, men started eating 'several' meals in one sitting and developed gastrointestinal upset and headaches as a result. They described feeling hungrier and using binge-eating and purging behaviours during the re-feeding period.

(4) They collected food-themed items and rummaged through garbage to find food.

(5) They tried to create the illusion that they had more food on their plates than in reality, cutting food into small pieces, and making their meal consumption last for hours.

(6) Increase in the use of spices and salt to add flavour to meals.

(7) Social isolation, describing themselves as feeling socially inadequate.

(8) During the semi-starvation and the rehabilitative phases, participants developed new anxiety and depressive symptoms.

(9) Experienced new issues with gastrointestinal discomfort, dizziness, headaches, decreased need for sleep, oedema, hair loss, and cold intolerance.

(10) In the semi-starvation period, the volunteers' weight dropped by 25 per cent and their muscle mass decreased by 40 per cent.

The Minnesota Starvation Experiment is probably the most cited study of starvation. But during the same period of the 1940s, a much more realistic study was carried out by the Jewish doctors in the Warsaw Ghetto, where the

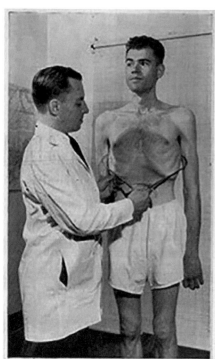
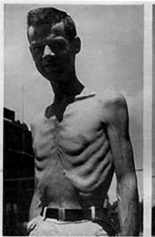
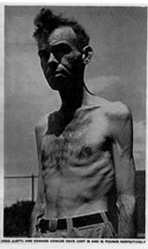

MEN STARVE IN MINNESOTA

CONSCIENTIOUS OBJECTORS VOLUNTEER FOR STRICT HUNGER TESTS TO STUDY EUROPE'S FOOD PROBLEM

Above:
Conscientious objectors during starvation experiment.
Life magazine - July 30, 1945. Volume 19, Number 5, p. 43.
Credit: Wallace Kirkland/Time Life Pictures/Getty Images.
Left:
Dr Ancel Keys measures the chest width of James Plaugher.

The Minnesota Experiment. (BBC Magazine, *20 January 2014*)

Jewish population was put on a diet of 200 calories per day. Some people were able to eat more through stealing, trading and other means. The study was started in February 1942 by twenty-six doctors led by Dr Israel Milejkowski. This is probably the only study of starvation where the researchers/ doctors were part of the starving population, so the researchers were suffering the same as the subjects of the study. The study ended in the summer of 1942, when the Jews in the Warsaw Ghetto were removed and sent to death camps. The doctors studying starvation in the Ghetto had their last meeting in August 1942, and a short time later, most of them were dead. Their research was saved and hidden. Their study was published in 1946 and an English version in 1979.[4]

The Warsaw Ghetto study emphasised the effects found in the Minnesota study. The starving people displayed very aggressive behaviour to obtain food, and there were reports of theft, murder and cannibalism. Force was needed to restrain violent people. This was followed by a period of apathy, where the mad interest for food not only declined but almost disappeared. We sometimes see pictures of starving people in this apathetic phase with very little energy. The report of theft and murder in the Ghetto study highlights the effects of starvation in a natural setting rather than the laboratory setting of the Minnesota study. Chapter 7 reports the violence in the American South during the Civil War as food became scarce, and perhaps surprisingly, some of the violence to seize food was carried out by women.

The mention of cannibalism within the Warsaw Ghetto study brings up this interesting facet of starvation – the appearance of cannibalism, as discussed by Nash in Chapter 21. Here I am referring to the eating of humans, dead or alive, for the purpose of survival, which is different to cannibalism as a part of ritualistic behaviour in some cultures. Much has been written about the presence of cannibalism in many animals, and the occurrence of cannibalism in many human cultures globally. Large-scale cannibalism has been documented in the settlement of Jamestown in America in the seventeenth century.[6] Also in Russia, during the state-imposed famine in which 5 million died (1921–2), and again during the Second World War, and among prisoners

Russians during the great famine, selling children's body parts for consumption.[5]

of war held by the Japanese during the Second World War. In the latter case, there were many reports of cannibalism of live prisoners. It is interesting to note the instances of starvation associated with some of these same events by Nash in Chapter 6, including Russian and Japanese prisoners.

The limited research on extreme hunger and starvation shows strong effects on feelings and behaviour. The initial aggressiveness gives way to apathy. Starving people have to contend with the very restricted access to food, and also with the abnormal behaviour of other starving people around them. Both the aggressive behaviour and the following apathy observed in starving people are related to the social and military disorder during periods of extreme hunger, as reported by Tank Nash in this very interesting book.

Herbert L Meiselman

Dr Herbert L. Meiselman is an internationally known expert in sensory and consumer research on food and other consumer products. He received his training in Psychology and Biology at the University of Chicago, University of Massachusetts, and Cornell University. He retired as Senior Research Scientist at Natick Laboratories, where he was the highest-ranking Research Psychologist in the United States Government. His accomplishments were recognised with a 2005 Award from the President of the United States.

Dr Meiselman is the author of over 220 research papers and eight books. He has worked in a broad range of fields in sensory and consumer science: basic academic research, product development (food and clothing), institutional food service design and evaluation. He has served as President of the Research Committee of L'Institut Paul Bocuse, Lyon, France, and served on the Research Committee for the Culinary Institute of America, Hyde Park, New York, and the food service programme at Orebro University, Sweden. He has served as Visiting Professor at Bournemouth University, UK; Reading University, UK; Orebro University, Sweden; and Charles Sturt University, Australia.

Notes

1. Keys, A., Brožek, J., Henshel, A., Mickelson, O. & Taylor, H.L., *The Biology of Human Starvation* (Vols 1–2) (Minneapolis, MN, University of Minnesota Press, 1950).
2. Redman, L.M., Martin, C.K., Williamson, D.A. & Ravussin, E., 'Effect of Caloric Restriction in Non-obese Humans on Physiological, Psychological and Behavioral Outcomes' (*Physiology and Behavior*, 2008), pp. 94, 643–8.
3. Gil, C., *The Starvation Experiment* (Duke Health/Center for Eating Disorders, online, accessed December 2022).
4. Habicht, J.-P. (1979), *Cases of Starvation: Hunger Disease, Studies by the Jewish Physicians in the Warsaw Ghetto*, translated from the Polish by Martha Osnos, Myron Winick (ed.) (Wiley-Interscience, New York, 1979), pp. xiv, 262.
5. Stromberg, J., *Starving Settlers in Jamestown Colony Resorted to Cannibalism* (Smithsonian, online, accessed December 2022).
6. Dean, S., *The Communist Cannibals: Shocking images reveal the depravation suffered by peasants forced to eat human flesh during the 1920s Russian famine* (*Daily Mail*, 2016, accessed online, January 2023).

Bibliography

Adam, P., *How did the Convoy System help in the War against U-boats?* (www.Quora, 9 April 2022).

Allard, P., *Les Énigmes de la Guerre* (Paris, Editions des Portiques, 1933).

Allen, L., [1984] *Burma: The Longest War 1941–45* (London, Phoenix Press, 2000).

Andreas-Friedrich, R., *Battleground Berlin* (London, Paragon House, 1990).

Appy, C.G., [2003] *Vietnam: The Definitive Oral History Told from All Sides* (London, Ebury Press, 2006).

Army Order No. 35 of 1941.

Arnold, D., *Famine: Social Crisis and Historical Change* (New York, NY, Wiley-Blackwell, 1991).

Arctic Convoys (Imperial War Museum, iwm.org.uk).

BAMA R W 19/166, pp. 25, 36.

Barber, N., *The War of the Running Dogs: Malaya 1948–1960* [1971] (London, Arrow Books, 1989).

Barker, A.J., *The First Iraq War, 1914–1918, Britain's Mesopotamian Campaign* [1967] (New York, Enigma, 2009).

Bartov, O., *Hitler's Army: Soldiers, Nazis and War in the Third Reich* (Oxford, Oxford University Press, 1991).

Bayly, C. & Harper, T., *Forgotten Armies: Britain's Asian Empire and the War with Japan* (New York, NY, Penguin Books Limited, 2005).

Bazaine, *Proces, Capitulation of Metz* (Paris, 1873).

Bazaine-Leboeuf, 30 July 1870 (*Guerre* III).

Bearss, E.C., *The Campaign for Vicksburg* (Dayton, OH, Morningside House, 1985), Vol. 3.

Beevor, A., *Berlin: The Downfall 1945* (London, Penguin, 2002).

Belcham, J., *Industrialisation and the Working Class: The English Experience 1750–1900* (Aldershot, Scolar Press, 1990).

Beres, I.R., 'On Assassination as Anticipatory Self-Defense: The case of Israel' (*Hofstra Law Review*, 1991).

Bergeron, A.W. (ed.), *The Civil War in Louisiana* (Lafayette, University of Louisiana, 2002).

Bevin in a memorandum, Foreign Office, TNA FO371/76549.

Bird, K.W., *Erich Raeder, Admiral of the Reich* (US Naval Institute Press, 2006).

Blair, C., *Hitler's U-Boat War: Vol. 1* (London, Cassell, 1996).

Blücher, Princess E., *An English wife in Berlin* (New York, Button & Co., 1920).

Boog, H.W. et al., *Der Angriff auf die Sowjet Union* (Stuttgart, Deutsche Verlags-Anstalt, 1985).

Brennan, L., 'Government Famine Relief in Bengal, 1943' (*The Journal of Asian Studies*, 1988, 47).

Britannica, The Editors of Encyclopaedia, 'Dreadnought', *Encyclopedia Britannica*, 5 March 2020.

Bronsart, S.P., *Geheimes Kriegstagebusch 1870–1871*, (ed.) Rassow, P. (Bonn, 1954).

Brown, A., 'What Percentage of White Southerners Owned Slaves?' (*The Moguldom Nation*, August 2020).

Brown, J.M., *Gandhi: Prisoner of Hope* (New Haven, CT, Yale University Press, 1991).

Bullock, A., *The Life and Times of Ernest Bevin* (London, William Heinemann, 1960–83).

Burkman, T.W., *Japan and the League of Nations* (University of Hawaii, 2008).

Burleigh, M., *Small Wars Faraway Places: Global Insurrection and the Making of the Modern World 1945–1965* (New York, Viking-Penguin Group, 2013).

'Burma Operations Record: 15th Japanese Army in the Imphal Area and Withdrawal to Northern Burma' (Office of the Chief of Military History, US Army, 1957).

Burnett, J., *Plenty and Want: A Social History of Diet in England from 1815 to the Present* (London, Routledge, 1966).

Caldwell, A., Jr., 'Air Force Maritime Missions' (United States Naval Institute Proceedings, October 1978).

'Camp Sumpter/Andersonville Prison' (US National Park Service).

Cant, S. & Dunkley, M., 'The Naval War' (*Logistics of the First World War*)

Carter, S., *The Final Fortress: The Campaign for Vicksburg 1861–1863* (New York, St Martin's Press, 1980).

Chamberlain to Hardinge, 9 and 16 December 1915 (Chamberlain papers, 62/2).

Chesnut, B.B.M., *A Diary from Dixie*, (eds) Martin, D. & Avery, M.L. (New York, Appleton & Co.).

Chesson, M.B., 'Harlots or Heroines? A New Look at the Richmond Bread Riot' (*Virginia Magazine of History and Biography*, 92/2, 1984).

Christopher, P., '*Malaya, 1948–55: Case Outcome: COIN win*' (Paths to Victory: Detailed Insurgency Case Studies, 2013).

Churchill, Sir W.S., *The Second World War* Vols V & IV (Boston, Houghton Mifflin, 1950).

Churchill, Sir W.S., *The Grand Alliance: The Second World War* Vol. 3 (Boston, Houghton Mifflin, 1950).

Churchill, W.S., *Marlborough: His Life and Times* [1933] (University of Chicago Press, 2002).

Churchill, W.S., *The Gathering Storm* (Boston, Houghton Mifflin Co., 1948).

Churchill, W.S., *The River War: A Historical Account of the Reconquest of the Sudan* (London, Longman & Green, 1899).

Cincinnatus (C.B. Currey), *Self-Destruction: The Disintegration and Decay of the United States Army During the Vietnam Era* (New York, WW Norton, 1981).

Clark, R.W., *Works of Man* (New York, Penguin, 1985).

Clarke, M., *The Sunday Times*, 23 October 2022.

Clarks, D., 'Soviet-British Plane Collision Kills 15; Russian Apologizes' (*The New York Times*, 6 April 1948).

Collidge, R.H., *Report* (11 September 1862, O.R. Ser. 1, Vol. 19, Pt. 2).

Collier, R., *Bridge across the Sky* (London, Macmillan, 1978).

Collingham, L., *The Taste of War* (London, Penguin Group, 2011).

Conquest, R., *The Harvest of Sorrow: Soviet Collectivisation and the Terror-Famine* (New York, Oxford University Press, 1986).

Cooper, N., 'French Indochina' (Academia.edu).

Costello, J., *The Pacific War 1941–45* [1981] (New York, Harper Collins, 2009).

Coulter, E.M., 'Effects of Secession upon the Commerce of the Mississippi Valley' (*The Mississippi Valley Historical Review*, December 1916, Vol. 3, No. 3).

Cunningham, Admiral Sir Andrew, *Despatch on Mediterranean Convoy Operations*, 1941.

Dahl, E.J., 'From Coal to Oil' (Washington, *Joint Force Quarterly*, Winter 2000–1).

Daily Southern Crisis, 23 February 1863.

Daily Telegraph, The, 7 July 2022.

Daily Vicksburg Whig, 15 November 1861.

Dattel, E.R., 'Cotton and the Civil War' (*Mississippi History Now*, July 2008).

Davis, B.J., *Home Fires Burning: Food Politics, and Everyday Life in World War 1 Berlin* (London, University of North Carolina Press, 2000).

Davis, L.E. & Engerman, S.L., *Naval Blockades in Peace, and War: An Economic History since 1750* (Cambridge University Press, New York, 2006).

De Bow, J.D.B., *The Industrial Resources of the Southern and Western States* (New Orleans, Office of De Bows Review, 1852, Vol. 2).

Defence Committee minutes, 13 October 1940, TNA CAB 66/13/2kl.

Desmarest, J., *La Defence National* (Paris, 1949).

Dimbleby, J., *The Battle of the Atlantic* (London, Penguin, 2016).

Dower, J.W., *Embracing Defeat: Japan in the Aftermath of World War II* (London, Penguin, 2000).

Dutch, S.I., 'The Largest Act of Environmental Warfare in History' (*Environmental & Engineering Geoscience*, 2009, 15 (4)).

Ebbert, J., Hall, M-B. & Beach, E.L., *Crossed Currents* (London, Brassey, 1991).

Eggenberger, D., 'Peleliu – Angaur', *An Encyclopedia of Battles – Accounts of Over 1,560 Battles from 1479 B.C. to the Present* [1967] (New York, Dover Publications, 1985).

Eicher, D.J., *The Longest Night: A Military History of the Civil War* (New York, Simon & Schuster, 2001).

Fall, B.B., *Hell in a Very Small Place: The Siege of Dien Bien Phu* [1966] (New York, Da Capo Press, 2002).

Famine Inquiry Commission 1945.

Favre, J., *Gouvernement de la Défense National*, 3 Vols, Vol. 1 (Paris, 1871–75).

Finlayson, A.R., *Killer Kane* (Jefferson, South Carolina, MacFarland, 2013).

Forsdike, M., *The Malayan Emergency* (Barnsley, Pen & Sword, 2022).

Frank, R.B., 'The Horribles: American Strategic Options Against Japan in 1945' (nationalww2 museum.org, 2020).

Frederick III, *The War Diary of the Emperor Frederick III, 1870–1871* [1927] (ed.) Allinson, A.R. (Worcestershire, UK, Home Farm Books, 2006).

Freedman, L., *Command: The Politics of Military Operations* (London, Allen Lane, 2022).

Gates, P.W., *Agriculture and the Civil War* (New York, Alfred Knopf, 1965).

General Assembly of Pennsylvania, 'An act for the Gradual Abolition of Slavery' (1780).

Gerlach, C., *Kalkulierte Morde. Die deutsche Wirtschafts- und Vernichtungspolitik in Weissrussland 1941 bis 1944* (Hamburg, Hamburger Edition, 1998).

GGS, Vol. 3, pp. 176–9, Vol. 5.

Ghosh, S., 'Famine, Food and the Politics of Survival in Calcutta, 1943–50', in Sarkar, T. & Bandyopadhyay, S. (eds) (Abingdon, Routledge, *The Stormy Decades*, 2018).

Glantz, D.M., *The Battle for Leningrad 1941–1944: 900 days of Terror* (London, Cassell, 2004).

Glantz, D.M., *When Titans Clashed: How the Red Army Stopped Hitler* (University Press of Kansas, 1998).

Goff, R.D., *Confederate Supply* (Durham, NC, Duke University Press, 1969).

Gould, D., 'Hardinge and the Mesopotamia Commission' (Cambridge University Press, *The Historical Journal*, December 1976).

Grant, U.S., *Personal Memoirs of U.S. Grant, Vol. 1* (New York, Charles Webster & Co., 1885).

Greenough, P.R., 'Indian Famines and Peasant Victims: The Case of Bengal in 1943–44' (*Modern Asian Studies*, 1980), 14 (2).

Grey, J., *A Military History of Australia* (Cambridge, Cambridge University Press, 1999).

Grindal, P., *Opposing the Slavers* (IB Tauris, London, 2016).

Hack, K., 'Devils that Suck the Blood of the Malayan people' (*War in History*, Sage Journals, 2018).

Hacker, J.D., 'A Census-Based Count of the Civil War Dead' (*Civil War History*, No. 57, Dec 2011).

Hardinge to Chamberlain, 31 December 1915 (*Hardinge papers*).

Hardinge to Cox, 28 December 1915 (*Hardinge papers 94*), No. 155.

Harper's Weekly, 6 June 1862.

Harries, M. & Harries, S., *Soldiers of the Sun* (London, Heinemann, 1991).

Harriman W.A. & Abel, E., *Special envoy to Churchill and Stalin 1941–46* (London, Random House, 1975).

Harris, Sir Arthur, *Bomber Offensive* (London, Greenhill Books, 2005).

Hastings, Sir M., *Nemesis: The Battle for Japan 1944–45* [2007] (London, Collins, 2016).

Hattaway, H. & Jones, A., *How the North Won: A Military History of the Civil War* (Urbana, University of Illinois Press, 1983).

Hays papers, IWM 20927.

Heathcote, A., *The British Field Marshals 1736–1997* (Barnsley, Pen & Sword, 1999).

Hitler, A., *Mein Kampf* (Munich, Franz Eher Nachfolger GmbH, 1925).

Horne, A., *The Fall of Paris: The Siege and Commune 1870–71* (London, Macmillan, 1965).

Hough, R., *The Great War at Sea* (New York, Oxford University Press, 1983).

Howard, M., *The Franco-Prussian War* [1961] (Abingdon, Routledge, 2001).

Howley, F., *Berlin Command* (New York, G.P. Putnam's Sons, 1950).

Hoyt's New Encyclopedia of Practical Quotations (1922).

https://encyclopedia.1914-1918-online.net/article/food_and_nutrition_germany

Huegel, A., *Kriegsernahrungswirtschaft Deutschlands* (Konstanz, Hartung- Gorre Verlag, 2003).

Huff, G., 'Causes and consequences of the Great Vietnam Famine 1944–45' (*The Economic History Review*, 72, 2018).

J.D. Gladney to Jefferson Davis, 6 August 1861 (O.R., Set 4, Vol. 2).

Johnson, W.H., a free African American and valet to President Lincoln to Colonel L.B. Northrop, Commissary-General of the Confederate Army, 10 August 1863 (O.R. Ser. 1, Vol. 24, Pt. 3).

Jolinon, J., 'La Mutinerie de Coeuvres' (Paris, *Mercure de France*, 1920).

Jukes, G., Simkins, P. & Hickey, M., *The First World War: The War to end all Wars* (London, Osprey Publishing, 2013).

Kay, A.J., *Exploitation, Resettlement, Mass Murder* (Oxford, Berghahn Books, 2006).

Kazuo Tamayama & John Nunneley, *Tales by Japanese soldiers of the Burma Campaign 1942–5* (London, 2000).

Keegan, J., *The American Civil War* (London, Vintage, 2010).

Keegan, J.D.P., *The Second World War* (London, Arrow Books, 1990).

Keen, R.D., Doctoral thesis, *Half a Million Tons and a Goat: A Study of British Participation in the Berlin Airlift June 1948–May 1949* (University of Buckingham, 2013).

Kellogg, R.H., *Life and Death in Rebel Prisons* (Hartford, CT, L. Stebbins, 1865).

Kennedy, F.H. (ed.), *The Civil War Battlefield Guide* (Boston, Houghton Mifflin Co., 1998).

Keogh, E., *Southwest Pacific 1941–45* (Melbourne, Grayflower Publications, 1965).

Kirschenbaum, L., *The Legacy of the Siege of Leningrad, 1941–1995: Myth, Memories, and Monuments* (New York, Cambridge University Press, 2006).

Korn, J., *War on the Mississippi: Grant's Vicksburg Campaign* (Alexandria, VA, Time-Life Books, 1985).

Krivosheyev, G.F. (ed.), 'Russia and the USSR in the Wars of the Twentieth Century: Losses of the Armed Forces. A Statistical Study'.

Lapping, B., *End of Empire* (London, St Martin's Press, 1985).

Larson, D.W., 'The Origins of Commitment: Truman and West Berlin' (*Journal of Cold War Studies*, 13, No.1, Winter 2011).

Lawrence, T.E., 'The Science of Guerrilla Warfare', *Encyclopedia Britannica*, 1929.

Lehmann, J., *Agrarpolitik und Landwirtschaft in Deutschland* (Ostfildern, Scripta Mercaturae Verlag, 1985).

Liddell Hart, B.H., *History of the First World War* [1934] (London, Cassell, 1970).

Linder, D., 'Scopes Trial Home Page – UMKC School of Law' (Law2.umkc.edu).

Litwack, L.F., *Been in the Storm so Long: The Aftermath of Slavery* (New York, Alfred Knopf, 1979).

Lonn, E., *Desertion during the Civil War* (Lincoln, University of Nebraska Press, 1998).

Lunn, E., *Salt as a Factor in the Confederacy* (Tuscaloosa, University of Alabama Press, 1965).

Mackenzie, A., 'The Rebirth of the SAS: The Malayan Emergency' (St Martin's Publishing Group, 2012).

Maclean, M., *Vietnam's Great Famine, 1944–45* (History Reformatted in Archival Form Clark University, 2016).

Mahan, A.T., *The Influence of Sea Power Upon History, 1660–1783* (Boston, Little Brown & Co., 1890).

Major, G.C., *Berlin Airlift: Logistics, Humanitarian aid and Strategic Success*, archived 16 January 2007 at the Wayback Machine.

Mallett, J.W., 'The Work of the Ordnance Bureau of the Confederate States 1861–65' (Richmond, Va., Southern Historical Society Papers, Vol. 37, 190.

Marder, A., *From the Dreadnought to Scapa Flow, The Royal Navy in the Fisher Era, 1904–1919: The War Years to the eve of Jutland: 1914–1916*, Vol. II (London, Oxford University Press).

Massey, M.E., 'The Food and Drink Shortage on the Confederate Homefront' (*North Carolina Historical Review*, 1949).

Matuszczyk, A., *Creative Stratagems: Creative and Systems Thinking in Handling Social Conflict* (Kibworth, England, Modern Society Publishing, 2012).

McAulay, L., *To the Bitter End: The Japanese Defeat at Buna and Gona, 1942–43* (Sydney, Random House, 1992).

McNeill, W.H., *America, Britain, and Russia: their Co-operation and Conflict, 1941–1946* (London, Oxford University Press, 1953).

Merrill, J.M., 'Notes on the Yankee Blockade of the South Atlantic Seaboard 1861–1865' (*Civil War History*, Vol. 4, December 1958).

Military Institutions of the Romans AD 378 (trans. Clark, 1776).

Miller, R.G., *To Save a City: The Berlin Airlift, 1948–1949* (Texas A&M University Press, 2008).

Milton, G., *Checkmate in Berlin: The First Battle of the Cold War* (London, John Murray, 2022).

Moberly, F.J, *The History of the Great War: The Campaign in Mesopotamia*, Vol. 2 (London, HMSO).

Molkentin, M., *The Centenary History of Australia in the Great War*, Vol. 1 (Melbourne, Oxford University Press, 2014).

Moon, P., *This Horrid Practice* (Penguin Books, 2008).

Moore, J.N., *Confederate Commissary General: Lucius Bellinger Northrop and the Subsistence Bureau of the Southern Army* (Shippensburg, Pa, White Mane Publishing Co. 1996).

Mukherjee, J., *Hungry Bengal: War, Famine, and the End of Empire* (New York, NY, Oxford University Press, 2015).

Muscolino, M.S., *The Ecology of War in China: Henan Province, the Yellow River, and Beyond, 1938–1950* (Cambridge University Press, 2014).

Nash, N.S., *Betrayal of an Army* (Barnsley, Pen & Sword, 2016).

Nash, N.S., *Chitrál Charlie: The Rise and Fall of Major General Charles Townshend* (Barnsley, Pen & Sword, 2010).

Nash, N.S., *In the Service of the Emperor* (Barnsley, Pen & Sword, 2022).

Nash, N.S., *K-Boat Catastrophe: The Full Story of the Battle of The Isle of May* (Barnsley, Pen & Sword, 2009).

Nash, N.S., *The Siege that Changed the World: Paris 1870–1871* (Barnsley, Pen & Sword, 2021).

Nbg. Doc. 2718–PS, *Aktennotiz über Ergebnis der heutigen Besprechung mit den Staatssekretären über Barbarossa*, 2 May 1941 (International Military Tribunal, (ed.) *'Der Prozess gegen die Hauptkriegsverbrecher vor dem Internationalen Militärgerichtshof'*, Nürnberg, 14 November 1945–1 Oktober 1946, Vol. 31, Sekretariat des Gerichtshofs, Nuremberg, 1948.

New York Times, The, 4 April 1865.

Newsinger, J., *The Blood Never Dried: A People's History of the British Empire* (2nd ed.) (London, Bookmarks Publications, 2013).

O'Sullivan, C.D., *Harry Hopkins: FDR's Envoy to Churchill and Stalin* (Maryland, Rowman & Littlefield, 2014).

Oliver, M., 2017, *Agent Orange: 24 Haunting Photos of The War Crime The U.S. Got Away With* (https://allthatsinteresting.com/agent-orange-victims)

Ongkili, J.P., *Nation-building in Malaysia 1946–1974* (Oxford University Press, 1985).

Ooi Giok Ling, *Southeast Asian Culture and Heritage in a Globalising World – Diverging Identities in a Dynamic Region* (Farnham, Surrey, Ashgate Publishing Ltd., 2012).

Ooka, S., *Fires on the Plain* (trans. Morris, I., Tokyo, Charles F. Tuttle Co., 1957).

Owsley, F.L., *King Cotton Diplomacy: Foreign Relations of the Confederate States of America* (Chicago, University of Chicago Press, 1959).

Pace, R.F., 'It was Bedlam Let Loose: The Louisiana Sugar Country and the Civil War' (*Louisiana History*, Autumn, 1998).

Paine, S.C.M., *The Wars for Asia 1911–1949* (New York, Cambridge University Press, 2012).

Persico, J.E., *Wasted Lives on Armistice Day* (histornnet.com, 2006).

Power, T., *Lee's Misérables: Life in the Army of Northern Virginia from Wilderness to Appomattox* (Chapel Hill, University of North Carolina Press, 1998).

Price, M.W., 'Ships that Tested the Blockade of the Carolina Ports' (*American Neptune*, Vol. 8, July 1948).

Raich, B. (ed), *Franklin D. Roosevelt, Selected Speeches* et al. (Eastern Press, 1957).

Rashid, Rehman, *A Malaysian Journey* (published by Rashid, 1993).

Read, P.P., *Alive: The Story of the Andes Survivors* (Philadelphia, Lippincott, 1974).

Reagan, G., *Military Anecdotes* (Guinness Publishing, 1992).

Record, J., *The Wrong War: Why We Lost in Vietnam* (Annapolis, Maryland, Naval Institute Press, 1998).

Reeves, R., *Daring Young Men* (New York, Simon & Schuster, 2011).

Register of the Commissioned and Warrant officers of the Navy of the United States, including officers of the Marine Corps and others, for the year 1861.

Reid, A., *Leningrad: Tragedy of a City under Siege, 1941–44* (London, Bloomsbury Publishing, 2011).

Report of the Mesopotamia Commission, 1917.

Reports to the General Assembly of Illinois, twenty-second session, 7 January 1861 (Springfield, 1861).

Rhodes, J.F., *History of the United States from the Compromise of 1850*, Vol. 5 (New York, Harper, 9 Vols, 1904).

Richmond, K., *The Japanese Forces in new Guinea* (Monograph, Australian War Memorial, awm.gov.au., 2003).

Rooney, D., [1992] *Burma Victory: Imphal and Kohima, March 1944 to May 1945* (London, Cassell, 1992).

Roosevelt, E., *As He Saw It* (New York, Duell, Sloan & Pearce, 1946).

Roosevelt, E. (ed.), *The Roosevelt Letters Vol III, 1928–1945* (London, G. Harrap, 1952).

Roush, G., Vietnam Helicopter Pilots' Association, 2018.

Russell, Lord of Liverpool, *The Knights of Bushido* (London, Cassell, 1958).

Sadkovich, J., *The Italian Navy in World War II* (Westport, CN, Greenwood Press, 1994).

Salisbury, H.E., *The 900 Days: The Siege of Leningrad* (Da Capo Press, 1969).

Salter, J.A., *Allied Shipping Control* (Oxford, Clarendon Press, 1921).

Sandburg, C., *Abraham Lincoln* (New York, 2002).

Sarazin, C., *Récits sur la Dernière Guerre Franco – Allemande* (Paris, 1887).

Shankland, P., *Malta Convoy* (London, Fontana Press, 1989).

SHAT Lt, 12, Metz, 31 October 1970, Major F.A. Léveillé.

SHAT Lt, 12, Metz, 23 September 1870, *'un member de l'armée'*.

Sheridan, P.H., to Grant, 7 October 1864 (O.R. Ser 1, Vol. 43, Pt. 2).

Sherman, W.T., *Memoirs of General William T. Sherman* (New York, D. Appleton & Company, 1889).

Sherwood, R.E., *The White House Papers of Harry L. Hopkins*, Vol. 1 (London, Eyre & Spottiswoode, 1948).

Simpson, H.R., *Dien Bien Phu: The Epic Battle America Forgot* (London, Brassey's, 1994).

Smith, A.F., *Starving the South* (St Martin Press, New York, 2011).

Sorley, L. *Westmoreland: The General who Lost Vietnam* (Boston, Mariner Books, 2012).

Spector, R.H., *Eagle Against the Sun: The American War with Japan* (Free Press, 1985).

Standish, M., *A Life Apart: The English Working Class 1890–1914* (London, Thames & Hudson, 1977).

'Startling Exposure of the Milk Trade of New York and Brooklyn' (*Frank Leslie's Illustrated Newspaper*, 8 May 1858), pp. 353–4, 359.

Stephens, I., *Monsoon Morning* (London, Ernest Benn, 1966).

Streit, C., *Keine Kameraden* (Bonn, Dietz, 1997).

Swami, V., 'Hangry in the field: An experience sampling study on the impact of hunger on anger, irritability, and affect', Hochstöger, S., Erik Kargl, E. & Stefan Stiege, S. (*Plos One*, July 2022).

Tanaka, K., *Hidden Horrors: Japanese War Crimes in World War II* (Oxford, Westview Press, 1996).

Tans, J.H., 'The Hapless Anaconda: Union Blockade 1861–1865' (*The Concord Review*, 1995).

Taylor, J., *The Generalissimo Chaing Kai-shek and the Struggle for Modern China* (Cambridge, Mass, Belknap Press of Harvard University, 2009).

Terkel, S., *The Good War: An Oral History of World War Two* (London, Hamish Hamilton, 1985).

Tetlow, E., 'Russia had Planned to Get Us out of Berlin by 1 August (*The Daily Telegraph*, 9 July 1948).

The Battle of Indochina (*Time* magazine, 28 September 1953).

Thompson, J., *Forgotten Voices of Burma* (London, Ebury Press, 2010).

Thornton, M. & Ekelund, R.B., *Tariffs, Blockades, and Inflation: The Economics of the Civil War* (Wilmington, DE, Scholarly Resources Inc. 2004).

Tilden, A., *The Legislation of the Civil War Period* (Los Angeles, University of Southern California Press, 1937).

Tilman, R.O., 'The Non-lessons of the Malayan Emergency (*Asian Survey*.1966 6 (8)).

Tolland, J., *The Rising Sun: The Decline and Fall of the Japanese Empire 1936–45* [1970] (New York, Random House, 2003).

Tombs, Prof R., 'How Bloody was La Semaine Sanglante of 1871?' (Cambridge University Press, *The House Journal*, Vol. 55, No. 3, September 2012).

Tooze, A., *The Wages of Destruction* (London, Allen Lane, 2006).

Townshend, Maj Gen. C.V.F., *My Campaign in Mesopotamia* (London, Thornton Butterworth, 1920).

Trefalt, B., *Japanese Army Stragglers and Memories of the War in Japan, 1950–75* (London, Routledge, 2003).

Tucker, T., *The Great Starvation Experiment: Ancel Keys and the Men Who Starved for Science* (New York, Free Press, 2007).

Tunner, *Over the Hump* (New York, Duell, Sloan & Pearse, 1964).

Turner, H.A., *The Two Germanies Since 1945: East and West* (Yale University Press, 1987).

Vat, D van der., *The Atlantic Campaign: The Great Struggle at Sea 1939–45* (London, Hodder & Stoughton, 1988).

Vincent, C.P., *The Politics of Hunger: The Allied Blockade of Germany 1915–19* (London, Ohio University Press, 1985).

von Clausewitz, C., *On War*, 1832 (trans. by J.J. Graham, revised by F.N. Maude).

Wagner, S.C., 'Biological Nitrogen Fixation' (*Nature Education Knowledge*, 2011).

Waite, R., papers KCLMA.

Watt, R.M., *Dare Call it Treason* (London, Chatto & Windus, 1963).

Wavell, FM, Lord *Soldiers and Soldiering* (London, Jonathan Cape, 1953).

Wawro, G., *The Franco Prussian War: The German Conquest of France 1870–1871* [2003] (New York, Cambridge University Press, 2010).

Welch, J.M., 'Without a Hangman, Without a Rope' (*International Journal of Naval History*, 1 (1), 2002).

West, R., *War and Peace in Vietnam* (London, Sinclair Stevenson, 1995).

Wheeler, R., *Voices of the Civil War* (New York, Meridian, 1976).

Wheeler, R., *Voices of the Civil War* (New York, Meridian, 1976).

White, T.H. & Jacoby, A., *Thunder out of China* (London, Victor Gollancz, 1947).

Williams, P., *The Kokoda Campaign 1942* (Melbourne, Victoria, Cambridge University Press, 2012).

Wilt, A.F., *Food for War: Agriculture and Rearmament in Britain before the Second World War* (Oxford, Oxford University Press, 2001).

Winters, J.D., *The Civil War in Louisiana* (Baton Rouge, Louisiana State University, 1963).

World War I Casualty and Death Tables, Public Broadcasting System (U.S.A.), based on U.S. Justice Department statistics, at: http://www.pbs.org/greatwar/resources/casdeath_pop.html.

Woznicki, A.N., 'Endocannibalism of the Yanomami' (*The Summit Times*, 1998, 6).

Index